MAIN LENDING   **3 WEEK LOAN**   DCU LIBRARY

Fines are charged **PER DAY** if this item is overdue.
Check at www.dcu.ie/~library or telephone (01) 700 5183 for fine rates and
renewal regulations for this item type.
Item is subject to recall.
Remember to use the Book Bin when the library is closed.
The item is due for return on or before the latest date shown below.

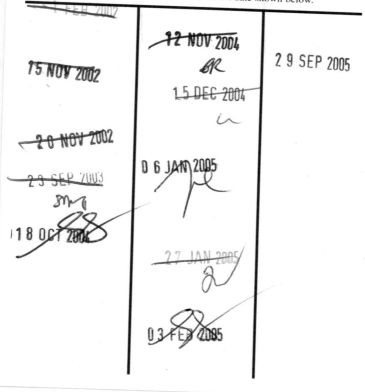

~~11 FEB 2002~~	~~12 NOV 2004~~	2 9 SEP 2005
~~15 NOV 2002~~	*BR*	
	~~15 DEC 2004~~	
~~20 NOV 2002~~		
~~29 SEP 2003~~	0 6 JAN 2005	
18 OCT 2004		
	~~27 JAN 2005~~	
	0 3 FEB 2005	

International Relations Theory

New Normative Approaches

Chris Brown
Keynes College, University of Kent at Canterbury

HARVESTER WHEATSHEAF

New York London Toronto Sydney Tokyo Singapore

First published 1992 by
Harvester Wheatsheaf
Campus 400, Maylands Avenue, Hemel Hempstead
Hertfordshire, HP2 7EZ
A division of
Simon & Schuster International Group

Typeset in 10/12pt Baskerville
by Witwell Ltd, Southport

Printed and bound in Great Britain by
BPCC Wheatons Ltd, Exeter

British Library Cataloguing in Publication Data

A catalogue record for this book is available from
the British Library.
0–7450–1534–4 pbk

2   3   4   5   96   95   94   93

Contents

Acknowledgements

I am grateful to David McLellan, Terry Nardin, Nick Rengger and Steve Smith, each of whom read the whole of this text and made many helpful suggestions, some of which I have adopted. Stephen Chan, Alan Carruth, Richard Disney, Martin and Pat Kane, Richard Sakwa and Keith Webb read parts of the text and, again, made useful suggestions, some of which have seen the light of day in the final version. Colleagues in the Board of Studies in Politics and International Relations at the University of Kent have been uniformly supportive and encouraging. Elizabeth Dorling and her colleagues in the Keynes Secretarial Office – Carol, Marilyn, Yana, Lucy and Tracy – have seen this text through several drafts with great efficiency and good humour. Clare Grist and Christopher Glennie at Simon and Schuster have been unfailingly helpful. William Lana and Jarrod Wiener have been of great assistance at the proof stage.

The ideas contained in this book, and the ways in which these ideas are presented, have been tried out on successive generations of MA students at the University of Kent. Bearing in mind that any errors that remain are largely their fault, and in order that future generations at Kent will have someone to blame other than me, I dedicate this book to them.

Chapter 1

Introduction: Theory and International Relations

It ought to be the case that the likely content of a book is signalled by its title, and in at least some of the social sciences this would indeed be the case for a work with the word 'theory' prominently displayed. In the case, for example, of economics, a work bearing the title 'economic theory' would unambiguously convey to any competent member of the profession the general nature of what was to follow; questions would remain concerning the orientation of the author – neo-classical or neo-Keynesian? – but what constitutes theory as such is no longer contestable within mainstream economics. Whether this degree of intellectual consensus is or is not desirable is a matter of opinion but what cannot be denied is that it does make easier the author's task: the use of a few generally understood codewords conveys to all likely readers the nature of what is to come, and the writer can concentrate his or her energies on the real task in hand.

Unfortunately, the current state of development of thinking in international relations makes it impossible to take this sort of short cut. There are virtually no neutral descriptive terms which can be employed to signal the content of a work, and each writer is more or less obliged to re-invent the subject from scratch or to risk serious misunderstanding. This is perhaps particularly the case when it comes to the theory of international relations, because theory is a term which is used in international relations with a bewildering number of different meanings. What is at stake here is not so much different orientations towards the subject matter of international relations – although there are, of course, equivalents within international relations of the neo-classical/neo-Keynesian divide in economics – but rather different senses of what the term theory might mean and different expectations about what a book on theory might contain.

A primary distinction here might usefully be made between 'empirical' and 'normative' theory – although, as will be suggested below, the term 'normative' is in many ways unsatisfactory. Since this is not a

1

work of empirical international relations theory it may be helpful first of all to say something briefly about this category before moving on to the more relevant contests over the meaning of normative theory.

Empirical international relations theory is here understood as encompassing both the attempt to create sets of interconnected law-like statements about international relations and the creation of intellectual frameworks within which such sets of statements can be situated – frameworks such as the 'paradigms' of realism, pluralism and structuralism identified by, *inter alia*, Michael Banks, or the 'perspectives' made famous in the best and most useful collection of readings in the field edited by Richard Little and Michael Smith.[1] In principle, at least, empirical theory is descriptive, explanatory and predictive. It attempts to provide an accurate account of how the world works. It is 'positivist' in aspiration, albeit with the proviso that to aspire to the status of the natural sciences in the late twentieth century involves taking seriously the burgeoning literature of the philosophy of science which in turn entails a refusal of the idea that there can be simply one satisfactory description of reality – hence the seriousness with which modern works of empirical international relations theory take the idea of perspectives or paradigms.[2] However, while accepting that all knowledge is theory-based, that theory-free observation is not possible, the empirical theorist is still concerned to provide as accurate an account of how things really are as the current wisdom of the philosophy of sciences warrants.

Since for the most part the rest of this book will not be concerned with empirical international relations theory it ought to be made clear from the outset that this avoidance is not based on any principled objection to such studies or, indeed, to the project of empirical theory as such. On the contrary, it will at times be argued that some so-called normative questions ought more accurately to be seen as empirical; to take one example examined in depth below, the issue of the rights and duties of rich and poor countries in their relations with one another cannot be sensibly discussed without bringing into play a considerable volume of empirical theory; equally, the older but still open question of the propensity to war of liberal states is, in principle, something that can be examined by empirical means even if, again as will be argued below, to date no satisfactory empirical test has been suggested.[3] Further examples would be redundant: the point is that although this is a work which focusses on normative theory, there is no suggestion here that this is the only respectable focus for an international relations scholar, nor that there is anything fundamentally wrong with an empirical approach, nor that for some ineffable reason international relations are peculiarly resistant to empirical theory. The only reason it is worth making this point is that it is clear that some 'normative' theorists do hold some or all of these positions, seeing their kind of theory as the only kind of theory. This is not a position that will receive any support from what follows.

This is, then, a work of 'normative' theory and it is now time to take the scare-quotes away from the term 'normative'. By normative international relations theory is meant that body of work which addresses the moral dimension of international relations and the wider questions of meaning and interpretation generated by the discipline. At its most basic it addresses the ethical nature of the relations between communities/states, whether in the context of the old agenda, which focussed on violence and war, or the new(er) agenda, which mixes these traditional concerns with the modern demand for international distributive justice.

To call this kind of theory 'normative' is to risk misleading the reader, because of the connotations of the term. The usual meanings of normative revolve around the idea of standard setting and prescription, and the danger is that two different kinds of intellectual activity will be confused: the setting of standards, and the study of how (and what and by whom) standards are set. Part at least of the resistance to normative theory emerges out of this confusion, and in particular out of the belief that normative theorists claim to possess some special knowledge which enables them to solve the difficult moral dilemmas of the day. Clearly, no such claim could be sustained: in so far as normative theorists do actually try to prescribe norms, it can only be by virtue of their role as citizens who happen to have thought about a particularly difficult issue for longer than most of their fellows, and who have at their disposal knowledge of the ways in which similar problems have been thought about in the past – none of which amounts to any kind of right to prescribe.

A more serious problem with the term 'normative' theory is that it implies the existence of 'non-normative' theory. Is it, in fact, possible to have theory that is not in some sense concerned with the business of standard setting and norm creating? Rhetoric aside, yes, it is possible to have that kind of theory – but a very great deal of what is traded in international relations as non-normative theory is steeped in normative assumptions.[4] Such recent mainstream concoctions as the 'theory of hegemonic stability' or the neo-realist account of the balance of power, or Wallerstein's 'World-systems' approach are clearly grounded in normative positions, whether acknowledged or not.[5] The danger is that by using the term normative theory to refer to a limited range of work, the non-normative nature of other writing will be tacitly, and wrongly, conceded.

However, all this is rather too late. Possibly, 'interpretive' theory would be better, but normative is a term that is so widely used now to describe the broad area in question that it is futile to try to resist – although the language of the rest of this work will be specifically oriented towards undermining any idea that normative theory is some kind of cordoned-off area separate from the rest of the discipline of international relations. But for the moment a more substantial question – indeed, the most substantial question posed by this book – comes into focus. Given the aspiration to create normative theory, what kind of questions will be examined and what sources will be expected to assist with the answers to these questions? This is highly controversial, because it applies to the nature of international relations as an academic discipline. Is there a worthwhile, free-standing body of 'international theory' from which both appropriate questions and convincing answers can be drawn, or should 'international relations theory' be seen as simply one dimension of a wider project of political and social theory, drawing both its coherence and its legitimacy from this context? The rest of this book depends on the latter of these two positions, and most of the rest of the introduction is devoted to explaining this choice and the reasons for rejecting 'international theory'.

ON INTERNATIONAL THEORY

The grammatically dubious but undeniably useful term international theory seems to have been coined by the British scholar Martin Wight and, in this instance at least, it makes sense to focus the argument on British international relations.[6] Until the revival which is the subject of this book, North American international relations theory tended towards the empirical, and the project of normative international theory has been predominantly British, in striking contrast to other areas of the discipline. In any event, Wight was one of the foremost intellectual figures of the 'English School' of international theorists, and the writer who did most to promote the idea of international theory.[7] In the late 1950s Wight was a leading figure in the British Committee on the Theory of International Politics, to use the title awarded by the Rockefeller Foundation to a group of philosophers, historians and diplomats who met regularly to explore international theory. The first paper presented to this group came from Wight, and was subsequently published as the lead essay in the single most influential collection to be produced in Britain on international theory, the Butterfield and Wight edited *Diplomatic Investigations*.[8] In spite of its deliberately provocative title – 'Why is there no international theory?' – this paper remains the best account of what international theory as a free-standing intellectual exercise might look like, and the reasons why Wight's arguments are unsatisfactory are of considerable importance to the shape of the rest of this book.

Wight's basic point is easily conveyed. He begins by defining international theory as 'a tradition of speculation about relations between states' and immediately denies the existence of 'classical' texts within this tradition.[9] On the one hand, international lawyers, peace theorists, Machiavellians and diplomats have contributed works of international theory which have not attained the status of classics; on the other hand, the great political philosophers – Wight instances, *inter alia*, Hume, Rousseau, Burke and Mill – have written works on international theory but only at the margins of their interests. Only in the case of Machiavelli is it possible to doubt that a first-rate thinker was not primarily a writer on domestic politics. Wight concludes this part of his thesis dismissively – 'I believe it can be argued that international theory is marked, not only by paucity but also by intellectual and moral poverty.'

Why so? Because of the 'intellectual prejudice' imposed by the sovereign state, and because of 'the belief in progress'. The former – state centricity, to use a word Wight would have hated – emerges from the collapse of medieval feudalism. In a period in which the loyalties of human beings both narrowed (from the universal church) and widened (from the local liege-lord), the sovereign state came to be the focus of Western politics and political thought, to the detriment of international theory.[10] More interesting is Wight's point about the role of progress in Western thought. Plausibly, Wight sees much of Western political thought as dominated by this notion; his point is that international politics is, by its very nature, not susceptible to a progressivist interpretation.

> International politics is the realm of recurrence and repetition; it is the field in which action is most regularly necessitous . . . [international] theory that remains true to diplomatic experience will be at a discount in an age when the belief in progress is prevalent.[11]

He concludes by suggesting a kind of 'disharmony between international theory and diplomatic practice, a kind of recalcitrance of international politics to being theorised about'.[12] He suggests that to find the equivalent of political theory in international relations it is necessary to go to international history, and tentatively puts forward the equation, politics is to international politics as political theory is to historical interpretation.

Wight's denial of international theory has not been taken seriously by his followers, nor was it intended to be, but the key feature of his definition of the field remains highly influential and can be seen to be still at work in later studies by the English school. This feature is the identification of international theory as the potential twin of political theory. Political theory is speculation about the state ('its traditional meaning from Plato onward' (p. 11)); international theory, if it existed, would be speculation about relations between states – the two discourses run in parallel, or would do if the latter were not so impoverished. Instead there is asymmetry: on the one hand, a rich and powerful tradition of great works by great thinkers, on the other, a collection of essentially second-rate texts always on the verge of sliding away from theory into historical interpretation. The task of the international theorist is to make the best of this bad job, doing what he or she can to make sense of the limited materials to hand.

It should be said that international theorists have, indeed, made the best of what, from their perspective, can only be a bad job. Wight's own studies of systems of states and Western values in international relations, Hedley Bull's work on *The Anarchical Society* and a host of other individual and collective studies bear witness to the fact that even within the limitations that international theorists impose upon themselves serious and valuable work can be produced.[13] The question is whether these limits are sensible. The proposition here is that they are not. On the contrary, it will be argued that there is a rich and powerful body of work on the theory of international relations upon which theorists can draw both in order to refine thought on well-established problems and in order to find appropriate categories for handling new problems. The claim here is not that there is some variant of international theory overlooked by Wight and his followers but in fact capable of filling the space he declared vacant alongside political theory. The point is more fundamental: the theory of international relations is not a long-lost, newly invigorated twin of political theory but an integral part of the latter discourse. Wight's mistake was not to misunderstand international theory but to mischaracterise *political* theory.

These are strong claims; the rest of this book amounts to a positive elaboration of the positions sketched above and later in this introduction the shape of this elaboration will be outlined. But before moving to this it is necessary to examine briefly how and, more to the point, why Wight – and by extension his followers – defined the field in the constrictive way that they did. The 'how' is easy to see. Virtually the opening words of Wight's essay define political theory as speculation about the *state*, which later in the text becomes the *sovereign* state. If this really is what political theory is about then clearly it makes sense to think of a second realm of discourse running parallel with political theory dealing with speculation about relations between states. It also seems quite likely that this second realm will indeed be impoverished by comparison with the first, given the unique position of the sovereign state in Wight's thought. The existence and lowly status of 'international theory' follows more or less automatically from Wight's initial identification of the terrain of political theory, an identification he believed to be so obvious as to require no justification or explanation.

The point is, of course, that far from being self-explanatory and requiring no justification, Wight's definition of political theory is highly contentious – indeed, his description of this definition as its 'traditional meaning from Plato onwards' is particularly bizarre since one of the things we know for sure about Plato is that he had no experience of a 'state', much less a 'sovereign' state. This is not primarily a semantic point. Suppose, for the sake of argument, a definition of political theory that Plato would have understood were to be adopted – political theory as the study of the search for justice in society, say. The whole structure of the relationship between political theory and international theory would be transformed. On this definition there would be no need to specify in advance a distinction between international and domestic political theory; whether such a distinction was required, and of what kind, would depend on the ways in which different thinkers at different times set up the question of justice. Most of the classical Greeks seem to have seen justice as a feature of the *polis* rather than of relations 'outside the walls', but the Stoics looked to the universal city of all men.[14] Thomistic and other Christian thought of the Middle Ages certainly saw the relations between communities as governed by justice, if not with the same effect as within the community.[15] Enlightenment thinkers such as Kant redefined the notion of justice again and produced a different internal/external split, while modern theorists of distributive justice debate at length the international implications of their subject.[16] A plausible generalisation might be that over time the scope of 'justice' has steadily widened, coming more and more to incorporate international as well as domestic concerns, but in any event the key point is that a focus on justice – as opposed to the state – produces a very different, and richer, account of international theory. Moreover, even in those periods when the dominant political discourses have nothing to say about the international dimension of justice, this silence does not indicate an absence of international theory; the silence *is* the international theory of that time and place.

To recapitulate: Wight sets up political theory in such a way that international theory is inevitably a marginalised twin discourse, doomed to insignificance. But international relations theory is not something separate from, running in tandem with, political theory: it *is* political theory, seen from a particular angle or through a particular filter. How Wight misdirects himself is relatively clear. A better question is, Why? Since Wight was an international theorist of great distinction, he cannot have wanted to downplay the significance of his own project, which, even discounting the intention to provoke, is what he achieved by his work. The only way to understand the direction of his thought, and the reason why so many others moved in similar ways, whether influenced by him or not, is to situate this thought in time. It can then be seen that the sort of limits accepted by Wight were characteristic of the age: it can also be seen that modern work which transcends these limits is also characteristic of *its* age.

THE CHANGING CONTEXT OF NORMATIVE INTERNATIONAL RELATIONS THEORY

A later chapter of this book is given over to an account of the changes in international relations and social philosophy which, taken together, have made this century unfallow ground for normative international relations theory, but a short preview here of some of the arguments as they pertain to Wight's period – which was, of course, also the period in which the modern discipline of international relations came of age – may be useful. Certainly, it is clear that the intellectual climate of the 1950s and 1960s was particularly unaccommodating to virtually all variants of political philosophy including normative international relations theory.

This period was the time of the 'end of ideology' – the notion, proposed, with more irony than he is usually given credit for, by Daniel Bell, that the big questions of politics had proved obsolescent, suitable only to be replaced by the mundane tasks of piecemeal social engineering. It was a period in which the dominant school of Anglo-American philosophy was analytical and linguistic, devoted to ever more detailed investigation of the meaning of words and sentences. The prevailing philosophy in the social sciences – taken from economics but influential everywhere – drew a sharp distinction between positive and normative analysis, in effect eliminating the latter.[17] Normative concerns were translated into 'value-judgements'; it was deemed to be possible to study the effect of value-judgements on behaviour and action but impossible to subject their contents to rational analysis. Value-judgements were treated as data, an approach consistent with the dominant theories of ethics – emotivism and prescriptivism – which, in essence, treated morals as no more than expressions of preference.[18]

In this context an impoverished political philosophy is more or less unavoidable; even the most famous collection of papers of the period begins with the lament that 'political philosophy is dead'.[19] The prospects of international political philosophy are even less appealing. In the minds of many intellectual leaders of the era the preservation of a free political system required a commitment to a variety of individualism which was, correctly, taken to be opposed to nationalism and other doctrines that took seriously the loyalties that people, in fact, seem to show towards 'their' state. The history of the twentieth century showed the evils of nationalism – a phenomenon virtually always in this period associated with authoritarian or totalitarian forms of government. The idea of a study that would take seriously·the philosphical bases of those factors that constitute communities and divide them one from another ran contrary to the spirit of the age.

Political studies were for the most part either (in Europe and Britain) institution-oriented or (in the United States) behaviouralist. Political theory meant the study of a canon of 'classics' from Plato to Mill – but usually not including Kant and Hegel in any depth, which perhaps explains Wight's bizarre identification of the nazis and communists as the 'children' of these two writers.[20] Clearly, the resources available to an international theorist of this period would be highly limited. Wight displayed an aristocratic disdain for the new science of politics. His follower, Bull, was ready and willing to engage the scientistic enemy, and did so in a famous paper, 'International theory: the case for a classical approach', which, notoriously, was rather more effective as the case *against* behaviouralism than as a case *for* anything.[21] The intellectual resources of the period simply were not oriented in such a way that normative international theory would be easy to construct.

The situation today is very different. A striking revival of political philosophy has taken place, and on terms that are highly favourable to a political theory oriented towards international relations. In part, these changes were simply a reflection of the working through of the limits necessarily entailed by the stunted conception of social enquiry dominant in the 1950s and early 1960s. The so-called 'postbehavioural' revolution is a case in point – the sudden discovery by American social scientists that they had been ignoring the real problems of American society did not lead to much work of substance but it did serve the purpose of relegitimising the study of normative questions.[22] But the developments of most significance for normative international relations theory came from two other directions, one very much 'real-world' and the other theoretical in the grand sense of the term.

The real-world events were wars – most particularly Vietnam but also, of greater salience than its scale alone would suggest, the Arab-Israeli 'Six Days War' of 1967. In the case of Vietnam disillusionment with the use made of American power in South-East Asia led to a striking growth of philosophical interest in the legitimate use of force by states. Very old topics in the laws of war came to be discussed in new journals (such as *Philosophy and Public Affairs*) and by scholars who, in previous times, would have been most unlikely to have situated themselves within this particular branch of ethics. Much of the impetus of this work was, predictably, hostile to the American effort in Vietnam, and it is in this context that the Six Days War plays an important role. A significant number of anti-Vietnam War philosophers were supporters of Israel, and thus obliged to acknowledge that war could, in certain circumstances, be justly fought. Their work was dedicated not simply to condemnation of the United States but to exploring their own concerns about Israel – the best book produced out of this experience, Walzer's *Just and Unjust Wars*, perfectly exemplifies this dual focus.[23]

The point about this new work is not that it was strikingly original – which it was not – but that it was grounded in the belief that moral reasoning was possible, that values are not simply statements of preference and that ethics can be 'practical' – that what is important is not the epistemological status of ethical statements, but the practical question of what ought to be done in particular concrete circumstances. All this was in stark contrast to the previous consensus. Parallel with this movement was one less event-driven but of greater long-term salience, the return of Grand Theory to political philosophy. This was most clearly signalled by the publication of Rawls' *A Theory of Justice* in 1971 – a book which revived not simply an old theme (the Social Contract) but a traditional mode of presentation, as a tightly reasoned treatise extending over six hundred pages.[24] The impact of this book has been immense, not so much through the power of its specific arguments, which have been heavily criticised, but through the power of its example, and the force of its central position. The proposition that social arrangements are unjust unless the inequalities they inevitably involve can be rationally defended is now widely accepted in a way that simply would not have been the case a generation ago.

A Theory of Justice argues for a limited notion of international justice, defending a strong distinction between inter- and intra-societal relations, but this is a feature of his work that has been criticised by writers such as Barry and Beitz, who have argued that international inequalities are every bit as much in need of justification as domestic inequalities. Such thinking in the 1970s and 1980s ran in parallel with the demand for a New International Economic Order (NIEO) and along with revived utilitarian and Kantian reasoning offered by, *inter alia*, Singer, Hardin and O'Neill has turned international distributive justice into one of the central concerns of modern normative international relations theory. The old issue of the membership of international society – states, individuals or both – has given way to a concrete question: what obligations do rich states/societies/people have towards poor states/societies/people?[25]

These changes, taken together, have created a very different climate for normative international theory from that prevailing in the first half of the postwar era. The work of the philosophers indicated above and of a number of international relations theorists such as Beitz, Frost, Nardin, Kratochwil, Linklater and Vincent has created a new international relations theory, in contact with, but intellectually different from, the older schools of 'international theory' in Britain and the United States.[26] The points of contact are clearly present.[27] The notion of a 'society of states' or 'international society' is at the heart of international theory and receives its most impressive defence in Bull's *The Anarchical Society: A study of order in world politics* and the sort of questions posed by the use of the term 'society' in this context remain at the head of the agenda of the new normative international relations theory. The difference is that the new agenda is less likely to look to the work of classical international lawyers or the notion of balance of power in order to flesh out the meaning of 'society'. Instead, the point of reference is more likely to be political philosophers such as Kant or Hegel, or political issues such as starvation in Ethiopia or mass murder in northern Iraq. Modern normative international theory claims a richer intellectual inheritance than does international theory, and, rather more diffidently, a less scholastic, Eurocentric focus of concern.

THE PURPOSE AND STRUCTURE OF THIS BOOK

The primary purpose of this work is to describe, annotate and evaluate the main debates generated by the new normative theory of international relations, examining a reasonable selection of the best work produced in recent years. Comprehensiveness is not a goal – this would require a different kind of book on a different scale – but the intention is that the reader should have a clear picture of the scope of the field by the end of the book. The heart of the book consists of a number of chapters, described in more detail below, which examine such topics as the moral status of state autonomy, the ethics of interstate violence and the requirments of global justice. However, before this heartland can be reached some quite extensive preparations have to be undergone, and once the heartland has been delineated some of its newest and most radical critics need to be heard: the heartland is, therefore, part II of the work, part I consisting of the necessary preparations, and the (one-chapter) part III of the new critics.

The extensive preparations are needed because a great many modern writers on international relations theory are not using concepts and theories drawn from the intellectual inheritance of international relations scholars. Their work instead grows out of – sometimes in reaction to – the main lines of moral philosophy, social philosophy and ethics as they have developed over the last hundred years, in turn on the basis of the broad theories of the previous century. In order to extract full value from writers such as Walzer and Nagel, Beitz and Nardin, Barry and Sandel, or Habermas and Rorty it is necessary to have rather more of a background in these areas than is common amongst students of international relations. The aim of part I of this work is to provide that background in sufficient depth to make sense of the authors involved, but without providing more detail than is strictly necessary.

The number of positions that have to be handled here is quite considerable, and to simplify the task the material is largely gathered under two headings: 'cosmopolitanism' and 'communitarianism'. These terms are not unproblematic but they are widely used in the modern literature and therefore it makes sense to establish the reference back. They are terms which have many points of contact with moral and social philosophy taken in general, unlike such distictively international relations categories as 'realism' or 'pluralism'. The cosmopolitan/communitarian divide relates directly to the most central question of any normative international relations theory, namely the moral value to be credited to particularistic political collectivities as against humanity as a whole or the claims of individual human beings. Communitarian thought either denies that there is an opposition here, or is prepared explicitly to assign central value to the community; cosmopolitan thought refuses this central status to the community, placing the ultimate source of moral value elsewhere. Some cosmopolitan thinkers believe that there ought to be one political community coextensive with mankind, but the cosmopolitan position is perfectly compatible with the pragmatic acceptance of a world of divided jurisdictions, and in this work the term 'cosmopolitan' is *never* used to refer exlusively to adherents of a world-government position.

Cosmopolitan is a word with classical Greek roots, and communities have existed throughout history; there is, therefore, no natural recent starting point for an examination of thought on these themes. Here the starting point is taken to be Enlightenment and post-Enlightenment thought, with Kant and Hegel as central figures, which entails passing over many figures taken as central by 'international theory' – Machiavelli, Hobbes, Grotius, Pufendorf and Vattel. This involves some loss, especially in the case of the first two names, but in so far as these writers retain influence on modern thinking it is by virtue of their impact on later thinkers whose work will be treated at some length. As far as the lawyers are concerned, there are, in any event, a number of good studies available – Linklater, in particular, provides an excellent account of these 'sorry comforters', as Kant characterised them.[28]

At the other end of the heartland of modern normative international relations theory can be found the work of postmodernists and critical theorists. These writers have set their sights on neo-realist theories of international relations and have not been primarily concerned to engage with normative theorists. However, the scope of their critique is such that it has implications throughout the field, and no work on international relations theory can safely disregard the thought that is emerging from this direction. Hence the brief part III of this work is devoted to these writings.

Before moving to a brief chapter-by-chapter outline, this may be the place to record omissions and self-imposed limits. There is no extended discussion of human rights taken as a separate subject: there are many excellent studies of this subject and, in any event, the issues it raises permeate the work as a whole.[29] This is a work which emerges out of Western political thought, and although this orientation is subjected to critique in part III the charge of ethnocentrism remains unanswered. The only answer that can be given, with all due humility and acknowledgement of potential ignorance, is that no alternative body of non-Western thought appears to come close to the level of sophistication exemplified by the authors considered in this book. This ought not to be surprising – for better or worse, the modern world has been created by Western Europeans and their offspring, and thinkers of this part of the world have a head start for the task of understanding their creation. To deny this may be 'politically correct' but, for the time being, flies in the face of history. A more serious

omission is that of the newly burgeoning body of feminist international relations theory. Given the extent to which modern political
theory has been transformed by gender studies it is predictable that
something similar will happen to international relations theory.
However, this transformation lies in the future, and, rather than make
the attempt to summarise and condense the diverse materials currently
available, this study will make only the occasional reference to
feminist work.[30]

CHAPTER OUTLINES

Chapter 2, the first of part I, examines cosmopolitan thought. It
locates the origin of modern cosmopolitanism in the Enlightenment,
and gives the most extended treatment to the thought of Kant. Kant is
taken to be the first great thinker to realise the need for a full
characterisation of political philosophy as not simply concerning the
relations of human beings to their communities but as equally
concerned with relations between these communities and between
individuals and humanity taken as a whole. Moreover, this complete-
ness is situated within the context of his wider philosophy and is
comprehensible only in this context. Kant is the greatest of all theorists
of international relations, not on the strength of *Perpetual Peace* but
because of the role of international relations in his work taken as a
whole. Other variants of cosmopolitan thought – utilitarianism and
Marxism – are examined at the end of this chapter.

Chapter 3 examines the communitarian alternative to cosmopolitanism. Following a brief literary excursion to show why this notion
seems to present problems to Anglo-American thinkers, the discussion
focuses on reactions to Enlightenment universalism. After a cursory
look at Rousseau and the German Romantics, the main body of the
chapter is devoted to an exposition of Hegelian thinking, Hegel and
the English Idealists being taken to offer the most complete account
of the world from a communitarian position, and the best available defence of the moral worth of the autonomous sovereign state.
The remainder of the chapter considers briefly the relationship between communitarianism and nationalism as it emerged in the
nineteenth century, in both its liberal, Millian and illiberal, Treitsch-
kean versions.

In the (briefer) fourth and final chapter of part I the story is told of
how the cosmopolitan and communitarian thought set out in chapters
2 and 3 came to be pushed to one side in the twentieth century, the
victim of two trends. In moral philosophy the linguistic and analytical

'turn' of the first half of the twentieth century shifted attention towards meta-ethics and away from the application of moral reasoning to practical ethical issues such as those posed by international relations. At the same time, in reaction to the slaughter of the war of 1914–18 a new discipline of international relations was set up with the ambition of developing its own theories and concepts and with a sweeping critique of the thought of the past. The final section of the chapter examines the way in which these trends have been partially reversed.

Part II begins with an introduction (chapter 5) which overviews the most central of all issues addressed by normative international relations theory, the question of the moral value to be assigned to state autonomy. Recapitulating the debate of chapters 2 and 3, and linking this to modern general studies of the topic, both by political philosophers and by international relations theorists, the role of this chapter is to emphasise the links between parts I and II and to prepare the way for the more detailed, issue-oriented work examined in the next two chapters by highlighting the general concerns which underlie these issues.

Chapter 6 is devoted to recent work on the ethics of interstate violence. Modern uses of just-war doctrine are examined. Employing terminology from Walzer's *Just and Unjust Wars*, *jus ad bellum* and *jus in bello* are reconceptualised in terms of the 'Legalist Paradigm' and the 'War Convention', and recent studies discussed under these headings. The literature generated by the Vietnam War remains central here and 'deontological' and 'consequentialist' thinking on the limits of action in warfare are examined. At the end of the chapter consideration is given to the particular problems posed by nuclear and other weapons of mass destruction and by deterrence strategies. One of the conclusions of this chapter will be that although modern work on the ethics of violence has clarified many issues, little that is actually new has emerged.

This is in contrast to the theories of justice examined in chapter 7, the longest of the book. After briefly presenting empirical evidence on the inequality that exists in the world, and after outlining some of the problems involved in doing anything about this inequality, the rest of the chapter is devoted to studies examining the obligations that the rich of the world have towards the poor. Utilitarian and neo-Kantian thought is given some attention but the main body of the chapter is given over to the debate on global distributive justice set off by Rawls' *A Theory of Justice*. After examining Rawls' reasons for developing two theories of justice with that between societies operating at a largely procedural level, the arguments of, *inter alia*, Beitz, Barry and Sandel will be considered, the tentative conclusion being that Barry's approach seems most likely to offer a way of linking domestic and international approaches to justice without either ignoring or over-stating the differences between these two dimensions.

Part III consists of one chapter, chapter 8, which is given over to an examination of critical and postmodern theories of international relations. These are approaches which self-consciously distance themselves from previous modes of thought, and a full appreciation of what they have to say requires the development of a wholly new orientation towards the meaning (or lack of meaning) of such central notions of Western thought as 'truth' and 'representation'. Such a reorientation is hardly possible on the basis of this chapter, the aim of which is simply to give a sense of what this writing is about along with a tentative judgement as to which areas of postmodern/critical thought are likely to prove to be fruitful in the future. The argument goes somewhat against 'deconstruction' but in favour of Foucauldian genealogy and the 'dialogism' of Bakhtin and his followers.

The ninth and final chapter is a brief conclusion, recalling the themes with which this study began, drawing attention to the ways in which these initial themes have, and have not, proved valuable guides to the later work, and, tentatively, looking to the future of interna-tional relations theory.

How to Read this Book

The aim of this book is to tell a coherent story and there is, thus, something to be said in favour of starting at the beginning and working through to the end. However, life is short, and, in any event, social-science scholars at all levels appear to have build-in resistance to the disciplines of the narrative, so it may be only realistic to provide a few shortcuts, however much one may hope that readers will not (over)use them.

Some readers of this book may be, in the first instance, political theorists/philosophers rather than students of international relations, and such readers may find that the discussion of Kant and Hegel in part I is rather more than they need – or alternatively rather less, not reaching a level of sophistication that would tell them anything they did not already know. Such readers may safely skip these chapters. Chapter 4 is less easy to work round since it interweaves a story about moral philosophy as a pursuit with a story about the claims of international relations to disciplinary status, and few will be familiar with both stories. For the political philosopher parts II and III will be of greatest interest. Chapter 5 is more or less essential, but 6 and 7 stand separately, and someone primarily interested in theories of justice could move past chapter 6 without great loss. Chapter 8 on postmodernism presupposes familiarity with the modernist writings of parts I and II.

Students and scholars of international relations are less likely than philosophers to be aware of the background to the material covered in part II and it is for such readers that the accounts of Kant and Hegel are particularly designed. These chapters could be skipped, but the later chapters will work much better if the reader is familiar with the basic lines of argument set out in chapters 2 and 3. For international relations scholars chapter 4 is essential because its discussion of twentieth-century moral philosophy introduces and defines a number of technical terms which will be freely employed in parts II and III and which will cause confusion if their meaning is not established early in the day. Again, chapter 5 is important for the rest of part II, but chapters 6 and 7 stand independently of each other. Once again, chapter 8 presupposes familiarity with the rest of the book.

NOTES

1. M. Banks, 'The inter-paradigm debate', in M. Light and A.J.R. Groom (eds) *International Relations: A handbook of current theory* (Frances Pinter, London, 1985). R. Little and M. Smith (eds) *Perspectives on World Politics*, 2nd edn (Routledge, London, 1991).
2. For an overview of the philosophy of science literature oriented towards international relations see M. Nicholson 'Methodology' in Light and Groom, *op cit*.
3. See, respectively, chapters 7 and 2 below.
4. The purist view that *all* theory is normative can be defended, but such a strong claim is unnecessarily controversial.
5. See R.O. Keohane, *International Institutions and State Power* (Westview Press, Boulder, Colo., 1989); K. Waltz, *Theory of International Politics* (Addison-Wesley, Reading, Mass., 1979): I. Wallerstein, *The Politics of the World Economy* (Cambridge University Press, Cambridge, 1984).
6. Useful general studies of Wight's work include B. Porter 'Patterns of thought and practice in Martin Wight's "International Theory" ' in M. Donelan (ed.) *The Reason of States: A study in international political theory* (Allen and Unwin, London, 1978), and H. Bull 'Martin Wight and the theory of international relations', *British Journal of International Studies*, vol. 2, no. 2 (1976). Wight's major works are being posthumously published, in some cases from lectures and other notes: see *Power Politics*, 2nd edn (Leicester University Press/RIIA, Leicester, 1978), *Systems of States*, ed. H. Bull (Leicester University Press/London School of Econ-

omics, Leicester, 1977). His influential lectures on 'international theory' will soon appear, edited by B. Porter.

7. On the English School see S. Grader, 'The English school of international relations: evidence and evaluation', *Review of International Studies*, vol. 14, no.1 (1988) and the reply from P. Wilson, 'The English school of international relations: a reply to Sheila Grader', *Review of International Studies*, vol. 15, no.1 (1989).

8. H. Butterfield and M. Wight (eds) *Diplomatic Investigations: Essays in the theory of international politics* (Allen and Unwin, London, 1966).

9. 'Why is there no international theory?', p. 17.

10. This processs is described in Wight, *Power Politics*, Ch. 1.

11. 'Why is there no international theory?', p. 26.

12. *ibid.*, p. 33.

13. *The Anarchical Society: A study of order in world politics* (Macmillan, London, 1977). Of the great many other texts that might be referred to here, special attention should be paid to the collections produced by the nearest successor group to the British Committee of the 1950s, the London School of Economics based Seminar in International Political Theory; see Donelan, *op. cit.*, J. Mayall (ed.) *The Community of States* (Allen and Unwin, London, 1982), and C. Navari (ed.) *The Condition of States* (Open University Press, London, 1991).

14. David Sylvan's draft paper for the International Political Science Association Fifteenth World Congress in Buenos Aires 1991, 'Insides, outsides, and walls in classical Greece' suggests that his forthcoming book on the genealogy of sovereignty and trade will shape future thinking about Greek 'international' thought.

15. For a brief introduction to these writers see F. Parkinson *The Philosophy of International Relations* (Sage, Beverly Hills, Calif., 1977).

16. See chapters 2 and 7 below.

17. M. Friedman, 'The methodology of positive economics', *Essays in Positive Economics* (Chicago University Press, Chicago, 1953) was an influential text here.

18. The issues raised in this paragraph are dealt with at greater length in chapter 4 below.

19. See P. Laslett, Introduction, p. vii, to Laslett (ed.) *Philosophy, Politics and Society*, 1st Series (Blackwell, Oxford, 1956). These fallow years for political philosophy are well described in B. Barry, 'The strange death of political philosophy' in *Democracy, Power and Justice: Essays in political theory* (Clarendon Press, Oxford, 1989), and in R. Plant, *Modern Political Thought* (Blackwell, Oxford, 1991).

20. Wight 'Why is there no international theory?' p. 28.

21. A collection containing Bull's paper and replies is K. Knorr and J.N. Rosenau (eds) *Contending Approaches to International Politics* (Princeton University Press, Princeton, N.J., 1969). The best reply to Bull is not included in this collection, see M. Banks, 'Two meanings of theory in the study of international relations', *Yearbook of World Affairs* (1966).

22. The text usually taken to mark the emergence of postbehaviouralism is D. Easton, 'The new revolution in political science', *American Political Science Review*, vol. 63, no. 4 (1969).
23. Penguin, Harmondworth, 1980.
24. Oxford University Press, Oxford, 1971.
25. The issues raised in this paragraph and the authors named will be discussed in chapter 7 below.
26. C. R. Beitz, *Political Theory and International Relations* (Princeton University Press, Princeton, N.J., 1979); M. Frost, *Towards a Normative Theory of International Relations* (Cambridge University Press, Cambridge, 1986); T. Nardin, *Law, Morality and the Relations of States* (Princeton University Press, Princeton, N.J., 1983): F.V. Kratochwil, *Rules, Norms and Decisions* (Cambridge University Press, Cambridge, 1989): A. Linklater *Men and Citizens in the Theory of International Relations* (Macmillan, London, 1982; 2nd edn 1990); R.J. Vincent *Human Rights and International Relations* (Cambridge University Press, Cambridge, 1986). This is, of course, intended as an illustrative list only.
27. The special issue of *Millennium: Journal of International Studies*, 'Philosophical traditions in international relations', to some extent bridges the two approaches, but with an emphasis on the new normative international relations theory, see vol. 17, no. 2 (1988).
28. Linklater, *op. cit.* chs 4 and 5.
29. Vincent, *op. cit.*, is a key reference here.
30. The pioneering special issue 'Women and international relations', *Millennium: Journal of International Studies*, vol. 17, no. 3 (1988) gives some indication of what is to come; see also J. B. Elshtain *Women and War* (Harvester Wheatsheaf, Hemel Hempstead, 1987) and C. Enloe, *Bananas, Beaches and Bases: Making feminist sense of international politics* (Pandora, London, 1989).

Part I

Cosmopolitan and Communitarian International Relations Theory

Chapter 2

Cosmopolitan Theory

INTRODUCTION

In classical Greece the *polis* was at the centre of the lives of its citizens.[1]
The word is only weakly translated by terms such as 'city' or 'city-
state'; the *polis* was at the centre of the religious life of its members as
well as their social and political lives. Indeed, even this wide formulation is in a way misleading in so far as it separates the *polis* from its
inhabitants: this was not the Greek way – when writing of the action of
a city, Greek authors generally employed the collective term for its
citizens; thus, it is almost always 'the Athenians' who act rather than
'Athens'. When Aristotle refers to man as a 'political animal', the
frame of reference is not that of politics in the modern sense of the
term; Aristotle means that man is designed to live in society, in the
city, and those who live outside the city are either beasts or gods.[2]
Because of the importance of the *polis*, the collapse of the world of
independent cities after the Macedonian victory at the Battle of
Chaeronea (338 BC) amounted to a moral as well as a political crisis,
and saw the rise of new religious attitudes which attempted to make
sense of life in circumstances where the previous source of meaning
was no longer available.

The most important of these new religious attitudes – and it was a
'religious attitude' rather than a 'religion' in the modern sense of the
term – was Stoicism. The Stoics understood morals and the good life in
the context of their views on the nature of the universe (*cosmos*);
human nature is part of cosmic nature and governed by the divine law
of nature. The differences between men in different cities – crucial to
the old order – are of no account: 'There is one divine universe, one
rational human nature, and therefore one appropriate attitude to all
men. The Stoic is a citizen of the *cosmos* not of the *polis*.'[3] The desired
state of acceptance *vis-à-vis* the divine and natural law is available to
Emperors or slaves; being a free citizen of a *polis* is no longer an
essential precondition for a morally meaningful life – instead, the
attitude to be cultivated is that of a citizen of the one universal city.
One must be a 'cosmopolitan'.

The thinkers of the Enlightenment were steeped in the classics and employed many Greek and Roman terms in their own writings; the term 'cosmopolitan' was widely used in the eighteenth century, and has been part of the language ever since. Of course, it should be stressed that there was no continuity of doctrine between Stoicism and the Englightenment – the meaning of crucial notions such as 'natural law' changed dramatically in the intervening millennia. None the less, the Greek origins of the term are instructive in so far as they assist us to avoid two of the commonest confusions associated with cosmopolitan thought. In the first place, cosmopolitanism has no necessary connection with the desire for some kind of world government. The Stoics lived under a 'world' government; that was precisely the problem – how to make sense of life in a context in which the coming of Empire had eliminated the previous focal points of existence. Cosmopolitanism is compatible with a rejection of politics, or with a pragmatic acceptance of existing political structures such as the states of eighteenth-century Europe. What is crucial to a cosmopolitan attitude is the refusal to regard existing political structures as the source of ultimate value. Second, cosmopolitanism is a universalist principle but not all universalist principles are cosmopolitan. In the classical period the Greek cities were universally a source of value, but the values were differentiated. Similarly, it is possible, as will be shown, to hold the nation as a universal source of particularist values.

In this work 'communitarian' will be taken as the antonym of cosmopolitan, and the theory of international relations will be organised and presented around these two poles. The meaning of the term communitarian will be examined at the start of the next chapter, but before proceeding with cosmopolitanism it may be helpful to consider briefly two other classifications of international thought which have been rejected in favour of the cosmopolitan/communitarian dichotomy – Carr's classic distinction between 'realism' and 'utopianism' (which feeds into the realist account of international relations developed by Morgenthau and others), and Wight's more elaborate threefold classification into 'Machiavellian', 'Grotian' and 'Kantian' international theory.[4]

The most obvious problem with the distinction between 'realism' and 'utopianism' is that these are spectacularly loaded terms, more valuable in the polemical context in which they were deployed than in the more considered circumstances required of reasoned debate. The term 'realism' covers two distinct and very different attitudes: on the one hand, the belief that morals have no part in international (or perhaps any) politics; on the other, the belief that morals stem from the community, which latter view will be discussed below. 'Utopian' is used by Carr to refer to thought that fails to recognise what he took to be the material basis of all politics, and thus thought which promoted the possibility of a natural harmony of interest. At the time of writing *The Twenty Years Crisis* Carr was a Marxist of sorts, who believed in a materialist account of conflict. Writers who agreed with this were realist (i.e. right) while those who disagreed were utopian (i.e. wrong). This does not seem to be a satisfactory basis for a classification. On the account of international thought offered in this work, some, but not all, 'utopians' are cosmopolitan, as are some so-called 'realists' (including Carr, in so far as he is a Marxist); some in each of his camps are communitarian. This redivision occurs because the cosmopolitan/ communitarian divide relates to the broad issue of the source of values and meaning in political life and not to the narrow issue of the causes of conflict.

Wight's ideal–typical account of international theory as Machiavellian, Grotian and Kantian is more subtle and valuable; it relates to a wider range of concerns than Carr's simple dichotomy. However, Wight's account of Kant as a 'revolutionary' determined to transform the system is misleading, as will be shown below. Grotius cannot easily be translated into a rationalist reformer of international relations, while the placing of Machiavelli at the head of a realist doctrine can also be criticised as unhistorical – in any event the 'Machiavellian' category confuses the amoralist with the communitarian, as does Carr; this may be no accident – Anglo-American writers of their generation seem to have been unable to take seriously the most important modern communitarians. All this aside, Wight's ideas are useful and, sensibly handled, can be rescued from these problems. However, the cosmopolitan/communitarian divide requires less special pleading and, very importantly, as will become clear below, relates more readily to current work in political philosophy relevant to international relations. The Wightian threefold classification does not have this wider application, being currently employed only in some branches, mainly British, of international relations.

The main loss involved in employing a cosmopolitan/communitarian account of international thought is that there is no room for extended consideration of realism – understanding this latter term in a limited way as the belief that international relations is a field of study in which normative theory is inappropriate, that international relations is simply a realm in which the amoralism of a struggle for power dominates. The view that there is no role for normative theory in international relations has been extensively criticised in many recent works on international theory.[5] The strongest point against amoralism in international relations stems from the observable fact that individuals and states employ moral language – the language of rights and duties – in their relations with each other in such a way as to preclude any argument that this language is inappropriate. Any 'realistic' account of state practice must recognise and reflect the fact that this is so. It could, of course, be argued that such language is merely rhetorical, that states claim from others what they would not themselves grant, and, contrary to the arguments of, for example, Gewirth, such egoism is not inherently self-contradictory.[6] A consistent amoralist would be advised to try to disguise this orientation – but there is nothing inherently illogical in this kind of realism. The point is, there is nothing interesting in this position either. Realists *in this sense* of the term have very little to say about international relations; they simply express a negative to all kinds of theory which attempt to situate the relations of communities within some kind of moral order. Because realists have only one thing to say, they make boring conversationalists. In so far as they express the common-sense point that any kind of normative theory that does not address problems of compliance, or that works from an inaccurate account of how things are, is likely to do little good, their position is worthwhile. But once this caution is turned into a general assault on all normative theory, realism becomes a positive block to understanding.

These comments apply to that variety of realism which stresses the amorality of international politics. Another strand of realist thought is less concerned with the critique of ethical statecraft, and more with the group origin of values. Robert Gilpin, in his reply to Richard Ashley's critique of neo-realism, catches this well when he takes as one of his basic assumptions that 'the essence of social reality is the group' that the group is the 'foundation of political life'.[7] For Gilpin realism is the combination of this assumption with his other two assumptions, namely that international affairs are essentially conflictual, and that of the primacy in political life of power and security in human motivation.

Clearly, this is saying something rather more substantial than is to be found in the writings of those realists who are simply critics of international ethics and proponents of international prudence. However, what exactly it is that is being said is best seen as representing an attenuated version of the communitarian thought which is to be examined in the next chapter of this book. There is no need to treat this variety of realism as a separate approach to the theory of international relations, given its obvious links to communitarian thought – although it should be acknowledged that most realists of this persuasion (including, probably, Gilpin) would not relish being seen as watered-down communitarians.

The cosmopolitan/communitarian classification is more or less inclusive for the modern age – all variants of international relations theory can be seen as falling into one or the other camp without too much violence being done to the intentions of the theorist. This is not the case for other areas. For example, medieval thought on the problems of 'international' relations is, for the most part, neither cosmopolitan nor communitarian. Christian thought after Augustine is shaped by a theology whose conclusions lead in neither direction. Augustine 'shows the way in which all mankind is divided into the two cities, the terrestial and the heavenly. These are not separate groupings but represent the saved and the damned.'[8] The City of God is most definitely not a universal city; most of humankind, including most of those living in Christendom, are doomed to final destruction – only those saved by the grace of God constitute the City of God, and this includes some who have died, some now living and some yet to be born. This basis of inclusion and exclusion underlies most medieval thought, and is, indeed, especially stressed by the protestant reformers of the sixteenth and seventeenth centuries, who made more explicit the doctrine that the vast majority of mankind was doomed to eternal torture. The City of God is a community that is, through the grace of God, the ultimate source of value, but it is a community that is not politically separate from the rest of humankind.

It is only after this view of the world is overcome that a division between cosmopolitan and communitarian views came to be relevant. It is a matter of some dispute whether changes within the Christian religion or a critique from outside brought about a new attitude, but certainly it is during the Enlightenment that the old view of the world collapses and, as a by-product, modern theories of international relations can be, for the first time, discerned.[9] Hampson's judgement that 'With very few exceptions the men of the Enlightenment [were] cosmopolitan in both theory and practice' catches the change in mood (although Hampson uses the term as synonymous with 'universalist', which is not the usage here).[10] Such central figures of the Enlightenment as Hume and Voltaire produced notions of morality that both rejected traditional Christianity and transcended the limits of localism; they lived their lives as part of an intellectual elite that prided itself on its distance from the squalid politics of monarchs and princes and which supported – albeit with a degree of cynicism – the many and various peace proposals which were a feature of the age.[11]

In the later decades of the eighteenth century this sense of a universal elite became less clear and, as will be seen in the next chapter, a number of writers who may or may not be seen as part of the Enlightenment put forward ideas which formed the basis for a communitarian approach to the relations of nations. However, the last years of the century also saw the publication of a series of works on political philosophy and international relations by Immanuel Kant – works that amount to the most impressive statement of the cosmopolitan viewpoint in the literature of international relations, one of the two or three seminal contributions to the theory of international relations. Kant's most famous work on international relations is *Perpetual Peace: a philosophical sketch*; however, it would be a mistake to try to understand this text out of context.[12] Much confusion has been caused by the title of this work which seems to link it to the peace literature of the eighteenth century and in particular to the many commentaries on the Abbé St Pierre's *Project for Perpetual Peace* produced by Enlightenment thinkers (including, most famously, Rousseau).[13] Although, clearly, Kant is contributing to this literature, it is also – and more importantly – the case that his approach to international relations stems from his political philosophy, which emerges from his moral philosophy, which, in turn, is embedded in his critical philosophy taken as a whole: if his international theory is to be given the credit it deserves it must be placed in this wider context. The next section of this chapter will attempt the daunting task of providing this context; the section after will focus specifically on Kant's international theory; and the final sections will examine two very different bases upon which cosmopolitan international thought can be constructed – utilitarianism and Marxism.

KANT

Morals and politics

Kant's philosophy is difficult to summarise; fortunately, all that is necessary for the purpose of this work is that his *project* be grasped, along with some of his central concepts – the detailed reasoning behind these concepts can be put on one side.[14] Kant's project was to put Enlightenment on a sound footing. He was the greatest figure of the movement in Germany, and provides us with an account of the meaning of Enlightenment still regarded by many as seminal.[15] In his short essay 'An answer to the question: "what is Enlightenment?",' he offered the following definition; 'Enlightenment is man's emergence from his self-incurred immaturity.' In the past man has been unwilling to think for himself; now, 'The motto of Enlightenment is therefore: *Sapere Aude!* Have courage to use your *own* understanding.'[16] Human reason is to be applied to an understanding of the natural world; Kant was a strong supporter of Newtonian science – to

social life, morals and religion – although it should be noted that the
role of reason in the case of morals and religion is to provide a
foundation for conventional morality and a, slightly unorthodox,
Christianity. Kant did not wish to innovate in these areas, save by the
key innovation of replacing external authority by reason.

This understanding of Enlightenment places a great emphasis on
the sovereignty of reason – one of the reasons this text has been picked
up as seminal by postmodernist critics of the Enlightenment project.[17]
Clearly, reason stands in opposition to prejudice and bigotry, but
Kant's view that immaturity is self-incurred provides the answer to the
challenge posed by these forces; people can and must think for
themselves. In the second half of his life Kant came to believe that the
greatest challenge to Enlightenment came not from the forces of
prejudice and bigotry, but from within the movement, and in
particular from the philosophy of David Hume. Hume was without
doubt Enlightened, but he employed reason to delineate the limits of
reason, and to criticise metaphysics in ways regarded by Kant as
profoundly damaging.

Hume's philosophy is based on his refusal to recognise as meaningful all sentences which contain neither statements of logical
necessity nor statements of empirical fact. Famously, Hume invites us
to question any text put in our hands:

> let us ask; *Does it contain any abstract reasoning concerning quantity or
> number?* No. *Does it contain any experimental reasoning concerning
> matter of fact and existence?* No. Commit it then to the flames: for it can
> contain nothing but sophistry and confusion.[18]

This corrosive principle affects all areas of human reason. In the
area of science, the idea of causation must go – it can be nothing more
than constant conjunction. The same principles in the realm of ethics
also demonstrate the limits of reason; it is not possible to derive an
'ought' from an 'is' and thus morals cannot be controlled by reason.[19]
When Hume's anti-metaphysics is applied to religion, the results are
predictable. 'The Christian religion not only was at first attended by
miracles', concludes Hume, disarmingly, 'but even at this day cannot
be believed by any reasonable person without one.'[20]

Kant always showed deep respect for Hume's intellect but the aim of
his philosophy was to demonstrate that Hume was wrong. This meant
showing that there *could* be utterances that were meaningful yet
neither logically necessary nor based on experience. In the centrepiece
of Kant's philosophy, *The Critique of Pure Reason*, Kant believed that
he had succeeded in this task. The argument is beyond the scope of this
text: the central point – which has great relevance to Kant's moral

theory – is that it is the mind that gives order to nature rather than nature which reveals patterns to the mind. It is because the mind has the capacity to produce notions such as 'causation' which are neither logically necessary nor based on experience that knowledge, at least of the phenomenal world, is possible. Readers who wish to pursue this are referred to the commentaries.[21]

This concerns science and the investigation of nature, but Kant also wanted to investigate the moral world using similar arguments. For Kant moral action is a matter of choosing principles of action that reflect the demands of duty. For this we employ reason, but the difficulty is that of knowing when reason is telling us to act from duty and when from our interests. Hume argued that reason cannot be sovereign; 'Reason is, and ought only to be the slave of the passions, and can never pretend to any other office than to serve and obey them.'[22] Kant, of course, rejected this; he believed that just as we have within us the capacity to produce ideas such as 'causation' we have, within us, also the moral law, which he calls the 'categorical imperative', which tells us how to distinguish our duty from our interests. The categorical imperative is 'categorical' as opposed to 'hypothetical' –it imposes an absolute injunction to act in a particular way, whereas a hypothetical imperative would simply say 'Do this if you want to achieve that.' For Kant, this kind of consequentialist reasoning cannot provide a moral basis for action.

The content of the categorical imperative is discussed in the *Groundwork of the Metaphysics of Morals*.[23] Kant offers three formulations of the imperative; the first is formal and requires that maxims be universalisable – '*I ought never to act except in such a way that I can also will that my maxim should become a universal law*' (p. 67). Thus, for example, the maxim that promises should be kept is in accordance with this imperative, because if the negative principle were to be universalised, promising would be meaningless. As has often been remarked, however, any principle of conduct can be universalised if defined in a suitably restrictive way, and content is required if the imperative is to be more than purely formal. The second formulation provides this content by insisting that human beings should always be treated as ends rather than means; '*Act in such a way that you always treat humanity, whether in your own person or in the person of any other, never simply as a means, but always at the same time as an end*' (p. 91). The idea of humanity as an end in itself is related to what Kant calls the Formula of Autonomy, that the will is subject to laws it makes itself. The idea that every individual makes universal law for himself links to the idea of a 'kingdom of ends', a realm in which rational agents are all subject to laws they themselves make; this leads to the third formulation of the categorical imperative – '*So act as if you were through your maxims a law-making member of a kingdom of ends*' (p. 34 – Paton's formulation).

Since it is often asserted that Kant's categorical imperative is purely formal, it should be noted that Kant believes that 'the aforesaid three ways of representing the principle of morality are at bottom merely so many formulations of precisely the same law' (p. 97); therefore the formula '*Act on the maxim which can at the same time be made a universal law*' suffices for moral judgement (p. 98). The view that the second and third formulations are contained in the first is, however, contestable, and certainly not obviously true in the way that Kant seems to think it is.

The 'kingdom of ends' is a complete determination of all maxims. How does this relate to law and politics in real kingdoms? What is the relationship between morality and politics? Politics and law must be based on morals but this should not be taken to suggest that politics or law can make people good.[24] Morality is a matter of choice and cannot be imposed; a public legal order can only enforce rules of conduct, and would not be required if everyone were of good will and always followed the categorical imperative. But they are not and do not; humankind is fallen and therefore a public legal order is required to enforce the observation of moral ends that would be voluntarily observed if the kingdom of ends could be realised. Morals provide the principles on which the political/legal order should be based – 'public legal justice in Kant might be viewed as the partial realisation of what would happen if all wills were good', as Riley puts it, although it should again be stressed that whereas law is about the enforcement of rules, morality is about the autonomous choice of principles.[25]

What kind of political theory does this suggest? Kant's principles of politics are normative (they tell us what we should do) and based on *Recht* – a word that can only be translated as a mixture of the English notions of law and justice (and is occasionally left untranslated in this text to remind us of this fact). The moral requirement of universality determines that the political order should be based on the rule of law; only thus can the moral autonomy of individuals be reflected in social institutions. What is required is 'A constitution allowing the *greatest possible human freedom* in accordance with laws which ensure *that the freedom of each can co-exist with the freedom of all others.*'[26] States are formed by a contract, the terms of which are subject to the requirements of morality. The lawful state is built on *a priori* principles; 'The *freedom* of every member of society as a *human being*. 2. The *equality* of each with all the others as a *subject*. 3. The *independence* of each member of a commonwealth as a *citizen.*'[27] Kant elaborates the latter point by defining a citizen as a 'co-legislator'. Out of this substantive principles start to emerge. Despotism clearly breaches the requirements of the *a priori* principles; Kant regards democracy (which he understands as 'direct democracy') as a form of despotism. The lawful state must be 'republican', which to Kant means that it must be based on the separation of executive and legislative powers – it is because democracy, as he understands the term, fuses these powers that it is despotic.

The role of the state based on *Recht* is, essentially, negative; the state exists to allow free, equal and self-dependent people to find security for themselves and their property. It does not exist to make them moral (which is impossible because moral action is based on a good will) but to provide circumstances in which morality is possible. It does not exist to make people happy – although Kant suggests that if the greatest possible human freedom is achieved the greatest possible happiness will follow automatically.[28] The state's role is negative, but none the less exceptionally important within the context of Kant's philosophy; it is only within a lawful state that the categorical imperative can be even partially realised.

We are, thus, enjoined by the categorical imperative to create a lawful state in order that at least a partial realisation of the good will can be achieved. But, as Reiss puts it, 'Right, however, cannot possibly prevail among men within a state if their freedom is threatened by the action of other states. The law can prevail only if the rule of law prevails in all states and in international relations.'[29] Kant makes two points here; first, war kills people and destroys property and is, as such, a direct threat to security and justice. The Hobbesian notion that states are able to extend physical protection to their citizens is palpably false. But, second, war is a direct cause of despotism and tyranny which also destroys security and justice. Therefore, the same moral imperative that enjoins the creation of the lawful state, requires the abolition of war.

One way to abolish war would be to abolish states, by creating a single world-state, and this would seem to be a goal in keeping with the general tenor of Kant's philosophy, since all rational beings have the same capacity to make synthetic *a priori* judgements, and are governed by the same moral law. Equally, since the role of the state is negative, and the political community is not in itself a source of value, there would seem to be no principled reason why the existing order of sovereign states should be valued. In the sense in which the term is used in this book Kant is a 'cosmopolitan' and a world-state would be a *possible* cosmopolitan solution to the problem of war. Kant does develop a role for cosmopolitan *Recht*, as will be seen in the next section, but he rejects the notion of a world-state. There are objections to a world-state based on the linguistic and religious differences between states, and on the obvious point that princes will not agree to lose their sovereignty, but equally it is to be doubted whether a world-state would be viable on practical grounds. Scale is important; as Kant puts it 'laws progressively lose their impact as the government increases its range', and a world-state based on conquest and the establishment of a universal monarchy – which Kant seems to feel, surely correctly, is the only way a world-state could emerge – would soon deteriorate from a soulless despotism into anarchy.[30] In current circumstances a world-state is neither achievable nor desirable.

However, war must be abolished if lawful states are to provide a context in which free equal and self-dependent people can exist in security and with justice; since the establishment of a world-state is not the answer, a world without war must be achieved in a world of states. A system of relations must be developed which will prevent war without requiring the elimination of states. How this is to be achieved is outlined in *Perpetual Peace: A philosophical sketch*, which will be examined in the next section of this chapter, as will be those 'guarantees' that Kant believes removes this project from the realm of fantasy and situates it firmly within the bounds of reality. Before proceeding to this task, it may be useful to summarise again the purpose of this section. The aim has been to show that Kant's international theory is a response to the requirements of his critical philosophy taken as a whole. Clearly, the work we will now examine does come in a sequence of eighteenth-century peace theories, but to consider *Perpetual Peace* solely in this light is to ensure that it will be misunderstood – and indeed some of the adverse judgements passed on the text, such as Gallie's view that as a piece of literature it is a disaster, a 'fantastic literary farrago', are almost entirely to be explained in terms of a failure to place the work in its correct context.[31] *Perpetual Peace* is not the most important of Kant's works, but it is a text that represents the culmination of his moral and political philosophy. Unless he can provide a convincing answer to the problem of war, the rest of his moral and political philosophy turns to ashes; it is his realisation that this is so, that only with a satisfactory theory of international relations can he be said to have a satisfactory political and moral theory, that makes him one of the two or three most important figures in the history of international thought.

Perpetual Peace

Perpetual Peace: A philosophical sketch may not be a 'fantastic literary farrago' but it certainly is a peculiar text, being a mixture of a code of conduct and a philosophical debate, with two substantive sections apparently at odds with one another, and a set of supplements and appendices longer than the main work – and, moreover, with perhaps the heart of the work appearing in a footnote.[32] Clearly this is a text that needs to be unpacked and contextualised.

The first section consists of the Preliminary Articles of a Perpetual Peace between States. There are six of these:

1. No conclusion of peace shall be considered valid as such if it was made with a secret reservation of the material for a future war.
2. No independently existing state, whether it be large or small, may be acquired by another state by inheritance, exchange, purchase or gift.
3. Standing armies (*miles perpetuus*) will gradually be abolished altogether.
4. No national debt shall be contracted in connection with the external affairs of the state.
5. No state shall forcibly interfere in the constitution and government of another state.
6. No state at war with another shall permit such acts of hostility as would make mutual confidence impossible during a future time of peace. Such acts would include the employment of *assassins (percussores) or poisoners (venefici), breach of agreements, the instigation of treason (perduellio)* within the enemy state, etc. (pp. 93–6)

These articles clearly are 'preliminary': they obviously do not establish a system of perpetual peace, because article 6 assumes that wars will still occur. The six articles are best understood as a set of rules that could, and should, be applied in the absence of perpetual peace. A full system of peace requires that states be brought into a constitutional relationship with one another; as Kant acknowledges elsewhere, this will be a painfully slow process and in the meantime a set of rules which do not assume such a lawful arrangement are required. In another section of *Perpetual Peace* Kant refers to the classical international lawyers (Grotius, Pufendorf and Vattel) as 'sorry comforters' whose codes are actually cited in justification of military aggression (p. 103); of course, in the absence of a legal order this idea of justification is nonsense, but Kant's aim in the Six Articles is, surely, to outline a code which could *not* be used in this way. Indeed, the articles go further than this; if adhered to, they would push the system along in the right direction, towards perpetual peace – unlike the codes of the sorry comforters which, at best, attempt to civilise behaviour within the existing order. Given the acknowledged difficulties of achieving perpetual peace this code has a very important role to play.

What of its content? The set of principles it enjoins are strikingly modern. Open diplomacy, non-aggression, self-determination, non-intervention, the delineation of lawful means of making war (*jus in bello*), disarmament – these are the principles that constitute the settled norms of the modern international system, using the latter term in Frost's sense of a norm as settled 'where it is generally recognised that any argument denying the norm (or which appears to override the norm) requires special justification'.[33] They are the principles that are to be found in such programmatic statements of the modern system as the Charter of the United Nations – although it is noteworthy that Kant nowhere assumes that an organisation in support of these articles (or, indeed, of the Definitive Articles) is required. The only article of the six that is not a settled norm is number 4 on the use of national debt in connection with the external affairs of the state. Here Kant is being highly realistic in identifying the sinews of war; however, circumstances have left him behind and the changing role of the state in the management of the national economy makes a rule of this sort hard to either justify or enforce.

The second section of *Perpetual Peace* contains the three Definitive Articles of a Perpetual Peace between States. In the introduction to this section there is a short footnote that clarifies the distinction between the Preliminary and Definitive Articles, and, indeed, clarifies the nature of the project taken as a whole. In the text Kant explains that peace is not the same as the absence of war; a state of peace needs to be formally instituted, otherwise, in the absence of a system of guarantees, neighbours can treat each other as enemies. In the footnote to this point, Kant lays out the requirements of a 'legal civil state' in which this mutual hostility is barred. The state of nature (in the absence of such a state) is in itself a source of threat and must be overcome. 'All men who can influence one another must adhere to some kind of civil constitution' and it is on this postulate that the Definitive Articles are based.

But any legal constitution as far as the people who are under it are concerned will conform to one of the three following types:
(1) a constitution based on the *civil right* of individuals within a nation (*ius civatis*).
(2) a constitution based on the *international right* of states in their relationships with one another (*ius gentium*).
(3) a constitution based on *cosmopolitan right* in so far as individuals and states, coexisting in an external relationship of mutual

influences, may be regarded as citizens of a universal state of mankind (*ius cosmopoliticum*). (p. 98)

This is a necessary classification, says Kant. Everyone who is in a position to influence anyone else must be covered by one of these constitutions.

What Kant is doing in this footnote is bringing together two states of nature – one composed of people, the other of states. The requirement to establish a legal order, a constitution, applies to both people and states; people are enjoined to create a civil constitution, states a lawful international order and people and states together a system of cosmopolitan *Recht*. It is this inclusiveness that is the most impressive feature of Kant's international theory. The footnote leads into the three Definitive Articles of a Perpetual Peace which relate to, give content to, the three legal orders identified above.

The first definitive article reads that 'The Civil Constitution of Every State shall be Republican' (p. 99). Kant's definition of 'republican' – and his support for republican politics as the only basis for a free, equal and self-dependent politics – is outlined in the previous section. Republicanism is desirable for its own sake, but here Kant adds the important point that a republican constitution will be conducive to peace, since 'if, as is inevitably the case under this constitution, the consent of the citizens is required to decide whether or not war is to be declared, it is very natural that they will have great hesitation in embarking on so dangerous an enterprise' (p. 120). Unlike kings, who treat war as a sport, the citizens of a republic will have to bear the costs of war themselves and for this reason will be naturally peaceful. Since this argument is often criticised, it should be stressed first that for Kant a republic is not a democracy (which is a variant of despotism), and thus the oft-stated view that democracies are inherently warlike does not touch his argument, but second, that in any event the case for republican government is quite independent of the empirical proposition that such states are peaceful in intent. The reason that the civil constitution of states should be republican comes out of the general considerations of Kant's moral theory; that he believes such states will be peaceful is an uncovenanted bonus.

The second definitive article is that 'The Right of Nations shall be based on a Federation of Free States' (p. 102). A state of nature is a standing threat to the security of its members and the states that find themselves in a state of nature are entitled to insist of each other that they enter into a legal relationship. Only savages would want to cling to their lawless freedom – 'we regard this as barbarism, coarseness and brutish debasement of humanity' (p. 103). One might think states would take the point, but instead rulers cling to the 'glory' of not submitting to any legal restraint, and the 'depravity of human nature is displayed without disguise in the unrestricted relations which obtain between the various nations' (p. 103). In a sense the *Recht* of nations is such that they cannot be forced to abandon this state, but no reading of international right can justify war; any meaningful understanding of the term must be compatible with the establishment of a *pacific federation* based on a treaty to abolish all war. If international right encompasses the right to go to war it would mean that force could determine what is lawful, which, for Kant, would be a meaningless abomination.

It is clear that the *Recht* of nations poses problems for Kant. His argument from the state of nature would seem to lead to a clear argument for an imperative to create a world republic. He will later argue that this is an impractical goal; his point here is that while this is a positive ideal it cannot be realised 'since this is not the will of nations according to their present conception of international right' (p. 105). A peaceful federation, initially with a nucleus of republican states but gradually expanding, is a kind of second-best solution, holding in check man's inclination to defy the law, but with an ever-present risk of backsliding.

The third definitive article states that 'Cosmopolitan Right shall be limited to Conditions of Universal Hospitality' (p. 106). Kant makes the point that this is a matter of 'right' and not philanthropy – which is to say that while it might be good that foreigners be granted the opportunity to settle within a state, or conduct other activities, the only thing they have a *right* to is hospitality: 'the right of a stranger not to be treated with hostility when he arrives on someone else's territory' (p. 106). He may be turned away but so long as he behaves peacefully he should not be treated with hostility. This is a very limited position – far more limited than some modern Kantians would wish, although in keeping with late-twentieth-century custom, which is to allow automatic right of abode only to *bona fide* political refugees, a position which Kant also supports. However, it is clear that Kant regards the development of a universal community as a positive factor, and is particularly supportive of the promotion of economic intercourse – his point is simply that the only *right* strangers have is to hospitality.

The next sections of *Perpetual Peace* consist of two supplements and a two-part appendix. The problem with these texts is that they relate more closely to other writings of Kant on moral and political philosophy than they do to *Perpetual Peace* – although, of course, they address key problems within this latter text as well. The first supplement is headed 'On the guarantee of a perpetual peace' – obviously an important subject – and begins with the bald statement that 'Perpetual peace is *guaranteed* by no less an authority than the great artist *Nature* herself *(natura daedala rerum)*' (p. 108). There then follows a rather unhelpful discussion of the way in which nature conspires to promote the various notions of *Recht* outlined above, the most useful part of which being the practical arguments against a world-state referred to at the end of the previous section. To understand this supplement it is necessary to relate it to Kant's philosophy of history as expressed in, for example, the *Idea for a Universal History with a Cosmopolitan Purpose* of 1784 and the discussion on the problem of progress in *The Contest of Faculties* of 1798.[34] In the former work Kant sees a hidden plan of nature in the conflicts and antagonisms that exhaust people and states and ultimately will make them amenable to the dictates of reason, and lead them to republican constitutions and perpetual peace. A similar argument is found in the later text; the 'negative wisdom' of human beings, weighing the consequences of their evil natures, will lead them gradually to abolish war. The text here is worth quoting at greater length as an illustration of Kant's practical gradualism; human beings will find themselves 'compelled to ensure that *war*, the greatest obstacle to morality and the invariable enemy of progress, first becomes gradually more humane, then more infrequent, and finally disappears completely as a mode of aggression.'[35]

The second supplement is entitled 'Secret article of a perpetual peace'. Legal orders should be public; only one secret article is allowable – '*The maxims of the philosophers on the conditions under which public peace is possible shall be consulted by states which are armed for war*' (p. 114). This rather bizarre stipulation emerges out of Kant's belief in the power of reason and the necessity for its untrammelled exercise. Freedom of speech for philosophers is not simply desirable on its own terms, it is conducive to the peaceful settlement of disputes because philosophers have no axe to grind and can thus give disinterested advice – 'since the class of philosophers is by nature incapable of forming seditious factions or clubs, they cannot incur suspicion of disseminating propaganda' (p. 115). Kant is, perhaps, realistic in his assessment of the conspiratorial capacities of philosophers, but naive in assuming that this will be recognised. In any event, the article must be secret for fear of embarrassing rulers by making it clear that they are taking advice. The main interest of this supplement is again to draw attention to the fact that Kant realises only too well how difficult it will be to achieve perpetual peace.

The appendix to *Perpetual Peace* is in two parts: the first 'On the disagreement between morals and politics in relation to perpetual peace' (p. 116), the second 'On the agreement between politics and morality according to the transcendental concept of public right' (p. 125). Again, these writings relate to earlier studies on the relationship between theory and practice, as well as to the philosophy of history – of particular relevance here is *On the Common Saying: 'This May be True in Theory, but it does not Apply in Practice'*.[36] Kant's moral philosophy, taken as a whole, demands that theory produce practice, that politics give way to morality and yet is highly sensitive to the fact that given the evil in man's nature the demands of the categorical imperative will be resisted. This appendix is one more meditation on this subject.[37] Kant proves well aware of the seductive arguments of the anti-moralists, the so-called practical men of affairs. His basic point is that ultimately the sophistries of the latter are self-defeating, believed by no-one. Objectively, there can be no conflict between theory and practice, but the selfish disposition of man creates such a conflict. Ultimately Kant believes this selfishness can be overcome; not to believe this would lead to the 'desperate' conclusion that it would be impossible to justify 'the mere fact that such a race of corrupt beings could have been created on earth at all' (p. 124). Kant's conclusion is ultimately optimistic, but in a very guarded way. He concludes *Perpetual Peace* with the duty to bring about in reality a state of public right – *'albeit by an infinite process of gradual approximation'* (my emphasis) (p. 130).

No assessment of *Perpetual Peace* can be adequate that is not also a judgement on Kant's moral and political philosophy in general, and in particular of his view of the relationship of people and the state. Such a judgement makes most sense in the context of an examination of the most important alternative view, and thus requires the present-ation of communitarian approaches to be attempted in the next chapter. For the time being, comments will be restricted to one or two more limited questions raised by the international relations literature on *Perpetual Peace*.

Martin Wight describes Kant as a (indeed, *the* definitive) 'revolu-tionary' international theorist, because Kant wishes to see the transfor-mation of the international system into something else – as opposed to Machiavellians and Grotians, who are, respectively, satisfield with the status quo or seek only limited reforms.[38] This characterisation is clearly accurate, but also clearly misleading. Kant does want to see the emergence of a system of perpetual peace which would transform international relations; however, first, he sees this transformation taking place on the basis of international right, and not by the replacement of the system by a world republic, and, second, he sees this happening by 'an infinite process of gradual approximation' and not by any dramatic step. The 'revolution' – if such be the appropriate term – is limited in scope; moreover, it will be a 'long revolution'.[39] Placing Kant at the head of a tradition of speculation about international relations that includes, for example Gandhi and Lenin is more likely to confuse than to clarify thought.

Ian Clark, on the other hand, places Kant at the head of a tradition of optimism in international relations – as opposed to the pessimistic Rousseau.[40] This is far more satisfactory than Wight's attribution, but, again, although Kant is, ultimately, an optimist, his optimism is qualified and guarded. Kant's thought involves a drive to achieve a world in which the categorical imperative can be realised; he believes in progress – human life would be meaningless if human beings were to prove incapable of eliminating war and this would be intolerable. Even the bad things that happen are ultimately part of the hidden plan of nature. The difficulty comes in the explicitly Christian element in Kant's thought. Is the kingdom of ends achievable on earth? Surely not – the best that can be hoped for is a 'gradual approximation' to this state. Kant is an optimist in so far as he does not believe in the hopelessness of the human condition. Human beings have reason and can use it to better their conditions. Even the radical evil of human nature cannot frustrate this; 'the problem of setting up a state can be solved even by a nation of devils (so long as they possess understanding)' (p. 112). But there is no easy optimism here.

So, Kant is a revolutionary and an optimist, even though neither term does full justice to the complexity and sophistication of his thought. What of the empirical side of Kant's work? Is he, if not a realist, at least realistic in his approach? The main point that needs to be made here is that Kant's argument does not rest on empirical propositions although it does contain such statements. He does not argue that economic 'interdependence' will promote *Perpetual Peace* – and indeed could not make this argument since the relationship between state and economy was very different in his era from what it later became – but he does suggest that economic intercourse will extend the range of cosmopolitan right if allowed to do so. The internal order of states should be republican because only thus is the freedom, equality and self-dependence of men preservable, but Kant also argues that republican states will be peace-loving. How do these arguments stand up to empirical examination?

Conventional international relations deals harshly with arguments that are based on the proposition that foreign-policy behaviour can be related to the domestic structure of states. Waltz in his two major works characterises such arguments as 'second image' in *Man, the State and War* and 'reductionist' in *Theory of International Politics*.[41]

Singer's 'Correlates of war' project has produced data that suggests that involvement in war is a function of position within the international system – broadly, the more important the state, the more wars it has been involved in.[42] By contrast, in a recent study explicitly relating to Kantian international theory, Michael Doyle has argued that what he calls 'liberal states' have never gone to war with each other, although they have fought non-liberal states.[43]

What is moot is whether any of these arguments meet Kant's position. Doyle, for example, sees liberalism as coming in two varieties – laissez-faire and social welfare – neither of which corresponds to Kant's republicanism (although the former is closer than the latter), and then offers a long list of 'liberal' states which have yet to engage in war with one another. The problem is that Kant's notion of republicanism is far closer to a Hayekian view of liberalism than anything seen in the real world; his notion of property rights and the lack of an economic role for the state divorces his republicanism from really-existing liberalism. None the less, Doyle's work is suggestive, and his picture of an expanding Pacific Union within which war is no longer an instrument of policy – a 'security community' in the terminology of Karl Deutsch – is true to Kant's reasoning in *Perpetual Peace*.[44]

All in all, the best that can be said is that Kant's position is not obviously wrong or so far off-base empirically that it is not worth considering; on the contrary, there is at least some reason to think that his position – which it should be stressed again is *not* empirically based but the product of theoretical knowledge – is defensible. Moreover, since liberal states have always been forced to coexist with non-liberal adversaries, how a world solely composed of liberal states would work is a moot point. For the moment, the matter will be left at that, while other variants of cosmopolitan thought are examined.

UTILITARIAN ACCOUNTS OF COSMOPOLITANISM

Utilitarianism is usually and rightly seen as a moral philosophy which is totally at odds with Kantianism. Kant and Kantians are 'deontologists'; they believe that moral behaviour is a matter of acting on the basis of moral principles and with moral motives – the only thing that is good in itself is a good will, to paraphrase the opening of the *Groundwork of the Metaphysic of Morals*. Utilitarians are 'consequentialists'; they believe that the only factor determining whether an action is right or wrong is its consequences. Kantianism is not hostile to the consideration of consequences, but principles are always taken to 'trump' consequences in moral arguments, a position regarded as anathema to consequentialists, for whom principles are simply guidelines to action based on past experiences of consequences.[45] As will be seen below, there are different variants of consequentialism; utilitarianism is that variant, most commonly associated in its classical form with Jeremy Bentham, which asserts that moral actions are those which maximise 'greatest happiness'. Human beings are governed by 'two sovereign masters, *pain* and *pleasure*' and the greatest-happiness principle, the principle of utility, emerges from this.

> By the principle of utility is meant that principle which approves or disapproves of every action whatsoever, according to the tendency which it appears to have to augment or diminish the happiness of the party whose interest is in question.[46]

This is, of course, dramatically different from the Kantian position. For Kant, the fact that an action conduces to the happiness of an individual is a matter for suspicion, requiring close examination to ensure that it really is enjoined by duty. But the difference between Kantianism and utilitarianism goes deeper than this. Kantian ethics are 'agent-centred'; they are based on what an individual should do. In the last resort, utilitarianism views the greatest happiness *impersonally*. Whereas for Kant the role of the state is to provide for freedom, equality and self-dependence as goods in themselves for the individuals who are its citizens, for Benthamites the role of the state and all other social institutions should be simply to promote the general happiness, through whatever means are most likely to achieve this goal. Thus, for example, it may be in practice the case that representative government and a set of rights for the individual is the best way of promoting the general happiness – as Bentham came to believe – but this is at root an empirical rather than a principled observation.[47]

In spite of these differences, the tradition of classical utilitarianism is clearly cosmopolitan in the sense that this term is used in this work.[48] For Bentham there are, on the one hand, individuals who experience pain and pleasure and, on the other, situations which are characterised by lesser or greater happiness. Value comes from these two sources and not from the state or any other political community. Bentham did not write extensively on international relations – although he did, it seems, coin the term 'international' – but the main lines of his international theory are clear.[49] The basic duty individuals have is to the happiness of mankind in general; the citizen of a nation is also citizen of the world. Generally, utility is maximised by recognising that subsidiary institutions such as the state or the family have a claim on our duties but this is so only because it promotes the general happiness and not because states (or families) have claims on us which override utility. And again, governments have a responsibility to promote the happiness of their citizens, but this does not override their responsibility to promote the happiness of mankind in general, which could, in principle, involve action against the interest of one's own society.

These are radical thoughts – as radical in their requirements as Kantian morality, if not more so. A number of late-twentieth-century writers who are either explicitly utilitarian, or working 'in the shadow of utilitarianism', have employed these notions to develop elaborate arguments in international theory – as will be seen in later chapters of this book.[50] Bentham and the early Benthamites, on the other hand, do not provide more than a very thin international theory. Bentham believed international law could provide a code of conduct for international relations corresponding to the requirements of utility. It would need to be codified – codification of law was one of Bentham's firmest general principles – and he also supported the idea of an international tribunal to resolve differences between nations, although without coercive powers.[51] In general, Bentham believed that war was unlikely to be conducive to the general happiness and was thus to be opposed; major factors that contributed to war included other actions contrary to the principle of utility, such as colonialism and foreign entanglements in general. Bentham's account of the causes of war and of its remedy was essentially the same as his account of other evils in the world – insufficient attention was being paid to the principle of the greatest happiness; let this be the guiding point and all else follows.

Again it should be stressed that Bentham is not an advocate of world government – although he would be if he believed this to be required to promote the general happiness – but he is a cosmopolitan. The state has no value as such – indeed no feature of life has value *as such* for Bentham. The greatest-happiness principle of utilitarianism is both universal and cosmopolitan. Whether a strict utilitarian position can be defended is a moot point. It is interesting that when J.S. Mill comes to examine an important international issue in the essay '*A few words on non-intervention*', it is not clear that the case he makes in favour of a general principle of non-intervention in the domestic affairs of other states (the exception being where an oppressive government is itself receiving help from outside) is simply based on the utilitarian view that intervention is likely to be a source of disutility.[52] It can also be argued that he is supporting the (non-utilitarian) view that freedom looses value if given to individuals rather than taken by them.[53] In general, Mill attempts to mitigate the rigour of the utilitarian position, and comes close to endorsing the non-utilitarian, and noncosmopolitan view that communities can be a source of value independent of utility.

MARXISM, SOCIALISM AND COSMOPOLITANISM

If Kantianism and utilitarianism are in some sense polar opposites in terms of moral theory – deontological as against consequentialist – yet share a cosmopolitan conception of the world, a similar unity of opposites can be seen between, on the one hand, Kantian and utilitarian thought seen as variants of liberalism and the version of collectivist thought represented by Marxism and classical socialism. Again, radically different starting points lead to cosmopolitan conclusions. Kantianism begins with the moral agent, utilitarianism with an impersonal principle, socialism with a class perspective, but in each case the end point is to endorse an attitude towards international relations which is oriented away from particularistic sources of value and towards the global community.[54]

'Workers of all countries, unite!' and 'The worker has no country' are phrases that occur in the *Communist Manifesto* of Marx and Engels; similar sentiments can be found in most of the socialist writers of the nineteenth century.[55] The central premise of all variants of Marxian socialism is that the true interest of workers lies in their identity as a class – in classical Marxism defined by reference to ownership and control of the means of production – and that the interests of the working class in one country are in conflict with other classes in that country but in harmony with the interests of working classes elsewhere. As the writers of the *Manifesto* acknowledge, politics actually takes place in a specific location and conquest of power by the working-class will, in the first instance, be of *national* power – but this is purely a product of the contingencies of the struggle.[56] From a Marxian perspective there can be no real conflict of interest between workers of different countries, because political conflict emerges out of class struggle, and the workers of different countries share a common class interest.

Several points need to be made about this basic position – which, it should be stressed, is common to most variants of nineteenth-century socialist thought. In the first place, it might seem that the emphasis on class is in some respects analogous to the main lines of medieval Christian thought as outlined above, in so far as socialism also seems to envisage a division between the damned and the saved, this time in the form of the bourgeoisie and proletariat. Is this a genuinely cosmopolitan position if it makes this sort of distinction between human beings based on class? The answer given by Marx and echoed by other socialists is that the proletariat is a universal class even though not all human beings are members of it.[57] Unlike previous victors in the class war, the proletariat, when it conquers, will establish a society without classes and therefore without class oppression; salvation is available to all. The dictatorship of the proletariat will be a phase preceding the withering away of the state and therefore of the divisions between human beings. Whether this is a satisfactory answer to a serious question will be a matter of opinion, but the cosmopolitan *intentions* of Marxian socialism are clear.

The second point that should be made about this variant of cosmopolitanism is that it assumes away some of the most obvious problems with the doctrine; in particular, the possibility that a consistently cosmopolitan attitude might involve the sacrifice of real interests is discounted from the start. From a Kantian perspective a clash between duty and self-interest is a permanent feature of moral life – indeed, the absence of such a clash is inherently suspicious, suggesting the possibility that duty is not being pursued: utilitarians stress that the real interests of individuals, communities and humankind may be different, and provide an impersonal criterion that privileges the latter. By contrast, Marxist approaches require that all clashes of interest are to be understood as the product of class society – the idea that *workers* of different countries might have genuinely different interests is ruled out by the assumptions made about the way in which interests are formed.[58]

In principle at least, cosmopolitanism comes cheap to socialist thought – the costs of taking the global view are seen as likely to fall on the oppressing class; the workers are deemed to have nothing to lose from the adoption of a cosmopolitan perspective on international relations. It could well be argued that this position has presented real problems for Marxists when faced with the practical problems of dealing with nationalism as political force. Nairn's judgement that 'The theory of nationalism represents Marxism's great historical failure' is not excessively harsh.[59] Some Marxists have responded to nationalism by simply refusing to take seriously its claims, and have generally been rewarded by exclusion from political power; others have allied their socialist principles with the national cause only to see the former wither on the vine and the demands of the nation take over. The point could well be made that neither Kantians nor utilitarians have been conspicuously successful in putting into practice their political principles in the international arena, but in these cases there has been, at the very least, an awareness of the existence of a problem that has often not been present with Marxian thought – liberal cosmopolitans are, on the whole, only too well aware that the policy is not without its costs, at least in the short to medium run. Liberals (Kantian or utilitarian) believe that a harmony of interests is achievable but it is something that has to be worked for rather than built into the assumptions of the case. From a Kantian perspective, the most serious problem with Marxism in general is that it assumes too readily that a 'universal kingdom of ends' could be achieved by social action and the victory of a class; Kant would have argued that the blocks to such a kingdom lie within the nature of people and cannot be overcome by this sort of of political struggle.

The final point that should be made about Marxian cosmopolitanism – and here Marxism does to some extent diverge from much of the rest of at least the nineteenth-century socialist tradition – is that because Marxist ethical thinking is consequentialist, judging action in accordance with its contribution to the achievement of socialist revolution, the issue of war and peace does not have the centrality it does in other variants of cosmopolitan thought.[60] A contrast here with another variant of consequentialism – utilitarianism – is instructive. For utilitarians the case against war is based on considerations of utility; in principle, there is no reason why war should not contribute towards the general happiness, and if it does it cannot be opposed from a utilitarian perspective. Marxism must make much the same judgement, but with this crucial difference; whereas it is difficult to see how, except in very restricted circumstances, war could be conducive to general happiness, it is much easier to see how war might be thought to lead to revolution. Marx and Engels certainly believed that some wars would have this effect and supported them accordingly; famously, Lenin from 1914 to 1917 saw the war as a source of opportunity – he called not for the end of war but for its conversion to revolution, and he believed, correctly, that by weakening the hold of the state in tsarist Russia war would make the revolution easier of achievement.[61]

These features of Marxian cosmopolitanism distinguish it from liberal variants, but the distinction should not be overstressed. As with Kantian and utilitarian thought, socialism and Marxism accept no sources of value other than those stemming from mankind in general, even if the way in which value is constituted differs widely as between the three doctrines.

CONCLUSION

This chapter has examined three sources of cosmopolitan thought; Kantian thought has been examined in most detail because it is in the works of Kant that the most elaborate and explicit theorising of cosmopolitanism is to be found. Kant's social philosophy is all of a piece; his international theory is an essential part of his political theory, which emerges out of his moral philosophy, itself locked into his philosophy of science and 'pure reason'. In the case of alternative sources of cosmopolitanism such as utilitarianism and Marxism, a cosmopolitan perspective is an implication of a general philosophical position. In the case of Kant, cosmopolitanism is more than this; it is at the heart of his understanding of humanity and the meaning of a 'transcendant' – universal and necessary – philosophy. However, the intellectual centrality of Kant should not be allowed to disguise the fact that, as we shall see, late-twentieth-century cosmopolitanism owes much to Bentham and Mill.

To some theorists of international relations, placing Kantianism, utilitarianism and Marxism in the same camp will seem perverse; these three positions are the main sources of political programmes and ethical stances that are in contest in, at least, the Anglo-American world. To see them as essentially on the same side would seem strange. Other theorists will be less surprised, regarding these three approaches as different variants of 'utopianism', to be contrasted with a power-oriented 'realism' uninterested in the sort of concerns generated by these doctrines. Both these positions are mistaken. These three variants of cosmopolitanism cover only a limited range of possibilities for normative international relations theory; there is an approach based on alternative positions which are neither cosmopolitan nor realist in the conventional sense of the term – and it is to this tradition that the next chapter is devoted.

NOTES

1. See, for example, A. MacIntyre, *A Short History of Ethics* (Routledge and Kegan Paul, London, 1967), chs 1–7, for an account of the meaning of the *polis* to the Greeks.
2. Aristotle, *The Politics*, ed. S. Everson (Cambridge University Press, Cambridge, 1988), pp. 3ff.
3. MacIntyre, *op. cit.*, p. 107.
4. E.H. Carr, *The Twenty Years Crisis* (Macmillan, London, 1939). At the

moment no extended account by Wight of his classification is available, but see B. Porter 'Patterns of thought and practice in Martin Wight's "International Theory" ', in M. Donelan (ed.) *The Reason of States: A study in international political theory* (Allen and Unwin, London, 1978), and H. Bull 'Martin Wight and the theory of international relations', *British Journal of International Studies*, vol. 2, no. 2 (1976).

5. For good statements of the centrality of normative theory from different perspectives see C.R. Beitz, *Political Theory and International Relations* (Princeton University Press, Princeton, N.J., 1979) and M. Frost, *Towards a Normative Theory of International Relations* (Cambridge University Press, Cambridge, 1986).

6. A. Gewirth, *Reason and Morality* (University of Chicago Press, Chicago, 1978).

7. R. Gilpin, 'The richness of the tradition of political realism', cited from R.O. Keohane (ed.) *Neo-Realism and its Critics* (Columbia University Press, New York, 1986), p. 304.

8. G. Leff, *Medieval Thought from Saint Augustine to Ockham* (Penguin, Harmondsworth, 1958), p. 45.

9. See the Introduction to N. Hampson, *The Enlightenment* (Penguin, Harmondsworth, 1968).

10. *ibid.*, p. 243.

11. On which see F.H. Hinsley, *Power and the Pursuit of Peace* (Cambridge University Press, Cambridge, 1963).

12. *Perpetual Peace* is one of the texts in H.J. Reiss (ed.) *Kant's Political Writings* (Cambridge University Press, Cambridge, 1979). Page references in the text to *Perpetual Peace* will be to H.B. Nisbet's translation in this edition.

13. See Hinsley, *op. cit*, and C.J. Carter, *Rousseau and the Problem of War* (Garland, New York, 1987).

14. It might well be argued that this is an unscholarly approach to an important thinker, but the alternative of requiring a full grasp of the critical philosophy before approaching Kant's political writings is certain to result in the neglect of these important works. This account of Kant is very heavily based on secondary sources, especially S. Korner, *Kant* (Penguin, Harmondworth, 1955), P. Riley, *Kant's Political Philosophy* (Rowman Littlefield, Totowa, N.J., 1983), R. Solomon, *Continental Philosophy since 1750* (The Oxford History of Western Philosophy, 7; Oxford University Press, Oxford, 1988), R. Norman, *The Moral Philosophers* (Clarendon, Oxford, 1983), The Introduction to Reiss, *op. cit.*, A. MacIntyre, *op. cit.*, and *After Virtue* (University of Notre Dame Press, Notre Dame, Ind., 1981).

15. MacIntyre in *After Virtue* identifies Kant and Mozart as the two supreme exemplars of Enlightenment (p. 36) unwilling to allow Hume preeminence even in depravity – for so MacIntyre regards the movement. On the Enlightenment in general see, for example, Hampson, *op. cit.*, P. Hazard *The European Mind 1680–1715* (Penguin, Harmondsworth, 1964),

and *European Thought in the Eighteenth Century* (Penguin, Harmondsworth, 1965).

16. Reiss, *op. cit.*, p. 54.
17. See M. Foucault, 'What is Enlightenment?', for an explicit use of Kant's text in this way: *The Foucault Reader*, ed. P. Rabinow (Penguin, Harmondworth, 1986).
18. *Enquiries Concerning Human Nature and Concerning the Principles of Morals*, ed. L.A. Selby-Bigge, 3rd edn (Clarendon, Oxford, 1975), p. 165.
19. *A Treatise on Human Nature* (Penguin, Harmondsworth, 1969), Book III, part I, section I, p. 521.
20. *Enquiries*, p. 131. Hume was one of the relatively few atheists of the Enlightenment, although many members of the movement were deists or highly unorthodox Christians. Hume's death in 1776 was accompanied by great interest to see if this enemy of revealed religion would suffer a last-minute relapse into faith; he did not, and died with great serenity. Hume's death is interestingly examined in M. Ignatieff, *The Needs of Strangers* (Chatto, London, 1984), ch. 3.
21. Extensive selections from the *Critique of Pure Reason* are to be found in L.W. Beck, *Kant: Selections* (Scribner Macmillan, New York, 1988). For commentary see the references in note 14.
22. *Treatise*, Book II, part III, section III, p. 662.
23. In Beck, *op. cit.*, but most helpfully with extensive analysis in H.J. Paton, *The Moral Law: Kant's groundwork of the metaphysics of morals* (Hutchinson University Library, London, 1948). Page references in the text are to this edition.
24. Much of this follows Riley, *op. cit.*
25. *ibid.*, p. 3.
26. Reiss, *op. cit.*, p. 191 (from *Critique of Pure Reason*).
27. *ibid.*, p. 74 (from *On the Common Saying: 'This May Be True In Theory But It Does Not Apply In Practice'*).
28. *ibid.*, p. 191 (following passage cited in note 26).
29. *ibid.*, Introduction, p. 33.
30. *ibid.*, p. 113 (from *Perpetual Peace*).
31. W.B. Gallie, *Philosophers of Peace and War* (Cambridge University Press, Cambridge, 1978), p. 11.
32. 'Literary farrago' is, perhaps, fair comment, but 'fantastic' is not – there are reasons for these peculiarities.
33. Frost, *op. cit.*, p. 121.
34. Reiss, *op. cit.*, pp. 41ff. and 176ff.
35. *ibid.*, p. 189.
36. *ibid.*, p. 61.
37. For a valuable recent contribution on this topic, using some Kantian notions, see N.J. Rengger, 'Serpents and doves in classical international theory', *Millennium: Journal of International Studies*, vol. 17, no. 2 (1988).
38. See references to Wight in note 4 above.

39. This term is Raymond Williams'; see *The Long Revolution* (Penguin, Harmondsworth, 1961).
40. I. Clark *The Hierarchy of States: Reform and resistance in the international order* (Cambridge University Press, Cambridge, 1989). See also A. Hurrell's 'Kant and the Kantian paradigm in international relations', *Review of International Studies*, vol. 16, no. 3 (July 1990).
41. Respectively, Columbia University Press, New York, 1959, and Addison-Wesley, Reading, Mass., 1979.
42. J.D. Singer and M. Small, *The Wages of War 1816–1965: A statistical handbook* (J. Wiley, London, 1972), Part D, ch. 11, 'The war proneness of nations'.
43. M. Doyle 'Kant, liberal legacies and foreign affairs', Parts I and II, *Philosophy and Public Affairs*, vol. 12, nos 3 and 4 (1983).
44. On security communities, see K. Deutsch *Political Community and the North Atlantic Area* (Princeton University Press, Princeton, N.J., 1957).
45. For more on deontological and consequentialist approaches to normative issues see chapter 4 below.
46. J. Bentham *An Introduction to the Principles of Morals and Legislation* (with *A Fragment on Goverment*), ed. W. Harrison (Blackwell, Oxford, 1960), pp. 125ff. Extracts from this text and works by J.S. Mill and J. Austin are helpfully collected in Mary Warnock (ed.) *Utilitarianism* (Fontana, London, 1962).
47. For the evolution of Bentham's position on this matter, see the Introduction to Harrison (ed.) *op. cit.*
48. The following discussion draws heavily on A. Ellis, 'Utilitarianism and international ethics', in T. Nardin and D. Mapel (ed.) *Traditions of International Ethics* (Cambridge University Press, Cambridge, 1992.
49. Bentham's most interesting writings in international affairs are the four essays on the *Principles of International Law* which were in his unpublished papers and are now available in *The Works of Jeremy Bentham*, vol. 2 (Russell and Russell, New York, 1962), pp. 535–60. In some respects this work anticipates Norman Angell with its stress on the pointlessness of war in a commercial age.
50. The phrase 'in the shadow of utilitarianism' is employed to describe his own position by R.E. Goodin in *Political Theory and Public Policy* (University of Chicago Press, Chicago, 1982). The recent work of utilitarians such as Hardin and Singer reflects the changing agenda of international theory; see chapters 4, 5 and 6 below.
51. On this tribunal see Essay 4 of *Principles of International Law, op. cit.*, p. 552.
52 J.S. Mill, *Essays on Politics and Culture*, ed. G. Himmelfarb (Anchor Doubleday, New York, 1963), p. 368.
53. See pp. 382ff.
54. Strictly for the purpose of this discussion, Marxism and socialism are taken as synonymous unless differentiated in the text; this procedure is not too distorting for these issues in the nineteenth century. On Marxism and

international affairs in general see C. Brown, 'Marxist approaches to international political economy', in R.J. Barry Jones (ed.) *The Worlds of Political Economy* (Pinter, London, 1988), and 'Marxism and international ethics', in Nardin and Mapel (eds), *op. cit.*

55. D. McLellan (ed.) *Karl Marx: Selected writings* (Oxford University Press, Oxford, 1977), pp. 221–47.
56. *ibid.*, pp. 235ff.
57. See *Towards a Critique of Hegel's 'Philosophy of Right': Introduction*, in McLellan, *op. cit.*, esp. at p. 72.
58. Lenin's notion of a labour aristocracy involves only a fragment of a working class – see *Imperialism* section VIII in *Selected Works* (Progress, Moscow, 1968). The idea that the interests of whole working classes in different countries could be radically opposed comes into the Marxist literature after 1945, especially through those influenced by Paul Baran; see, for example, Baran, *The Political Economy of Growth* (Penguin, Harmondsworth, 1973).
59. T. Nairn, *The Break-Up of Britain* (New Left Books, London, 1977), p. 329.
60. See Brown in Nardin and Mapel (eds), *op. cit.*
61. See Karl Marx, *The Eastern Question*, (ed.) E. Marx Aveling and E. Aveling (Cass Reprints of the Economic Classics, London, 1969), for an illustration of Marx's opportunist approach to war – the context here is the Crimean War. On Lenin see *Socialism and War* (Progress, Moscow, 1972).

Chapter 3

Communitarian Theory

INTRODUCTION: 'BUT I SHOULD STILL BE MYSELF?'

Kantian ethics are agent-centred; they impose duties upon individuals and these duties cannot be displaced to social structures – although such structures may also be agents. Utilitarian ethics are impersonal as opposed to agent-centred, but rest on the pains and pleasures of individuals, aggregated in an (allegedly) suitable way. The cosmopolitan nature of these two doctrines stems directly from the approach to the individual upon which they are based. Because of the nature of individuals and their role in the constitution of moral positions, the status of institutions that come between the individual on the one hand and mankind on the other is bound to be secondary and derivative. From a Kantian perspective, it is the inability of man to achieve on earth the universal kingdom of ends required by the third formulation of the categorical imperative, an inability stemming from the radical evil in man's nature, that legitimates the existing structure of separate political communities. For the utilitarian, the legitimacy of political communities rests on the contingent empirical judgement that the greatest happiness is best served by the existence of local jurisdictions. The Kantian moral agent and utilitarian maximiser of the general happiness have radically different psychologies, but share the cosmopolitan attitude that places the legitimacy of the state on a contingent and provisional basis; from both points of view, the state is, all things considered, the most satisfactory way of organising social life currently available, and as such deserves conditional support, dependent on its maintaining this contingent status. But the driving force of political, social and moral life lies elsewhere, in the pursuit of utility or in following the dictates of the categorical imperative wherever they may lead.

None of this, of course, precludes the possibility that individuals might develop a degree of affective loyalty towards 'their' society, but it does dictate that any such loyalty ought to be put continually to the question. From a Kantian or utilitarian perspective, particularist loyalties are always, at root, irrational. The Enlightenment notion of the immutability of human nature – 'man in general has always been what he is', as Voltaire put it[1] – underlies both cosmopolitan doctrines, and precludes the possibility that affective attitudes to the political community could be a rational response to the formation of the individual. From the cosmopolitan perspective, the role of the state is essentially instrumental and it is as such an inappropriate object for more than a conditional loyalty.

Is there a problem here? Clearly, many would say that there is not, that this is a healthy attitude to the state which in no way precludes the possibility of a satisfying political and social life – this position is particularly prevalent in the Anglo-American world; others would see in this response a degree of blindness, an inability to grasp certain features of what it means to live in a community. Positions here are easy to caricature and difficult to grasp in a nuanced way; initially, it may be helpful to approach them via an examination of a work of the imagination which is centrally concerned with community. Lawrence's *The Rainbow* is a study of a family in an organic community, a community that in the text is both endorsed as a source of value and continually challenged.[2] The founder of the family, Tom Brangwen, marries a Polish exile, Lydia Lensky, whose foreignness is a major part of her attraction to the owner of Marsh Farm, Cossethay; two generations later, 'The widening circle' describes the Brangwen grandchildren, Ursula and Gudrun gaining an education and a sense of the wider world. All through, the rural community is politically placed – the specificity of Lydia's exile from Poland is carefully described[3] – without being politically determined. Politics is there, providing a refuge for Poles, funding the crucially important school system, but without shaping or defining the lives of the individuals. Attitudes are made explicit in a dialogue between Ursula Brangwen and her cousin, Anton Skrebensky, an army engineer. It is the time of Kitchener's conquest of the Sudan; Anton would fight if necessary, a position Ursula challenges. Conquest of the Sudan, says Anton, is necessary to back up would-be colonists; he does not want to be a colonist:

'. . . but we've got to back up those who do.'
'Why have we?'
'Where is the nation if we don't?'
'But we aren't the nation. There are heaps of other people who are the nation'
'They might say *they* weren't either.'
'Well, if everybody said it, there wouldn't be a nation. But I should still be myself,' she asserted brilliantly.

'You wouldn't be yourself if there were no nation.'
'Why not?'
'Because you'd just be a prey to everybody and anybody.'

Ursula rejects this argument, unafraid of robbers who would 'take everything you'd got', she expresses her hatred of soldiers, 'so stiff and wooden'. Anton says he would fight for the nation, Ursula replies:

'For all that, you aren't the nation. What would you do for yourself?'
'I belong to the nation and must do my duty by the nation.'
'But when it didn't need your services in particular – when there *is* no fighting? What would you do then?'
He was irritated.
'I would do what everybody else does.'
'What?'
'Nothing. I would be in readiness for when I was needed.'
The answer came in exasperation.
'It seems to me,' she answered, 'as if you weren't anybody – as if there weren't anybody there, where you are. Are you anybody, really? You seem like nothing to me.'[4]

This splendid exchange is notable for two features: on the one hand, Ursula's flamboyant individualism; on the other, the weakness of Anton's defence. 'I should still be myself' is a striking claim against which nothing that Anton has to say can make headway. However, it would be a mistake to see this simply as a victory for Ursula's refusal to accept the nation as a moral category. What makes the exchange fascinating is that it is *Anton* who is saddled with a thin doctrine of the nation. His account of the nation is either instrumentalist – the nation as protector, a ludicrously inadequate argument in this context since the Sudanese seem unlikely in the near future to threaten Nottingham-shire – or based on an inarticulate patriotism. He asserts that Ursula would not be herself if it were not for the nation, but is unable to deliver an argument that would justify so strong a claim.

Ursula obviously has a powerful sense of self. On what basis? Clearly, she is not a calculating hedonist in the utilitarian mould – a position Lawrence detested – nor is she the Kantian individual in whom the struggle between duty and inclination rages. Her strength as an individual comes not from those immutable features of human beings worked up by the Enlightenment, but from her rootedness in an organic community. It is because she knows who she is and where she is from that she is able to assert so brilliantly her individuality. Lawrence's point, surely, is that this community, her community, is not the 'nation'. Anton is 'nothing', there is not anybody there, because he can only define himself as part of the nation and, on Lawrence's account, the nation is unable to provide the sort of roots that are needed if one is to be an individual. But, on the other hand, is the picture of Ursula's community complete without a political dimension that, perhaps, only the nation could supply?

The argument is unresolved, possibly because Lawrence did not want to resolve it – *The Rainbow* was written in the middle of the First World War, which Lawrence opposed, and his attack on unthinking patriotism is calculated accordingly – possibly because it is unresolvable without a different set of political theories coming into play.[5] Neither Ursula nor Anton – nor, perhaps, Lawrence – is thinking within a framework that would allow for the possibility of a 'nation-sized' organic community. The purpose of this chapter is to examine the ways in which such a framework could emerge – to look at those political theories that would on the one hand justify Anton's assertion that 'you wouldn't be yourself if there were no nation', while on the other provide Ursula with a fuller sense of what it is to be herself than her own position can offer. The aim is to examine 'communitarian' positions that, in contrast to cosmopolitanism, attempt to deepen an understanding of communal and social solidarity rather than theorise the relationship between the individual and humankind. The next section of this chapter will examine some of the ways in which these issues were set up in the eighteenth century, in the context of both the Enlightenment and anti-Enlightenment movements. The central sections of the chapter will then examine the Hegelian and English Idealist account of community, which will be followed by a brief examination of nineteenth-century nationalist and statist thought.

COMMUNITY, ENLIGHTENMENT AND ANTI-ENLIGHTENMENT

The root notion of communitarian thought is that value stems from the community, that the individual finds meaning in life by virtue of his or her membership of a political community. The thinkers of the Enlightenment were perfectly familiar with this notion; the political experiences of classical Greece and republican Rome were crucial to the intellectual formation of the enlightened, and, indeed, the Roman experience still shaped a live current of civic republicanism in political thought. However, in practice, most important figures of the Enlightenment were hostile to the communitarian idea. Their basic objection was nicely summarised by Voltaire; in his *Philosophical Dictionary*, the entry for 'Fatherland' contains the key observation: 'It is sad that to be a good patriot one often has to be the enemy of the rest of mankind.'[6] For this great opponent of superstition, the belief that one's country has some special virtue placing it apart from human-kind is firmly to be opposed.

The two great figures of the Enlightenment – Hume and Kant – would have agreed, albeit for different reasons. As we have seen, Hume was a sceptic in politics as in all else. His account of the state and political authority is instrumentalist; he rejects the notion of contract as obvious historical nonsense:

> Almost all the governments which exist at present, or of which there remains any record in history, have been founded either on usurpation or conquest or both, without any pretense of a fair consent or voluntary subjection of the people.[7]

However, justice, peace and order are required so that people can enjoy the benefits of society and, given their selfishness, such benefits can only be underwritten by government. Just as all people are much the same, so all governments have similar natures, being the site of 'a perpetual intestine struggle open or secret, between Authority and Liberty' neither of which can absolutely prevail.[8] In short, government is necessary and government authority should not be opposed – Hume is a conservative thinker in this respect, although on grounds the Tories of his age could hardly accept – but it would be foolish to regard the political community as a source of value; on the contrary, individuals have their own ends determined by the passions, and on the best construction the most positive role of government is to allow the pursuit of these ends to continue unhindered.

Kant's notion of the roots of individual action was very different, and he gave a slightly more positive account of the role of the correctly formed polity. As discussed in chapter 2 above, a 'republican' state – always bearing in mind Kant's definition of this term – can provide a framework within which the good can be pursued, and Kant endorses a contractualist account of the ideal origins of the state, unwilling to allow that the existing distribution of property rights is arbitrary – a fact upon which Hume insists. But for all this, it is clear that for Kant, as for Hume, the state is, in the end, a secondary institution. The only thing that is good in itself is a good will; the state cannot make men good, it cannot provide value to the human individual – the moral law, the categorical imperative, is within everyone, and the same for everyone, easier to come close to realising in a properly constructed state, but in no sense constituted by that state.[9]

A feature common to Romantic and post-Romantic thought has been to describe the Humean and Kantian account of the nature of man as, to employ a term of the first half of the next century, 'alienated' – separated from, set in opposition to, the community. It is worth stressing that Hume and Kant would have agreed with this description while rejecting its negative connotations. For each of them, 'freedom' – which, of course, they interpreted differently – meant precisely the state of being at an arm's length from the community. Freedom meant self-determination; moral autonomy for Kant, a free run for the 'passions' for Hume. Alienation is a precondition for this freedom.

The single figure who contributes most to a change in sensibility in this respect is Jean-Jacques Rousseau, a figure whose role in eighteenth-century thought is profoundly ambiguous.[10] As Hampson remarks, he can with equal plausibility be described as 'either one of the greatest writers of the Enlightenment, or its most eloquent and effective opponent'.[11] Rousseau's great theme is the corrupting effect of society. In the presocial state of nature, humans live an uncorrupted animal existence in which self-love (*amour de soi*), a positive force, does not turn into emulation (*amour propre*).[12] Society, arising out of the institution of property, corrupts the natural goodness of man – Rousseau's great work here is *Emile*, the philosophical account of an education uncontaminated by the greed and corruption of society.[13] The chains of society everywhere bind men, with appalling results in which the miseries of war feature prominently. States, with all the *amour propre* of corrupted beings, and, as Hoffman points out, with none of the residual compassion that one might look for in men, behave in ways that deserve Voltaire's strictures on the patriot.[14] Moreover, because it is society that corrupts, from Rousseau's perspective the development of a 'world society' will simply make things worse; whereas later Kant would see in the beginnings of economic interdependence a support for the extension of cosmopolitan *Recht*, Rousseau's profoundest thought on international relations is that exactly the opposite will be the case – interdependence will simply create the conditions for ever greater conflicts of interest and more damaging wars.[15]

Rousseau's diagnosis purportedly comes with a cure; in the opening lines of *The Social Contract* Rousseau claims to be able to render legitimate the change that has made free-born people slaves. His answer is not to look to some fanciful return to a presocial state of nature but to create a political community in which the unity of the body politic is a reflection of a 'general will' of the citizens and is thus not simply an external power to those citizens, but a force which reflects their true wills. In order to make sense of this position, some of the key passages in *The Social Contract* are devoted to the crucial issue of the relationship between the general will and the immediate and particular desires of the individual; Rousseau has to argue that the former corresponds to the real interests of the individual in a way that the latter cannot, to the point where ultimately 'anyone who refuses to obey the general will shall be forced to do so by the whole body, which means nothing more or less than that he will be forced to be free.'[16] This conclusion is for some the starting point for modern totalitarianism;[17] for Hume it would be a simple contradiction in terms, while for Kant it was a straightforward misconception; but for all subsequent variants of communitarian thought it is an obvious implication of Rousseau's key insight – that a satisfactory life lies in being in a right relationship with a community.

The problem with Rousseau's thought is that his account of the circumstances under which the general will can be realised is so restrictive as to have little practical relevance for modern conditions. His strictures against representative democracy commit him to small, face-to-face communities where all can legislate together, and, in the interests of peace, international trade must be kept to the minimum; taken together, these requirements dictate a world of small, agrarian, autarchic, communities of citizen farmers and artisans – Spartas without the Helots and transported to the Swiss Alps. This is hardly a solution to the problems of the modern world. On Rousseau's own account only one country in Europe was not already spoiled and therefore capable of 'legislation'. The island of Corsica would one day 'astonish' Europe – a famous presentiment since the birthplace of Napoleon Bonaparte did indeed provide a force that would spread to all of Europe a republican politics that its founders believed to be in part inspired by Rousseau.[18] However, the French Revolution's attempt to create a sense of community and wholeness through a phoney recreation of the Roman heritage – via devices such as the sometimes farcical ceremonies of Robespierre's Religion of the Supreme Being, or the republican iconography of David – bore only a warped relationship to Rousseau's account of the free state.[19]

In opposition to the universal claims of the Revolution, Burke posed a different notion of the organic community to that of Rousseau or the French republicans. 'A nation is . . . an idea of continuity which extends in time as well as in numbers and in space';[20] it is not something that can be created or recreated, nor is it based on abstract principles – the rights of Englishmen established over the centuries, based now on prescription, are real in a way that the abstract notion of the rights of man is not. Europe consists of a family of nations each with its own traditions, living together as virtually one great state with some diversity of customs until the barbarism of the French Revolution disrupted this state of affairs.[21] In view of the record of war in the eighteenth century it is tempting to dismiss this as pure polemic, but in fact Burke does have a rich notion of the practices and traditions in international society, which in a different context would deserve further study.[22] However, in the context of this book, Burke's thought leads to a dead end. He does not provide the basis upon which a general approach to communitarian international thought can be constructed; his specificity is a virtue in some contexts, but not for our purposes.

Rousseau and Burke are, one way or another, reacting to the Enlightenment in France; the German Enlightenment was always different, and the most important critic of the most important *Aufklärer* – Johann Gottfried Herder, the critic of Kant – produced a set of ideas distinct from anything produced outside of Germany, ideas that influenced the formation of the thought of the German romantics and of Hegel.[23] The importance of Herder lies in his exploration of the notion that individuals are shaped by cultures; the notion of an individual defined as such in contradiction to his culture is not simply undesirable, it is an impossibility. The individual is not prior to culture – as the Kantian position would seem to assume – but shaped by it, and culture in this context is not something that can be consciously created, as, say, the republican tradition might cultivate civic virtue, but something best expressed in language and folkways – the culture of the *Volk*, the 'people' or 'nation'. Herder is an important figure in German culture by virtue of his promotion of the study of German folk-culture, its songs, poems and stories, and the sense of community he espouses springs from these roots.

Herder's politics follow from this: 'Herder's central political idea lies in the assertion that the proper foundation for a sense of collective political identity is not the acceptance of a common sovereign power, but the sharing of a common culture.'[24] Nationality is crucial to politics; it is a common language and a shared culture that makes common citizens – as opposed to metaphysical notions such as the general will. However, the politics that Herder espouses is, in Barnard's phrase, 'anarcho-pluralist'; Herder wants to see power spread rather than concentrated and his system would not allow for central administrative organs or a state in the modern sense. His ideas are a curious – and attractive – mixture of communitarian and cosmopolitan notions. The *Volk* is a central notion but, unlike later theorists of the nation, Herder is a pluralist who values all cultures and refuses to rank them in any kind of order of significance – 'the culture of *man* is not the culture of the *European*: it manifests itself according to place and time in *every* people.'[25] This is admirable, but Herder's rich sense of community is, none the less, married to a weak sense of the political. As with Rousseau, the political system he espouses is less convincing than the sensitivity with which he perceives the nature of political identity.

Herder was in revolt against the notion that the richness of cultural experience could be replaced by the cold light of reason. Following from this perception, 'German Romanticism became largely a revolt against reason.'[26] The German Romantics, took over Herder's notion of culture without his pluralism and cosmopolitanism, endorsing a variety of hierarchical political utopias constructed on relativist ethics and, in sharp contradiction to Herder, incorporating strong state structures. The most interesting of these theorists, Fichte, produced a vision of the 'closed commercial state', in which the state regulates the activity of the citizens, 'protecting' them, to such an extent that Bosanquet's judgement that this text is 'perhaps the earliest document of a rigorous State Socialism' seems reasonable.[27]

In reaction to the individualism of the mainstream Enlightenment – as embodied in writers such as Hume and Kant – all these writers propose notions of the community designed to promote or reflect the idea of an organic relationship between individuals, which relationship they see as desirable or already nascently existent. The problem with this approach is twofold. On the one hand, the political arrangements proposed bear no relationship to reality, nor, in the view of the most perceptive of these writers, Rousseau, could they bear such a relationship. On the other hand, if they could be brought into existence there seems good reason to fear that the positive gains of Enlightenment thought would be lost as the price of the construction of an affective organic community – the freedom of the individual would be submerged in order to give him or her a meaningful place within the community. A satisfactory political theory of the community ought to meet these points; it should be an interpretation of reality rather than a utopian construction of how things should be, and it should preserve individual autonomy, the great achievement of Enlightenment thought, while situating this individuality in a communitarian context.[28] This may seem to be a tall order, but it is the claim of the Hegelians that they can meet this set of specifications. This claim will now be examined.

HEGELIAN ACCOUNTS OF POLITICS

At the centre of one of the most important attempts to understand the notion of political community lies the work of Hegel. A generation ago this judgement would have been inconceivable, at least within the Anglo-Saxon world, but over the last twenty-five years there has been a remarkable revival of interest in Hegelianism.[29] This revival has been closely related to the fortunes of Marxism; in the 1960s interest in the young Marx led scholars to study the Hegelian sources of his early writings, while in the 1980s the failures of Marxism in eastern Europe and the former Soviet Union redirected interest towards Hegel's notion of civil society.[30]

However, none of this interest has made Hegel any easier to understand, or his system any easier to expound – although the multiplicity of good secondary studies does make for a fuller set of 'further readings'. There are many problems that have to be overcome in a presentation of Hegel's thought. The difficulty with his ideas is not simply a function of language and style, as is largely true with Kant; the obscurity is real and sometimes impenetrable. Hegel offers a total system of philosophy; his aim is Absolute Knowledge – for once, capitalisation seems appropriate – and his thoughts on politics and international relations are embedded in this 'total system'; it is a matter of debate whether they can be understood in isolation from the system.[31] However, since those writers most favourably disposed towards Hegel reject his notion of the Absolute even while asserting his great contemporary relevance, it seems reasonable to at least try to present a 'demythologised' account of his politics. The problem of presentation remains.

One way out of this difficulty would be to adopt the strategy of employing a, more sober, Hegel substitute – for example, in his study *The Moral Philosophers*, Richard Norman takes as his text for the Hegelian approach to ethics Bradley's chapter 'My station and its duties' from *Ethical Studies* rather than Hegel's *Philosophy of Right*.[32] The problem with this particular example is that Bradley has rather less to say about international relations than some other Hegelians; however, the basic principle of an indirect approach to Hegel will be followed here. In this section an eclectic account of Hegelian politics will be offered, drawing on the *Philosophy of Right* but also *Ethical Studies*, Bosanquet's *Philosophical Theory of the State*, and recent studies of an essentially Hegelian disposition such as those of Charvet and Frost.[33] In the next section, the international thought of Hegel and the English Idealists will be examined, and here the presentation will be less eclectic, linking particular positions to particular writers in a much closer way.

Hegel's mature writings of the first decades of the last century were formulated in reaction to the German Romantics and, more important in this context, to Kant and Kantian philosophy. Hegel's objection to Kant's moral philosophy is that it is purely formal – 'Duty for duty's sake' as Bradley puts it – and based on an incorrect view of the nature of persons; the two critiques go together.[34] Kant sees the individual as a moral agent existing prior to society, driven by the moral law, the categorical imperative. The Hegelian position denies that it is possible to think of individuals in this way in isolation from the community that has shaped them and constituted them as individuals – following Herder in this but, as will be seen, assigning a non-Herderian importance to the state within the community. Hegel draws a sharp distinction between morality (*Moralität*) which is abstract, based on conscience, and the Kantian 'good will', but lacks content, and ethics (*Sittlichkeit*), which is 'the concrete morality of a rational social order where rational institutions and laws provide the content of conscientious conviction'.[35] Some such distinction is commonplace in moral philosophy; the distinctiveness of the Hegelian position is that because individuals are constituted by the community, the demands of social ethics override – and should override – the imperatives of conscience. This position is nicely expressed by Bradley in a clear, and to some, shocking, passage in 'My station and its duties':

> [conscience wants] you to have no law but yourself, and to be better than the world. But [an ethic in the above sense] tells you that, if you could be as good as your world, you would be better than most likely you are, and that to wish to be better than the world is to be already on the threshold of immorality.[36]

No clearer contrast with an ethic based on the categorical imperative – which insists on the irrelevance of the 'world' in matters of moral judgement – could be imagined, and indeed Bradley in his subsequent essay on 'Ideal Morality' backs away from the implications of his statement.[37] Hegel did not.

The notion that to be out of step with one's world is to be on the 'threshold of immorality' might seem to sanction an extreme cultural and moral relativism. This is not Hegel's intention, and his *Philosophy of History* and *Philosophy of Right* purport to show that the modern state is the culmination of history, superior to all previous social forms, because it is only within the modern state that an ethical life which allows freedom for all is realised.[38] It is never possible to be better than one's world, but not all worlds are of equal value, and the modern (Hegel says 'Germanic') realm is superior to its predecessors.

Ethical life is based on three institutions, described in the third part of the *Philosophy of Right* – the family, civil society and the state. The ethical family – and not all families are ethical; in Rome, for example, the power of the father reduced children to slavery – provides a context within which each family member is valued and loved for his or her own sake, and the recognition that this provides for children is an important first step in the constitution of individuality.[39] However, love is based on feeling, not reason, and a person in a family is simply a family member – the constitution of individuality requires that persons leave this context and make their way in the wider world.

This wider world, Hegel terms civil society.[40] There are three elements to civil society in the account given in *Philosophy of Right*. First, there is 'a system of needs'; this refers to the economic life of the community, making one's way in the world, owning property, entering into economic relations with others similarly placed. Second is 'the administration of justice', the set of rules required by the system of needs. Third is civil society constituted by 'the police and the corporation'; police here is a misleading term since in English it is now more or less divorced from the notion of 'policy', which is what is meant here. The police and the corporation could be interpreted without too much distortion as the public and private institutions of policy-making. It should be noted here that much of what is usually thought of as the state falls, according to Hegel, within civil society. If we think of the state as an external set of rules for the 'authoritative allocation of values' in the terms of modern political science, or as an instrument that performs the task of social co-ordination made necessary by the clash of individual interests and passions as Hume would have it, or in Kantian terms as the product of a contract which makes it possible for individuals to act morally, then the state as a whole falls within the Hegelian notion of civil society.

Hegel's point is that this is inadequate. In civil society, as members of corporations and as property owners, persons develop their individuality to an extent not possible within the family. Within the family, identity is tied up with being a family member – filling a specific, limited role in a relationship based on love not reason. In civil society by contrast, the sense of individuality is all-powerful – people develop as individuals as against all others and the rules of civil society are designed to regulate a relationship which is distant and non-affective. In civil society these rules are external to the individual; they are experienced as constraints on freedom, as indeed they are. The third element of ethical life is the state, and it is the role of the modern state to provide the context within which the external rules needful for relations between individuals can be internalised, no longer experienced as constraints. The state provides the element of unity necessary if the individual is to overcome the separateness inherent in civil society.[41]

There is a potential problem here. On the one hand, the state is to provide a context within which persons become truly individual, but on the other, the claims that Hegel makes for the state would seem to threaten this individuality. Thus the state is the 'actuality of the ethical idea' and 'an absolute unmoved end in itself', which means 'this final end has supreme right against the individual, whose supreme duty is to be a member of the state.'[42] It is not difficult to see how, on a superficial reading, this could be seen as a warrant for authoritarian if not totalitarian control. However, for Hegel the ethical state is a constitutional state – more precisely, what he calls a 'constitutional monarchy'; the crown should have power of ultimate decision, in a system with separate executive, based on the universal class of civil servants, and legislature, based on the representation of the various estates in society.[43] The state constitutes its citizens as true individuals precisely because, although the ultimate expression of unity, it is also limited – not by any external force but by its own logic. Critics of the Hegelian approach have not found this convincing, and argue that the constitutionalism which Hegel definitely espouses is undermined by the claims he also makes on behalf of the state.[44]

The unity of the Hegelian state is clearly related to Rousseau's general will, but with striking differences.[45] The key difference is that Rousseau's general will can only be realised in small-scale autarchic societies and is, as such, at best an unattainable ideal, at worst a utopian fantasy. Hegel, by contrast, believes that he is describing in his philosophy not what ought to be but what is. The famous, much maligned and misunderstood sentence 'What is rational is actual and what is actual is rational' makes the point.[46] By this Hegel does not mean to assert the obvious untruth that all states in the 1810s are constitutional monarchies of the sort he describes – indeed, his assertion that Prussia itself was such a state can only be described as an aberration. What the 'rationality of the actual' statement means is that in the *Philosophy of Right* Hegel believes he has outlined a rational interpretation of the nature of the individual and the modern state, the only interpretation that makes sense of the chaotic contingent features of the states that actually exist.

It should be noted that it is at this point that the attempt to provide a 'secular interpretation' of Hegel's politics runs into difficulties.[47] From the non-metaphysical perspective adopted here, this interpretation of the state can only be an 'interpretation' – a more or less plausible account of the salient features of modern states; it cannot be the only possible interpretation. Likewise, the institutions of a constitutional monarchy can be described as those most conducive to freedom, but the idea that these institutions are the *only* way that freedom can be achieved cannot be supported. Hegel's account of his own position is in terms of the unfolding of spirit (*Geist*), its self-realisation in the world reaching complete self-knowledge in the modern state; it is in these terms that he believes himself to be describing what is, and not simply an ought-to-be.[48] Clearly, this guarantee is only available to someone who accepts Hegel's position in full; others, including the majority of modern 'Hegelians', will have to be satisfied with arguments which attest to the general plausibility and heuristic value of his position but which cannot provide the certainty with which he wrote.

The ethical family, civil society and the corporation, and the institutions of a constitutional state provide, according to Hegel, a context in which the freedom of the individual is fully achievable without that loss of affective community thought unavoidable on the Enlightenment account of the conditions for human autonomy. To the thinkers of the Enlightenment freedom involves separation from traditional communities which swamp and stifle individuality; critics of the Enlightenment argue that the individual that such a freedom creates, cut off from all sense of rootedness in the world, will be a tortured and wretched being. It is crucial to realise that Hegel's position does *not* represent a compromise between these two extremes. He believes that in the modern state both positions are met in full; absolute freedom is combined with absolute unity – these notions are not in contradiction to one another; on the contrary, each is implied by the other.[49]

It should be clear by now why Hegel can be taken as the most important 'communitarian' thinker as opposed to the cosmopolitanism of Kant. However, it should be stressed that Hegel does not regard his position as implying that there are fundamental differences between human beings in different communities. In a note to section 209 of the *Philosophy of Right*, a section on the administration of justice in civil society, he remarks: 'A man counts as a man in virtue of his manhood alone, not because he is a Jew, Catholic, Protestant, German, Italian &c. This is an assertion which thinking ratifies and to be conscious of it is of infinite importance.' However, he continues that this assertion goes wrong when turned into a critique of the modern state; thus 'It is defective only when it is crystallised e.g. as a cosmopolitanism in opposition to the concrete life of the state.'[50] This provides a convenient jumping-off point for a discussion of Hegelian international relations theory.

HEGELIAN THEORIES OF INTERNATIONAL RELATIONS

Hegel's account of international relations is set out in sections 321–40 of the *Philosophy of Right* supplemented by observations at a number of other points in the text. The essential points are simple. The state is in the full sense sovereign; there can be no higher authority than the state. Thus the notion of an international law that controlled state behaviour must always remain at the level of an ought-to-be rather than an actuality. The individuality of citizens demands the preservation of the individuality of the state; this is not, as it were, negotiable. One of the roles of the state in its external aspect in civil society is to promote and protect the economic interests of the population, and a specific civil society will be driven by its inner dialectic to 'push beyond its own limits and seek markets and so its necessary means of subsistence, in other lands which are either deficient in the goods it has overproduced, or else generally backward in industry'.[51] This is one of the causes of conflict and war – although Hegel makes the point that the final end of the state is to be found in protecting its own substantive individuality rather than the security of individual life and property, the latter being a demand that arises from civil society, not the state in its internal aspect.[52]

War is not an external accident but a necessary feature of a world in which the individualities of states cannot be limited. War is not to be regarded as an absolute evil. War contributes towards the maintenance of the ethical health of peoples; 'perpetual peace' – Hegel specifically refers to Kant here – is not simply unattainable; it would be if attained positively undesirable.[53] War provides a context within which individuals can demonstrate their individuality in the most dramatic way by acts of courageous self-sacrifice in which they endorse the values that have made them true individuals, recognising the state as the source of their individuality.[54] This is an opportunity peace does not provide.

States recognise themselves as states even in war, and Hegel believes it important that the states-system be preserved; the individuality of any one state depends on the existence of the individuality of other states and this should not be threatened. Hence:

> in war, war itself is characterised as something which ought to pass away. It implies therefore the proviso of *jus gentium* that the possibility of peace be retained (and so, for example that envoys must be respected), and, in general, that war be not waged against domestic institutions, against the peace of family and private life, or against persons in their private capacity.[55]

The rest of international law is a matter of the customs of nations, valuable but of a different status.

All this would seem to be related to 'realist' or 'power-politics' approaches to international relations. Clearly, there is some affinity here, but it cannot be stressed too strongly that Hegel is *not* suggesting that might is right. Sections 341–60 of the *Philosophy of Right* – on world history – make this clear. 'World history is a court of judgment' and 'world history is not the verdict of mere might'.[56] Once again, there is a problem here with any secular account of the Hegelian position; when Hegel writes of history as a court he is employing a metaphor but not a rhetorical device. History will indeed ensure that the movement of events will bring about the achievement of absolute freedom through the self-realisation of spirit in the world. In his Preface to the *Philosophy of Right* Hegel remarks 'To recognise reason as the rose in the cross of the present and thereby to enjoy the present, this is the rational insight that reconciles us to the actual';[57] some such solace is needed here, but of course, available only to those who think with Hegel on the subject of spirit.

Hegel's picture of international relations and war is an account of how things actually are, how they must be and how they always will be. The modern state brings about the full realisation of reason and freedom and cannot be transcended. Vincent and others have pointed to a passage in *Philosophy of History* in which Hegel appears to be suggesting that the Germanic realm will be followed by a new kind of realm in America, but Plant is surely right in regarding this position as incompatible with Hegel's overall account of freedom and reason.[58] Whether it makes sense to think in terms of an 'end of history' is a matter of some controversy,[59] but that Hegel believed that there was no higher stage than the ethical state seems certain – he is specific that philosophy is possible only in retrospect, we can see the movement of spirit only because it is complete; in his famous phrases 'When philosophy paints its grey on grey then has a shape of life grown old. . . . The owl of Minerva spreads its wings only with the falling of the dusk.'[60] The ethical state may be spread throughout the world but cannot be transcended by a world government; just as no individual could be an individual without other individuals, so the state cannot be a state without other states, and without the state there can be no individual citizens. The preservation of a world of states is an ethical necessity hence the stricture against cosmopolitanism reported above. It seems to follow conclusively from the first premises of the Hegelian approach to ethical life that the state cannot allow supremacy to any other body – which is not to say that existing states could not be replaced by some new state, merely to assert that there must be a plurality of states accepting no superior. What is less clear is that it follows from this that war is a necessary – let alone desirable – feature of international relations. It is instructive here to examine the work of two of the English Idealists who devoted some space to this question and came up with different conclusions from those of Hegel.

T.H. Green's *Lectures on the Principles of Political Obligation* were first delivered in 1879 and published posthumously in volume II of his *Philosphical Works.*[61] Along with Bradley's *Ethical Studies* and Bosanquet's *The Philosophical Theory of the State* this is one of the key texts of the influential school of English Idealists – until the last two decades the most important group of writers to have been influenced by Hegel. Green establishes an essentially Hegelian view of the state and then in a series of lectures examines the rights this perspective attributes to the state and to individuals. The most important of these for our purposes is Lecture K, 'The right of the state over the individual in war'.[62] After discussing a number of issues concerning the destructiveness of war, wars for liberty, and wars of religion, and while acknowledging that there can be no authority over states, that the state is the institution 'through which alone the freedom of man is realised', Green denies that there is any necessity for war:

> It is nothing then in the necessary organisation of the state, but rather some defect of that organisation in relation to its proper function of maintaining and reconciling rights, of giving scope to capacities, that leads to a conflict of apparent interests between one state and another. The wrong, therefore, which results to human society from conflicts between states cannot be condoned on the ground that it is a necessary incident of the existence of states.[63]

He goes on to argue that the equation of public-spirited patriotism with military aggressiveness is invalid and that the individuality of states, which must be preserved, does not require conflict with other nations. His vision is of a 'bond of peace' emerging and deepening among the nations, without ever submerging their separate identities.[64]

Bosanquet arrived at similar conclusions in his *The Philosophical Theory of the State.* This work was first published in 1899, but the third edition was revised for publication in 1919, which, of course, gave Bosanquet the opportunity to reflect on the Great War of 1914–18 – and, in view of the criticism attached to Hegelianism as an alleged cause of German aggressiveness, some such reflection was mandatory.[65] The first edition had stressed that the state was the supreme community, and although its actions could be morally wrong they are not the subject of law. Bosanquet leaves this position unchanged, merely underlining the point that a guilty state 'would be judged before the tribunal of humanity and of history.[66] To reiterate an earlier remark, the judgement of history, of course, is something to be taken very seriously by a Hegelian. In his 1919 Introduction, Bosanquet insists again that 'states are diverse embodiments of the human spirit, in groups territorially determined through historical trial and failure.'[67] They are part of an 'ethical family of nations' each with its own mission; sovereignty is an inherent feature of this mission.

> On these premises it is ridiculous to ask if sovereignty and the state are favourable to war. Plato already pointed out that war springs from that disease of the state which leads to policies of expansion. In order to reinforce the organisation of rights by other states the main thing which each has to do is to perfect its own.[68]

States have wills and personalities and more responsibility. The state is 'the guardian of moral interests and must be faithful to its duty';[69] the state can enforce its rights and cannot pass off this moral responsibility to the new League of Nations. However, and explicitly following Green, there is no reason to believe that war is an inherent part of the relations of states or could be a good in itself.[70]

Clearly, Green and Bosanquet see things differently from Hegel, and the extended quote from Bosanquet precisely picks out the difference, without, apparently, noticing that this is what it is doing. Bosanquet writes of 'that disease of the state which leads to policies of expansion', but Hegel explicitly endorses expansion as a policy made necessary by virtue of the duty of the state to protect its citizens and promote their interests (see above).[71] However, Green and Bosanquet have a point here; the expansionary policies of the state are for Hegel an aspect of the state in its external dimension as a regulatory organ within civil society and not of its ethical nature as the unifying feature of ethical life. In this sense Hegel's comments on colonisation and expansion in the *Philosophy of Right* need to be placed in context not as a necessary feature of state policy, but as a contingent judgement as to what, in certain circumstances, state policy will be. This is a judgement that can be challenged without undermining Hegel's political philosophy taken as a whole.

This is not to say that Hegel's judgement is not sound. It could be argued quite reasonably that Hegel's account of an expanding economy generating conflict is a realistic assessment of the driving forces of civil society as opposed to the counter assertions of Green and Bosanquet. Certainly a 'Marxist–realist' such as Carr would be bound to point out that Green and Bosanquet were intellectual luminaries of the greatest economic empire the world had then seen, and perhaps their assessment of the 'diseases' of the state reflects that fact.[72] None the less the central feature of Hegelian international theory that comes out of this is that, however plausible Hegel's account of conflict is, it does not follow that war *is* a *necessary* feature of the relations between Hegelian states. Nor, it should be stressed – and here Green and Bosanquet are surely right – is there any substance to the view that the 'cleansing' feature of war, its roles in forming citizens, is a necessary feature of communitarian international thought. The best that can be said of this view is that it does identify a real phenomenon, as the Dunkirk spirit or the solidarity of the Blitz suggests; but this cannot be taken as a justification for war, it is merely an observation that not all the side effects of war are disastrous.[73]

In coming to terms with this theory, it is necessary to make clear two distinctions. The first has been addressed in the last paragraph; it is the distinction between those aspects of Hegelian international theory that are necessary in so far as they define the approach and those that are merely contingent interpretations of these necessary features. The real distinction here is between statements which assert the supremacy of the state, the inadmissability of accepting any superior authority to the state, which are, indeed, definitive and unavoidable given the first premises of the theory, and those statements which involve assertions about the behaviour of states towards one another, which will always be a matter of opinion and judgement. The reason why it is important to keep this distinction always in mind is because critics of Hegelian international thought frequently confuse the two different kinds of assertion, using problems with the contingent aspects of the theory to undermine the necessary. As was seen in chapter 2, much the same problem arises in connection with Kantian international thought.

The second distinction that needs to be kept in mind is between those justifications for the Hegelian position that stem from Hegel's own philosophy of absolute knowledge, and those which rest on what one might term 'common-sense' reasoning. The essential point here is that Hegel's belief that the state guarantees freedom and that world history has a meaning that undermines any equation of right with might rests on foundations unavailable to those who do not accept his idea of history as the self-realisation of spirit – and, nowadays, this means pretty well everyone. Whether or not Hegel's position is satisfactory is going to depend on the general plausibility of the account he gives of ethical life; it will not be judged in the terms he would have considered appropriate. This need not be a major handicap; it merely means treating Hegelian theory as exactly that – 'theory' and not 'knowledge'. At various points in the argument it has proved necessary to introduce the wider system in order to explain how it is that Hegelians hold particular positions and for this purpose a completely demythologised Hegel is impossible. However, it is still possible to hold that a secularised Hegelian account of international relations is the best available to us without accepting the full system – in much the same way that it is possible to believe Kant to be one of the greatest thinkers on international relations without believing that he has given a convincing account of the making of synthetic *a priori* judgements.

COMMUNITARIAN THEORIES OF INTERNATIONAL RELATIONS IN THE NINETEENTH CENTURY

In the examination of cosmopolitan thought in chapter 2 it was shown that while the Kantian position was undoubtedly the most elaborate account of cosmopolitanism available, it was not the only sophisticated version on the market. Benthamite and Marxist accounts of cosmopolitanism provide an alternative focus on the subject to the Kantian account of *Perpetual Peace*. The utilitarian position in particular, with its impersonal outcome-oriented focus, offers a stark contrast to the agent-centred Kantian approach – indeed, the only reason for taking Kant rather than Bentham as the archetypal cosmopolitan is because Kant offers a more elaborate series of texts on the subject than his consequentialist opponent.

In the case of communitarian theory, the situation is rather different. Most nineteenth-century communitarian thinkers are either working from intellectual origins that have affinities with the Idealist and Romantic movements discussed above, or are simply reflecting an intellectually unrigorous mixture of patriotic traditionalism with a simplified version of Machiavellian statism. Contemporary social theory does offer communitarian theory that is neither idealist nor romantic, but the tradition only prefigures this work at a limited number of points – in particular, in the writings of J.S. Mill.

The most important non-Hegelian contribution to the communitarian tradition is the cluster of ideas – associated with no particular writer – that make up the theory of nationalism.[74] The doctrine that the world divides naturally into nations, that nations are the source of value for human beings and should therefore be the basis for political organisation is clearly one of the most influential notions of the last two centuries, and is now firmly embedded in the settled norms of the international system. This doctrine clearly builds upon notions of patriotism and love of one's own folk that are premodern and

prepolitical, but it also builds upon the inellectual movements discussed above. Rousseau's insistence on the importance of love of one's
country as one of the factors that can preserve a just society comes
through clearly in writings such as the *Considerations on the Government of Poland,* and the republican cult of the nation was clearly an
important factor in the French Revolution, which in turn was
instrumental to the spread of nationalism throughout Europe.

Nationalism as a political doctrine also owes a great deal to Herder
and the German Romantics. As discussed above, Herder's own view on
political organisation was anarcho-pluralist rather than nationalist.
His notion of the *Volk* was not intended to identify the basis of a
nation–state; from his perspective politics is something that should be
organised around national groupings but not in the form of a state as
conventionally understood. It is also the case that Herder refuses to
argue that one people are superior to another; his argument is that all
peoples have something to offer, their own distinctive contribution to
the human family. Some at least of the early theorists of nationalism –
Mazzini, for example – adopted this perspective of a nationalism that
is non-competitive and implies no judgement as to the relative worth
of different nations in the wider scheme of things.[75] This position
could reasonably be described as a politicised or 'statised' version of
Herder's vision. It also could be regarded as an excessively optimistic
account of the socio-psychology of nationalist thought; in practice,
most nationalism *is* competitive and directed against others – those
theories (the majority) which regard nationalism as a modernising
ideology which is in some sense based on the desire to 'catch up' would
say that nationalism is inevitably and inherently based on competition
and emulation.[76]

Early-nineteenth-century nationalism in Germany was also heavily
influenced by Fichte, whose *Addresses to the German Nation* combined a national appeal with a statist position – Fichte was a
Machiavellian who advocated the application of Machiavellian methods to the task of achieving German liberty.[77] A similar mix is to be
found in the writings of Treitschke later in the century, although in
this case the attempt to place the growth of a national power-state in
an ethical context 'cast a radiance upon power in the state which
excessively transfigured it', to quote the judgement of a writer whose
sympathy towards Treitschke was greater than the latter has usually
been granted in the twentieth century.[78]

In this brief examination of the basis of nationalism it should be
noted that no reference has been made to Hegelian thought. This is
because although Hegel's thought emerges from the same roots as
nationalism, and although it can be, and has been, made compatible

with the doctrine, there is no necessary link between the two. For Hegel the ethical state is not necessarily a national state, nor, *a fortiori*, is the national state necessarily ethical. The ethical nature of the state rests upon its role as the point of unity, where citizens internalise the authority that faced them as an external force in civil society. There is no reason to think that this unity is a national unity – indeed, in so far as Hegel's assessment that Prussia was a constitutional monarchy of the type he favoured is to be taken seriously then an explicitly non-national model is being offered. Bosanquet later argues for the importance of language in the formation of political communities, and it may be that common nationality could buttress common citizenship, but the two notions are clearly separate.[79]

If early nationalist thinking owes much to the German counter-Enlightenment, and to the French republican tradition, later notions of a 'right to self-determination' come much closer to those twentieth-century versions of communitarian thought which rely on democratic legitimation. The key figure here, who, in a relatively few number of references to the subject, prefigures many of the arguments of twentieth-century communitarians, is John Stuart Mill. Mill's essay 'A few words on non-intervention' was briefly considered in chapter 2 above, in the context of utilitarian thought on international relations.[80] The point was made there that Mill appears to assign a value not simply to freedom, however it is achieved (which would be a consistently Benthamite position), but to peoples liberating themselves. In *Considerations on Representative Government* Mill explicitly endorses the national principle;

> Where the sentiment of nationality exists in any force, there is a *prima facie* case for uniting all the members of a nationality under the same government, and a government to themselves apart. This is merely saying that the question of government ought to be decided by the governed. One hardly knows what any division of the human race should be free to do if not to determine with which of the various collective bodies of human beings they choose to associate themselves. . . . Free institutions are next to impossible in a country made up of different nationalities.[81]

These are very strong statements and it is not clear that Mill is fully conscious of the extent to which this position is at variance with the (modified) utilitarianism he purports elsewhere to espouse. He follows the last remark about free institutions with a series of comments of an essentially utilitarian nature about the ease of communication between leaders and led which follows from the possession of a common language, but his assertion that any 'division of the human race' has a right to self-determination is difficult to defend on strictly utilitarian lines.

The real significance of Mill's position is that it prefigures much twentieth-century communitarian thought. Whereas contract theorists simply assume that some kind of community is pre-existent, and whereas, by contrast, nationalists emerging out of German Romanticism and Idealism assume that there is a cultural basis for the nation, Mill's position dodges the problems involved with both of these approaches. Mill's normative doctrine that the 'question of government ought to be decided by the governed' puts the issue of the shape and extent of the community on the agenda – unlike contractarian thought – while making it clear that what constitutes a 'division of the human race' for these purposes is determined by the choice of the people and not by some pre-existing cultural attributes. 'A nation is a nation if it believes itself to be one, and on the basis of this belief it is entitled to self-determination' would be a reasonable summary of this position, and it is some such reasoning that is at the root of a great deal of communitarian thought in the twentieth century – at least, of communitarian thought that is rooted in liberalism. Of course, Mill's position is not without problems. As the experience of nationalism over the last hundred and fifty years demonstrates only too clearly, subjectively determined divisions of the human race do not always – or even usually – coincide with geographically segregated communities, and the issue of determining which divisions have a right to self-determination is the source of endless problems. Equally, it is not clear what kind of rights communities which have determined themselves to be nations have other than the right to make this determination; does it follow, for example, that the right to form a nation entails the right to regulate the 'membership' of one's nation?[82] If so, is this right an absolute right or subject to limitations? It would be fair to say that Mill does not address these issues, or even pose them in any clear form. He seems to assume that the problem of nationalism is created by the existence of oppressive multi-national empires whose dissolution would remove the source of discontents – in fact, the experience of the twentieth century suggests that the destruction of entities such as the Habsburg Empire leads to more, not fewer, problems with nationalism as the liberated peoples contest with each other rather than the imperial authorities.

Although Mill does not work through the implications of his defence of the national principle – indeed, seems unaware that many of these implications exist – he does provide an interesting pointer to the way in which one branch of the communitarian tradition will develop in the next century. What is particularly interesting about Mill is that he endorses the nation from a progressivist standpoint. Up to this point in the discussion it might have been thought that the contrast between cosmopolitan and communitarian thought was a contrast between, broadly defined, 'left' and 'right' camps. Such a characterisation would have been somewhat tendentious – it would certainly be a mistake to see the English Idealists as thinkers of the political right without a great deal of qualification – but not self-evidently false. Even if Mill's thoughts on this subject are not fully developed, it is, none the less, significant that the author of *On Liberty* can be described as a communitarian. It highlights the point that these are notions which have no necessary link with particular political positions on the wider issues that divide modern societies. While there may be affinities between some varieties of communitarian thought and the political right, other varieties which rest on democratic notions of political legitimacy may point in the other direction. This point will take on particular significance when it comes to an examination of twentieth-century communitarian thought.

CONCLUSION

As is the case with cosmopolitanism, communitarian thought is complex and contains within itself more than one theory of politics. What we are dealing with here are two frameworks within which theories can be sited rather than two theories as such. Or, perhaps, communitarianism and cosmopolitanism can be best seen as background theories which provide the assumptions upon which those theories which attempt to give a direct account of how the world works are based. The 'background' nature of these approaches, and the varied theories they can generate, makes it difficult to assess their adequacy, whether they are looked at individually or set against each other. As some late-twentieth-century debates reveal, in the last resort the extent to which communitarian as opposed to cosmopolitan thought is convincing seems to depend more on the 'gut' feelings of individual authors than on the processes of reasoned argument.[83] It is not surprising that this is so: what is at stake here are questions that go to the heart of the ways in which individuals – whether in their capacities as citizens or philosophers or both – view the ultimate source of value in social life, and although such matters are accessible to reason they are rarely determined by debate and discussion alone. In a book such as this no-one – neither author nor reader – need feel called upon to declare outright for one or other approach.

However, what can be said is that the two approaches, taken

together, do offer a fairly comprehensive framework within which thought on international relations can be situated and, indeed, for much of the last century was so situated. In the nineteenth century there was no discipline of international relations but there were a number of discourses which revolved around international problems – strategy, international law, international history – and it seems clear that these discourses did indeed take as their foundation one or other of the variants of cosmopolitan or communitarian thought. This may not always have been explicitly recognised, but it was a feature of these discourses none the less. To take just one example, Azar Gat's recent, outstanding, study, *The Origins of Military Thought from the Enlightenment to Clausewitz*, demonstrates just how much the founders of strategy owed to the philosophical framework created by the German reaction to the Enlightenment, a framework described in the present work as communitarian.[84] Of course, this framework lay in the background of strategic discourse – such is the proper role of background theories – but it was available to provide answers to the more searching questions about strategy when or if these questions were actually posed. Most of the time they will not be posed. Most of the time a practical discourse such as strategic studies works within a carefully delineated area and is not required to explain and justify its most fundamental assumptions. Sometimes, however, fundamental questions do come to the surface, basic assumptions are challenged, and when this happens what is required is an overarching conception of the world which can provide a coherent account of the essentials of human existence. For much of nineteenth-century international thought either cosmopolitan or communitarian thought provided such an overarching conception.

This point can be made in another way, by posing the more general question about the role of political philosophy in political analysis. Wilfred Sellars helpfully defines philosophy as the study of 'how things, in the broadest possible sense of the term, hang together, in the broadest possible sense of the term', and this is a definition that can be applied with profit to the role of political philosophy.[85] Most of the time we do not need to ask ourselves how things hang together. Most of the time, when engaging, for example, in strategic analysis, it is possible to 'black-box' the big questions of international relations and proceed on the basis that all that is required is practical knowledge about how, starting from this point, one could best make it to there. But this process of black-boxing is rational only if we know that if we wanted to open the box we could do so, and find within some sort of anwer to the questions we have bypassed, some sort of account of how things hang together. For the nineteenth-century strategists, communitarian thought provided such a content for the black box, and played the same role for some of the international lawyers of the era, others resting more comfortably on Kantian or Benthamite roots.

Twentieth-century international thought has followed a different route from that of the nineteenth century, with the emergence of international relations as an academic discipline pulling together the diverse strands of nineteenth-century international studies and attempting to produce general theories of its own to link together these strands. However, such theories still require grounding, and there seems no intrinsic reason why communitarian and cosmopolitan thought could not have continued to perform their nineteenth-century role as the background theories of international relations. For example, realism is clearly the most influential of twentieth-century theories of international relations, and, as was argued at the outset of the last chapter, it is quite possible to see some variants of realism as representing an attenuated form of communitarianism. This, however, is not the way that international studies has actually developed in this century. Instead of stressing continuities with past international thought, the tendency has been to discount communitarian and cosmopolitan thought and to seek theories of international relations which do not rely on extra-disciplinary foundations. Instead of Kant and Hegel, or Bentham and Mill, those past thinkers who have received most attention have been chosen because of their alleged relationship to current theories, such as putative godfathers of realism like Machiavelli and Hobbes, or embryonic theorists of international society like Grotius and Vattel. It is only comparatively recently, and largely from outside the discipline of international relations, that the classical founders of cosmopolitan and communitarian thought have again become salient. Mainstream international relations has tried to exist without the aid of these background theories.

It is the thesis of this book that this approach is mistaken, and that as a 'free-standing' academic discipline international relations has not proved able to provide an adequate account of how things hang together. The discipline took a wrong turn earlier in this century, the consequences of which are only now beginning to be overcome. How – and, more importantly, why – this wrong turn was taken is the subject matter of the next chapter.

NOTES

1. Cited in the Introduction to F.M. Barnard (ed.) *J.G. Herder on Social and Political Culture* (Cambridge University Press, Cambridge, 1969), p. 35.

2. Penguin, Harmondworth, 1986.
3. See, for example *ibid.*, p. 86.
4. *ibid.*, p. 357.
5. In any event, it would, of course, be an obvious mistake to identify Lawrence's position with that of Ursula or any other character.
6. *The Portable Voltaire*, ed. B.R. Redman (Viking Penguin, New York, 1949).
7. D. Hume, *Political Essays* (Bobbs Merrill, New York, 1953), 'Of the original contract', p. 47.
8. *ibid.*, p. 41, 'Of the origin of government'.
9. For Kant's position see pages 28–33, ch. 3, above.
10. For Rousseau's contribution to international theory see, especially, S. Hoffmann 'Rousseau on war and peace', in *The State of War* (Praeger, New York, 1965) and C.J. Carter *Rousseau and the Problem of War* (Garland, New York, 1987).
11. N. Hampson, *The Enlightenment* (Penguin, Harmondsworth, 1968), p. 9.
12. These notions are best elaborated in the 'Discourse on the origins of inequality', in *The Social Contract and the Discourses*, translated and with an Introduction by G.D.H. Cole (Dent, London, 1973).
13. Trans. B. Foxley (Dent, London, 1969).
14. Hoffman, *op. cit.*, p. 64.
15. *ibid.*, p. 62.
16. *The Social Contract and other writings*, ed. and translated F. Watkins (Nelson, London, 1953), ch. VII, P. 19.
17. See, for example, J.L. Talmon, *The Origins of Totalitarian Democracy* (Sphere, London, 1970), ch. 3.
18. *Social Contract*, book II, ch. 10, (Watkins edn, p. 54); see also in the same collection the 'Constitutional project for Corsica'.
19. On these matters see S. Schama, *Citizens* (Viking Penguin, London, 1989), ch. 4, 'The cultural construction of a citizen'. For an account of a civil religious festival see ch. 18(ii), p. 827.
20. Cited in the Introduction to B.W. Hill (ed.) *Edmund Burke on Government, Politics and Society* (Fontana, London, 1975), p. 59.
21. These positions are best expressed in the 'Letters on the proposals for peace with the regicide directory of France', in E. Burke, *Writings and Speeches*, vol. VI (The World's Classics; Oxford University Press, Oxford, 1907).
22. See R.J. Vincent, 'Edmund Burke and the theory of international relations', *Review of International Studies*, vol. 10., no. 3 (1984).
23. On Herder's political and social thought, see F.M. Barnard, *op. cit.*, and *Herder's Social and Political Thought: From Enlightenment to nationalism* (Clarendon, Oxford, 1965).
24. Barnard, *J.G. Herder*, p. 7.
25. Cited in the Introduction *ibid.*, from *Letters for the Advancement of Humanity*, p. 24.

26. H.J. Reiss, Introduction to *The Political Thought of the German Romantics 1793–1815* (Blackwell, Oxford, 1955). From Editor's Introduction, p. 3.

27. Extracts from *The Closed Commercial State* are in Reiss, *Political Thought*. Bernard Bosanquet's comment is in *The Philosophical Theory of the State*, 4th edn. (Macmillan, London, 1965) p. 229.

28. This account of Hegel's project draws heavily upon C. Taylor *Hegel* (Cambridge University Press, Cambridge, 1975), ch. 1.

29. See, for example, Taylor, *ibid.*; R. Plant, *Hegel: An introduction* 2nd edn (Blackwell, Oxford, 1983); Z. Pelczynski, *Hegel's Political Writings* (Oxford University Press, Oxford, 1964); Z. Pelczynski (ed.) *Hegel's Political Philosophy* (Cambridge University Press, Cambridge, 1971); S. Avineri, *Hegel's Theory of the Modern State* (Cambridge University Press, Cambridge, 1972); R. Norman, *Hegel's Phenomenology: A philosophical introduction* (Sussex University Press, Brighton, 1976); A. MacIntyre (ed.) *Hegel: A collection of critical essays* (Anchor, New York, 1972); P. Singer, *Hegel* (Oxford University Press, Oxford, 1973). For the older view of Hegel as a forerunner of authoritarianism, if not worse, see K.R. Popper, *The Open Society and Its Enemies* (Routledge and Kegan Paul, London, 1945), and the debate in W. Kaufman (ed.) *Hegel's Political Philosophy* (Atherton Press, New York, 1970).

30. On Hegel and the young Marx see R.C. Tucker, *Philosophy and Myth in Karl Marx* (Cambridge University Press, Cambridge, 1961), and D. McLellan, *The Young Hegelians and Karl Marx* (Macmillan, London, 1969), and *Marx before Marxism* (Macmillan, London, 1970). On civil society see J. Keane (ed.) *Civil Society and the State: New European perspectives* (Verso, London, 1988), and his *Democracy and Civil Society* (Verso, London, 1988).

31. Plant strongly argues for the necessity to place Hegel's political views in their philosophical context, against, for example, Pelczynski.

32. Norman (Clarendon, Oxford, 1983), ch. 8; Bradley (Oxford University Press, Oxford, 1988), essay V.

33. *Philosophy of Right*, trans. with notes by T.M. Knox (Oxford University Press, Oxford, 1967); Bosanquet, *op. cit.*; M. Frost, *Towards a Normative Theory of International Relations* (Cambridge University Press, Cambridge, 1986), ch. 5; J. Charvet, *A Critique of Freedom and Equality* (Cambridge University Press, Cambridge, 1981). This account also draws heavily on Plant and Taylor, *op. cit.*, and, more critically, on W.H. Walsh, *Hegelian Ethics* (Macmillan, London, 1969).

34. Bradley, *op. cit.*, essay IV.

35. This quotation is from the translator's notes to section 33 of the *Philosophy of Right*, p. 319.

36. *ibid.*, p. 199.

37. *ibid.*, essay VI.

38. See *Philosophy of History*, translated J. Sibree (Dover, New York, 1956), and *Philosophy of Right*, part 3(iii)(c).

39. *Philosophy of Right*, part 3(i). On the ethical family see Charvet, *op. cit.*, and *Feminism* (Dent, London, 1982).
40. *Philosophy of Right*, part 3(ii).
41. *ibid.*, part 3(iii).
42. *ibid.*, sections 257 and 258, pp. 155-6.
43. *ibid.*, section 273. It should be stressed that Hegel's monarch is not simply a ceremonial figure; 'constitutional monarch' is not a term that conforms to current usage.
44. See, for example, Popper, *op. cit.*, Hegel's defence rests on the metaphysical underpinnings of his view of politics which guarantee freedom – on which see below.
45. The English Idealists make more of the link to Rousseau than does Hegel – see Bosanquet, *op. cit.*, chs IV–VIII, and T.H. Green, *Lectures on the Principles of Political Obligation* (Longman's London, 1941), lectures E and F and *passim*.
46. Preface to *Philosophy of Right*, p. 10.
47. 'Secular interpretation' is Frost's phrase: Frost, *op. cit.*, p. 168.
48. Taylor, Frost and Norman (*op. cit.*, ii) are the best guides to this claim.
49. See Taylor, *op. cit.*, ch. I.
50. *Philosophy of Right*, section 209, p. 134. There is no reason to read the final sentence as undermining the force of the rest of the paragraph.
51. *ibid.*, section 246, p. 151.
52. Hegel's note to section 324, p. 209.
53. *ibid.*, p. 210.
54. *ibid.*, sections 328 and 329, p. 211.
55. *ibid.*, section 338, p. 215.
56. *ibid.*, sections 341 and 342, p. 216.
57. *ibid.*, Preface, p. 12.
58. *Philosophy of History*, p. 86. Plant, *op. cit.*, p. 237.
59. See, for example, the controversy generated by F. Fukuyama, 'The end of history?', *The National Interest* (Summer 1989). Fukuyama's ideas are discussed briefly in C. Brown, 'Hegel and international ethics', *Ethics and International Affairs*, vol. 5 (1991).
60. Preface to *Philosophy of Right*, p. 13.
61. See note 45 above.
62. *op. cit.*, pp. 160ff.
63. *ibid.*, p. 173.
64. *ibid.*, p. 178.
65. See especially L.T. Hobhouse, *The Metaphysical Theory of the State: A criticism* (Allen and Unwin, London, 1918). Some indication of the spirit of the work can be found in the dedication to Hobhouse's son in the RAF, in the course of which responsibility for a recent German air-raid is laid at the door of 'the Hegelian theory of the god-state' (p. 6).
66. Bosanquet, *op. cit.*, p. 304.
67. *ibid.*, p. xlviii.
68. *ibid.*, p. xlix.

69. *ibid.*, p. 1.
70. P. Savigear, 'Philosophical idealism and international politics: Bosanquet, Treitschke and war', *British Journal of International Studies*, vol. 1, no. 1 (1975), argues on the basis of Bosanquet's correspondence and some wartime polemics, that he was prepared to accept that war played a positive role and in any event was not something that could be avoided. However, *The Philosophical Theory of the State* must be taken as his most important work on these matters, and here he seems to be doing no more than asserting the basic Hegelian position that no-one has the right to judge whatever the state does in pursuit of what it takes to be its interests – no-one that is, except the court of history.
71. Note 51.
72. See E.H. Carr, *The Twenty Years Crisis* (Macmillan, London, 1939).
73. Even this limited point may be undermined by the development of weapons of mass destruction.
74. The literature on nationalism is, of course, enormous. A selection representing different viewpoints might include: E. Kedourie, *Nationalism* (Hutchinson University Library, London, 1960); A.D. Smith *Theories of Nationalism* (Duckworth, London, 1971); E. Gellner, *Nations and Nationalism* (Blackwell, Oxford, 1983); H. Seton Watson, *Nations and States* (Methuen, London, 1977); J. Mayall *Nationalism and International Society* (Cambridge University Press, Cambridge, 1989); J. Plamenatz, *On Alien Rule and Self-Government* (Longman's, London, 1961).
75. G. Mazzini, *Essays*, ed. B. King (Dent, London, 1884).
76. For nationalism as a mobilising ideology, to assist the process of 'catching up' see Gellner, *op. cit.*, and T. Nairn, *The Break-up of Britain* (New Left Books, London, 1977).
77. See the discussion of Fichte as a Machiavellian in F. Meinecke, *Machiavellism* (Routledge and Kegan Paul, London, 1956).
78. *ibid.*, p. 408.
79. Bosanquet, *op. cit.*, ch. XI.
80. See page 43, ch. 2 above.
81. In J.S. Mill, *Utilitarianism, On Liberty, and Representative Government* (Dent, London, 1972), p. 361.
82. See the discussion of 'membership' in M. Walzer, *Spheres of Justice* (Martin Robertson, Oxford, 1983), ch. 2.
83. See, for example, the debate generated by M. Walzer's *Just and Unjust Wars* (collected in C.R. Beitz *et al.* (eds) *International Ethics* (Princeton University Press, Princeton, N.J., 1985)), where it is clear that reasoned debate can take the participants only so far. In the end, figures such as Walzer and David Luban are divided on matters of temperament as much as philosophy.
84. Clarendon, Oxford, 1989.
85. Cited in R. Rorty, *Consequences of Pragmatism* (Harvester Wheatsheaf, Hemel Hempstead, 1982), p. xiv.

Chapter 4

The Intellectual Context of Contemporary International Political Philosophy

INTRODUCTION

It was suggested at the end of the last chapter that the role of the theory of international relations is a special case of the role of philosophy in general; the aim is to show how things 'hang together'. International relations theory stands between philosophy in general and the specific, practical discourses of international relations. Diplomacy, strategy and international law have their own characteristic modes of thought, ways of approaching their particular segment of international relations. They are practices based upon shared rules of conduct and norms of behaviour which have persisted over time, but they are not self-validating; the details of their practices can and must make sense in their own terms, but the ultimate meaning of, for example, diplomacy, can only be in terms of some background theory that accounts for the existence of separate states, the fact that relations between these states is based on negotiation rather than command, and so on. There is a hierarchy of discourse; to use Kantian language, 'practical reasoning' must ultimately rest on 'pure reason'. Behind the practical considerations associated with diplomacy and international law is to be found a chain of reasoning that reaches through international relations theory as a special case of moral and political philosophy to the deeper questions of general philosophy. Most of the time there is no necessity to move along this chain of reasoning; specific practices of diplomacy or law or strategy are accepted in their own terms without the requirement that they be justified. But the fact that most of the time these references to background theory are not required does not mean that there will not be occasions when they become necessary, nor does it mean that, in the meantime, they are doing no work. The most successful background theories are those which so structure the foreground that their very existence is forgotten and it seems that the practices they validate are simple common sense.

Before the First World War a number of backgroud theories provided alternative validations for the practices of international relations. The previous two chapters of this work outlined these theories in terms of a dichotomy between cosmopolitan and communitarian theories; each of these categories can be broken down further, and in the case of cosmopolitan theory the distinction between Kantian and utilitarian accounts of international theory is of particular importance – as in the distinction in communitarian thought between the rich, but relatively uninfluential, Idealist tradition, and thinner, but perhaps more influential, notions of nationalism. The main point about these traditions is that they ground international relations theory within the wider projects of philosophy; they offer different and competing accounts of the way in which things 'international' are conceived and constituted within a wider understanding of how things hang together.

It was suggested at the end of the last chapter that the disciplining of international relations, its establishment as a recognised academic specialism with a claim to be a distinct branch of knowledge, could be seen as an attempt to reject, or at least lessen, this link to a wider account of the world. The academic ambition of international relations is to provide a basis for understanding the practices of international relations in terms of international relations and not in terms of anything else. The aim has been to provide a free-standing account of the world; in order to achieve this aim it has been necessary to stress the *sui generis* nature of international relations, and in order to sustain this position it has been necessary first to provide reasons why international relations should be defined and characterised in ways which set it apart from other objects of social theory, and second collectively to forget that this definition and characterisation is essentially arbitrary. It becomes necessary to define the objects of international relations theory abstractly, to stress the elements of regularity and necessity in international relations, and to deny that there is theory other than that created by the discipline itself.

It is, of course, the burden of this book that this was a great mistake. Before the formation of the discipline of international relations there existed a set of theories providing alternative accounts of the relationship between human beings, the state and humanity, and the contest of these different theories allowed a full characterisation of the richness and complexity of this wider dimension of social life. The replacement of this state of affairs by an undertheorised and limited conception of international relations as a regular academic discipline has been mostly loss. Whatever gains there may have been in terms of specialised knowledge have been more than counterbalanced by the consequences of the loss of contact between international relations and the wider issues of political and moral philosophy. It is only in recent years that recombining of the concerns of political philosophy and international relations has begun to recover the healthier state of affairs that once existed.

Much of the rest of this chapter will examine this recovery process, describing, amongst other things, the ways in which a lack of satisfaction with the methods and findings of the autonomous discipline of international relations produced a new attitude towards international relations theory. However, before proceeding with this task it will be necessary to correct a misapprehension that might arise on the basis of the above discussion: namely, that the rift between the new discipline of international relations and the philosophical roots upon which the old discourses were built was simply a matter of the former rejecting the latter. While it is certainly true that the new discipline of international relations did sometimes behave as though it had no significant roots, it would be a mistake to suggest that this was the only – or even the most important – factor in the changes that took place in the first half of the century. For it was also the case that major changes were taking place in the mainstream of Anglo-American philosophy in this period, changes which involved a dramatic down-grading of the status of moral philosophy. The rejection of philosophy by international relations was accompanied by the rejection of international relations – and other practical activities – by philosophy. If in recent years there has been a revival of philosophical interest in international relations this has been at least as much a function of changes in the world of philosophy as of changes in international relations. In order to understand the movements of thought which have created the modern interest in international political philosophy it is necessary to look at both sides of the process of convergence of international relations and philosophy. To do this it will be necessary to give a brief account of the main lines of moral philosophy in the Anglo-American world in the twentieth-century.

Ethics: Meta-, Normative and Applied

International relations relates to philosophy via the sub-disciplines of political and moral philosophy, and since political philosophy is itself best seen as a sub-division of moral philosophy it is with the latter that this section is most concerned.[1] Moral philosophy is about right action, human conduct in so far as it is devoted to the pursuit of the right and the good, and it is helpful to distinguish three ways in which moral philosophy – or the study of ethics – can be pursued.[2] First, we can think of 'meta-ethics', the study of the nature of moral judgement; second, there comes 'normative ethics', the study of general theories about good and bad, right and wrong; finally, there is practical or 'applied ethics', the study of right conduct in particular circumstances. Thus, if we think of a characteristic moral practice – say, promise-keeping – then meta-ethics asks what it means to say that promises *ought* to be kept, normative ethics places promise-keeping in some wider context such as utility or the categorical imperative and applied ethics asks whether in certain circumstances – usually involving harm to others – a particular promise should actually be kept. Separate processes of reasoning are involved here, but the major normative doctrines examined in the previous two chapters cover the whole range of ethical concerns – and it is for precisely this reason that doctrines such as Kantianism, utilitarianism and Hegelianism are of relevance. It is also, of course, the case that these doctrines are not simply moral philosophies, but accounts of the world in the widest sense, and thus these practical activities are linked to general philosophy.

The reason for stressing these distinctions is that in the first half of the twentieth century in Britain – and to a lesser extent in the United States – the study of meta-ethics came to dominate moral philosophy at the expense of both normative and applied ethics. The main interest in moral philosophy was the status of moral judgements; the prestige of moral philosophy declined, and the notion that philosophy had much to say about the great moral issues came to be discounted. Applied ethics was seen as an activity that was either suitable only for clergymen, politicians and leader-writers (C.D. Broad's characterisation),[3] or could be carried out by the philosopher without close reference to his or her professional concerns – in the way made famous by Joad or Russell.[4] Even normative ethics was in this period very much a task for the older generation, and the historians of philosophy. In so far as moral philosophy was a suitable subject for state-of-the-art professional philosophers at all, it was meta-ethics that attracted attention.

Why was this so? Partly, no doubt, because of a certain amount of complacency about moral behaviour; it sometimes seems as if actual codes of conduct were taken for granted and the only significant issue was not so much what ought to be done in particular circumstances but which of the alternative background justifications for a commonly agreed course of action made most sense. However, the more import-ant reason for the emphasis on meta-ethics came from the general trend of British philosophy in the first half of the century, which was towards 'analysis' – the role of the philosopher was seen as that of taking everyday sentences and rewriting them, either into sentences which more accurately 'pictured' the facts, or which revealed whether or not they were 'meaningful'.[5] The 'logical atomism' of Russell and the early Wittgenstein was based on the belief that the structure of the world could be revealed through the structure of the logic of mathematics, and that the role of philosophy was to rewrite statements in such a way as they could be seen to be composed only of simple 'atomic' propositions and logical constructions based on these propositions.[6] This reworking of the traditional empiricist agenda of Hume was in turn regarded as excessively metaphysical by 'logical positivists' such as Carnap and Ayer, and the role of philosophy under this school was solely that of determining which sentences were meaningful, because they contained verifiable statements of fact, and which meaningless, because they did not.[7] The dominant tendency was against speculative philosophy and in favour of the view that analysis was the main, or possibly only, business of philosophy.

The impact of these doctrines on ethics was twofold; on the one hand, the emphasis on meta-ethics followed naturally from the emphasis on analysis in so far as determining the true form of ethical statements could be seen as an obvious extension into moral philosophy of the tools of philosophical analysis; on the other hand, the result of this emphasis was to devalue the enterprise of ethics as a whole. This can be followed in some of the clearer – though not thereby more acceptable – passages of Wittgenstein's *Tractatus Logico-Philosophicus*. Wittgenstein declares the object of philosophy to be the 'logical clarification of thoughts'; the result is to 'make propositions clear', And 'All propositions are of equal value. Hence also there can be no ethical propositions. Propositions cannot express anything higher. It is clear that ethics cannot be expressed.' In the final words of the *Tractatus*, 'Whereof one cannot speak, thereof must one be silent', and clearly ethics comes into this category.[8] From the point of view of the logical positivist even this silence represented a kind of compromise. If the only meaningful sentences are those that can be verified or falsified and if ethical statements cannot by their nature be verified and falsified then ethical statements are meaningless – in Ayer's terms they simply express the preference of the speaker; thus to say 'X is good' is simply to say 'I like X'.

The major ethical doctrines in Britain in the first half of the twentieth century reflect this philosophical environment even if they attempt in some cases to escape from it.[9] It may be useful to mention briefly three of these doctrines – intuitionism, emotivism and prescriptivism. Intuitionism is associated with the work of G.E. Moore – although he resisted the term – and W.D. Ross.[10] Moore believed the role of philosophy was analysis; analysis of moral statements led one to a notion of the 'good' which Moore believed to be an objective but 'non-natural' quality. The 'good' could not be defined in terms of something else; indeed, it could not be defined at all. It could only be declared to be present or absent as a result of inspection – hence the term 'intuitionism', which Moore did not like because of its subjectivist implications, but which seems best to describe what is going on. Goodness is a 'non-natural' quality as opposed to, say, 'yellowness' or 'redness', and it must not be defined in terms of anything else – to do so is to commit the 'naturalistic fallacy'. Having defined (or refused to define) 'the good', Moore describes right action in essentially utilitarian terms; right action is whatever action maximises the amount of goodness in the world.[11]

Described in these terms, it is not easy to see why so many highly intelligent people took Moore seriously, but clearly this essentially aesthetic approach to 'goodness' struck a chord for the Bloomsbury group. It was, however, predictably, heavily criticised by the logical positivists, whose most influential moral theorist was C.L. Stevenson. In *Ethics and Language* Stevenson put forward the 'emotivist' doctrine according to which the role of moral statements is to evince the attitude of the speaker.[12] Moral statements have emotive meaning; they are designed to influence the adoption of a favourable or unfavourable attitude to the phenomenon in question. It is attitudes, not beliefs, that are affected. Hence, to return to the example quoted above, to say that 'X is good' is to express a favourable attitude towards 'X', not, as the intuitionist would have it, to express a belief in a non-natural quality possessed by 'X'.

As a development from this approach 'prescriptivism' as presented by Hare in *The Language of Morals* and *Freedom and Reason* argues that moral judgements are prescriptive.[13] To say 'X is good' is equivalent to saying 'do X' – in other words rather than simply expressing a favourable or unfavourable attitude, moral judgements attempt to influence action. Moral judgements are imperatives, but not all imperatives are moral; universalisability is crucial to this. Moral judgements are prescriptions based on certain features of a situation, on the principle that whenever these features exist the same judgement would follow. This doctrine is related not so much to logical atomism or logical positivism but to developments in analytical philosophy that followed on in the 1940s and 1950s from these theories. The new slogan 'Don't ask for the meaning [of a sentence] ask for the use' which came out of, in particular, the later Wittgenstein of the *Philosophical Investigations* leads readily to a prescriptivist notion of moral philosophy.[14] The 'use' of moral judgements – the kind of 'speech act' they were – is prescriptive; they announce a rule of conduct, moral because universalisable.[15]

Although the requirement of universalisability specified by Hare would seem to link prescriptivism, at least, with Kantian moral philosophy, even this tenuous connection is misleading; all the above doctrines are profoundly hostile to speculative metaphysics, which includes, of course, Kantian thought. Crucial to Kant's thought is the movement from a purely formal definition of the categorical imperative to definitions which contain substance and this move is condemned by those twentieth-century ethical theories influenced by analytical philosophy. Hence the point of this digression into contemporary moral philosophy, which is to highlight the break between the sort of theories discussed in chapters 2 and 3 above – which are genuine attemps to understand the relationships between individuals, states and humanity – and the characteristic twentieth-century stress on meta-ethics, which has had the effect of devaluing these exercises in normative ethics. Of the theories considered above only utilitarianism was taken at all seriously by analytical moral philosophers; although utilitarianism is based on metaphysical propositions about the nature of the good – that is, the pleasure/pain principle – this background is less obviously metaphysical than is the case with, say, Kantian moral theory, and easier to excuse or forget. With the partial and conditional exception of utilitarianism, all the doctrines discussed above were dismissed as meaningless by the logical positivists, or passed over in silence by the logical atomists.

This situation accounts, at least in part, for the breakdown of the relationship between philosophy and international relations theory. Although philosophers as citizens might have something to say about issues of war and peace, the dominant mood was to refuse to accept that these were, or could be, in any meaningful sense philosophical issues. Before moving on to discuss the rebirth of normative and applied ethics, it should be said that hostility to the old approaches was not simply current in Britain. In different ways in different places the philosophical climate in the first half of this century was generally unconducive to normative ethics as conventionally understood. British analytical philosophy was itself highly influenced by trends in German and Austrian philosophy, and, in turn, was influential in the United States. The native American pragmatist movement emerging out of the work of Pierce and James, and best represented in the period in question by John Dewey, was more oriented to issues of normative and applied ethics than its British equivalent but equally suspicious of speculative systems.[16] Developments in continental philosophy were no more hospitable to normative ethics; phenomenology and hermeneutics will be discussed briefly in chapter 8 in connection with critical theory and postmodernism – for the moment it need only be noted that the possibility of any direct connection between these movements and international relations theory is remote.

The final point that is worth noting in this connection concerns Marxism. Clearly, of all the positions discussed above Marxism was, in the first half of this century, the only doctrine with official status as the declared ideology of a major country; as such it might be expected that in the former Soviet Union and amongst social movements influenced by Marxism a concern with the agenda of chapters 2 and 3 would be at least present. That this was not the case is a product of the particular features of Soviet Marxism. There is within Marxism a bias against ethics on materialist grounds; although some variants of Marxist thought de-emphasise this bias, Leninism most definitely does not move in this direction. Soviet thought on international relations – and, through the great influence of the Third International, Marxist thought in general in this period – was resolutely materialist, anti-ethical and uninterested in the normative issues raised by its positions. The posititivist orientation of Soviet Marxism combined with its authoritarian politics, precluded serious consideration of the genuine problems raised by, for example, the apparent contradiction between commitment to the cosmopolitan goal of world revolution, on the one hand, and the interests of the Soviet state, on the other.[17]

What all this suggests is that the movement towards a self-contained discipline of international relations, abandoning the background justifications for the practical discourses of international relations previously provided by moral philosophy was not simply a matter of the new discipline fecklessly abandoning its roots; it was also a matter of moral philosophy turning away from the world and refusing to address the agenda that the new discipline, rightly, believed should be taken seriously. It will be suggested below that the attempt to provide a free-standing disciplinary base for international relations has not succeeded and that a return to the older traditions of speculation is now increasingly recognised to be necessary. However, such a return would only be possible if there was something to return to; it presupposes the revival of normative ethics that has taken place over the last quarter of a century. The next section is devoted to this revival.

THE REVIVAL OF NORMATIVE ETHICS

The revival of normative and applied ethics since around the mid-1950s has taken many forms; in some cases it has been a matter of the renaissance of particular schools of thought – utilitarian, neo-Kantian, neo-Aristotelean – but some of the most interesting work has been produced by scholars who are hard to classify; indeed, self-conscious members of 'schools' rarely produce work of great originality. The following comments – which will be related more closely to questions of international relations than was possible in the last section – are not intended to give a complete account of the new movements, but merely to outline some of the changes and provide a brief, situating account of theories and concepts which will recur in the next three chapters.

A good starting point for an account of the revival of normative ethics is the new life given to utilitarianism by a number of writers – for example Smart, Singer and, most recently, Parfit – who have restored the critical, cutting edge to this doctrine. For much of the first half of the century utilitarianism was the dominant system of normative ethics – dominating, it should be said, a thin field – but the role of the doctrine was taken to be that of the construction of defensible justifications for 'common-sense' morality. For example, it was taken more or less for granted that people should not tell lies; at the same time it seemed not too difficult to envisage circumstances in which the utilitarian goal of the greatest happiness would be maximised by a falsehood. Much of the time, utilitarian ethics was preoccupied with the task of removing the contradiction this generated, not by abandoning truth-telling, but by demonstrating, for example, that a rule in favour of truth-telling would maximise happiness if generally adopted and that in order to support such a rule it might occasionally be necessary to pass up the opportunity to maximise short-term happiness by telling a lie.[18]

This rather tame vindication of traditional morality was not what Bentham had in mind two centuries ago – utilitarianism was supposed to be a radical creed, challenging received wisdom and conventional notions of common sense. In the 1960s and 1970s this radicalism returned to the fore in utilitarian studies. J.J.C. Smart's attack on 'rule worship' and robust defence of 'act utilitarianism' was important here, as was the work of Peter Singer, whose defence of a limited practice of infanticide can stand as an extreme example of a willingness to challenge received opinion in the name of utility.[19]

One of the standard criticisms of utilitarianism concerns its impersonal approach: the charge is that a consistent utilitarian 'does not take seriously the distinction between persons'.[20] Individuals have one life to live and their own projects to pursue; to expect persons to devote themselves to the general good, sacrificing personal projects to do so, is to require too much, to the point of violating the integrity of persons.[21] One response to this criticism is to attack excessive concern with personal integrity at the expense of the general welfare;[22] another is to challenge in a radical way the notion of personhood. Derek Parfit's *Reasons and Persons* is, among many other things, an account of 'How we are not what we believe'.[23] On Parfit's account what matters is not personal identity but psychological connectedness and/or continuity; the differences between persons may be no more (nor less) significant than the differences between our present, past and future selves. The reasons for favouring our own interests may be far less compelling than is usually thought to be the case, especially since, borrowing the 'prisoner's dilemma' from game theory, Parfit also argues that a morality based on self-interest is often self-defeating.[24]

These are complex as well as radical ideas, and there is a limit to the extent to which they can be sensibly described within the compass of this work, but enough has been said to make it clear that radical utilitarian thought could have a major impact on the way in which we conceptualise international relations. Whereas nineteenth-century utilitarianism tended to assume that the existence of states was conducive to the greatest happiness, more radical modern variants are less conventional. Singer's account of the obligation to relieve poverty as a universal requirement is radical in its disregard of state boundaries, as will be seen in chapter 7 below.[25] Generally speaking, the strongest point against cosmopolitan international relations theory has always been that it fails to take sufficiently seriously the obligations we have to ourselves and to our immediate neighbours; the most effective modern defence of cosmopolitanism has come from the radical utilitarian refusal to give self-interest any more (or less) weight in determining action than the interests of others.

A movement in exactly the opposite direction to utilitarianism has been the revival of 'deontological' ethics. Deontology is a term coined by Bentham; it conveys the notion that there are certain kinds of duties on, and rights of, individuals which are absolute. The most famous deontological philosopher of the past was, of course, Kant, whose categorical imperative is a model of the idea of an absolute requirement on persons; but it is not necessary for deontological propositions to be formulated in Kantian terms.[26] The key opposition is to 'consequentialism' – the idea that the rightness of conduct is to be judged in accordance with its outcomes; by contrast, deontology asserts that certain acts are either mandatory or forbidden regardless of consequences.[27] It might be argued, for example, that individuals possess certain 'human rights' which entitle them to be treated in particular ways – or not treated in particular ways – regardless of the consequences of this treatment; thus, to take a famous example, an individual might be taken to have a right not to be tortured even if, *ex hypothesi*, torture was the only way to locate, say, a hidden bomb.

The impact of deontological thinking on international theory has been quite considerable. As suggested above, human rights are one issue area where deontology is crucial.[28] Equally, there has been a great deal of deontologically based reasoning on the proper conduct of war, and especially such issues as strategic bombing and nuclear deterrence. The idea that certain kinds of conduct are ruled out even if they can be deemed to be the only way to achieve a desired result is obviously a more promising basis for such rules as, for example, non-combatant immunity in warfare, than a utilitarianism that would enquire into the specific consequences of particular rules. However, the refusal to take into account consequences need not tell in the direction of limiting the means available in wartime. To return to the case of strategic bombing, a consequentialist account of this activity would weigh in the balance civilian casualties (a 'bad') against the contribution that this action would make to the achievement of victory (a 'good' if the war is just). A deontologist would be more interested in the goodness or badness of intentions, and if the intention is to attack a legitimate target then the fact that innocents might die – even that it is known that innocents *will* die – may be deemed irrelevant; this is, in essence, the burden of the doctrine of 'double effect'. The interplay between consequentialist and deontological accounts of justice in war is the theme of a number of excellent studies of the subject, on which see chapter 6 below.[29]

The basic premise of deontology – the notion that there can be absolute rights and duties independent of consequences – runs counter to the analytical tradition outlined above, and to the moral philosophies it generated, in a way that utilitarianism does not. Utilitarian accounts of the 'good' and the 'right', at least, seem to correspond to the widely shared intuition that the general welfare should be promoted. So also does the general prohibition on certain kinds of behaviour characteristically asserted by deontologists; but the idea that such a prohibition should be *absolute* seems more difficult to justify on non-theological grounds. The idea that a rule should be followed even if its consequences in a particular case are demonstratively bad seems perverse. However, part of the attraction of deontology may be found not so much in the absolute nature of the demands it makes, but in the fact that these demands do not cover all areas of human conduct. Deotonology allows for supererogatory conduct – acts which are neither strictly required nor strictly prohibited; thus, it might be said that, beyond a certain level, we are not obliged to make donations to the poor even though, on the whole, it would be good if we did. This category of action between the required and the forbidden seems to meet the point that persons be allowed a certain degree of autonomy in their lives, a point that poses difficulties for a strict utilitarian, who must see all human conduct as either obligatory or banned unless – a rather unlikely eventuality – it has no impact at all on the general good.[30]

Whether or not this feature of deontological moral philosophy makes it a more attractive approach than consequentialism, it does not respond to the obvious objection to this way of thinking, which is that there is no satisfactory account available of the ontological status of rights and duties. Why should we respect the rights of others when it is inconvenient to do so? It is possible to imagine a theological answer to this question on the lines that it is God's will that we should behave in this way, or that all human beings have rights by virtue of being part of God's creation. The Roman Catholic natural-law tradition approaches subjects such as the morality of nuclear deterrence on some such basis, as will be seen below.[31] However, the theologian's answer to this question is only compelling if the major premise is acceptable, which for many it will not be. Another answer might be 'conventionalist'; just as the rules of the road – to take a common example – are based simply on convention, but are none the less binding on all road users, so human rights are the product of convention and equally binding. The problem here, of course, is that the rules of the road are hardly a good analogy with disputed moral questions – the arbitrary conventions that govern traffic are acceptable precisely because no tricky moral problems are raised. The conventionalist argument may be the best available, but it hardly seems satisfactory.[32] Since it might be thought that this difficulty with deontology gives aid and comfort to consequentialism, it should be noted that consequentialist arguments are open to the same objection, albeit in a different form. Why, for example, should the goal of maximising the general happiness be binding on individuals? Utilitarians often seem to assume that it is obvious that happiness should be maximised, but this is clearly false; the fact that a course of action maximises my happiness, much less the general happiness, is not, in itself, a reason for adopting it. Only with an additional premise can the utilitarian position be compelling.

It was largely because of an awareness of these difficulties that the moral philosophies described in the previous section were formulated. Moore's position that the good is a quality that is discernible by inspection or intuition may not be very satisfactory, but it does at least have the merit of recognising that without some foundation ethics faces real problems. Emotivists and prescriptivists did not accept Moore's solution, but their accounts of moral statements as simply expressions of attitude, or as particular kinds of imperatives seem to miss an important point. The normal use of moral language surely suggests that when we say that something is 'good' we mean something rather more than 'I like this and so should you'. But what 'more' is it that we mean? One point upon which intuitionists, emotivists and prescriptivists are agreed is that this question cannot be answered in any way that would imply belief that goodness is a natural quality, a fact about people or situations. Moore calls this belief the 'naturalistic fallacy' (inaccurately, since although this belief may be mistaken, it is not necessarily fallacious); it is clear that although on his account 'goodness' is a quality, it is 'non-natural'. His later critics followed him on this matter, if not on others; the moral theories of analytical philosophy all reject the view that there are facts about morality that could be described as natural – in this they follow in the empiricist tradition; rejection of 'naturalism' is a modern version of Hume's distinction between 'is' and 'ought' statements and his rejection of the possibility of deriving an 'is' from an 'ought'.[33]

One of the most important features of the revival of normative applied ethics over the last two or three decades has been the re-emergence of 'naturalism', and in particular of the Aristotelean view that there are natural qualities of human beings – the 'virtues' – which are both objectively discernible and the basis for moral judgement.[34] Some of this work is explicitly neo-Aristotelean – see, for example, Galston, *Justice and the Human Good* – while other writers reject Artistotle's specific account of the virtues but build on the idea that there are natural qualities of human beings that can form the basis of moral judgement.[35] In very different ways, for example, Shue, Walzer and MacIntyre produce moral philosophies on the base of an authoritative account of what it means to be human.[36] The obvious problem with this approach is to find a foundation for a substantive account of human ends. Aristotelean teleology, which can give an account of human ends, is based on positions which have been destroyed by modern natural science. To design a moral theory on the basis of the 'virtues' – whether seen in Aristotelean terms or not – is to accept the separation of moral philosophy from the sciences. It becomes what Rawls (a non-Artistotelean) describes (following Hume) as 'the theory of moral sentiments' – a self-contained activity severed from general philosophy.[37]

From the perspective of the theory of international relations, the significance of the revival of naturalism is quite considerable. Partly, this is a matter of giving a better account of the basis of universal human rights than would be available without naturalistic backing – Shue's account of 'basic rights' is a good illustration of this point. But of greater significance is the support given by this kind of moral theory to the view that living in a community is a crucial part of what it is to be human. Artistotle's account of man as a 'political being', designed for the city, has resonances in the work of a number of modern naturalists. The importance of this position lies in the contrast with those consequentialist and deontological approaches which stress the cosmopolitan character of moral obligations. Whereas a utilitarian has an impersonal view of right conduct which, in principle at least, makes no distinction between obligations towards humanity and towards one's own community, and whereas deontological reasoning is also generally based on universal accounts of rights and duties, a morality based on the human virtues is more likely to give a higher status than either of these positions to the needs of the community. Some of the most important modern communitarians begin with a naturalist account of man and the community.[38]

Each of these features of moral philosophy over the last quarter of a century – the revival of radical utilitarianism, deontology and naturalistic ethics – has contributed to the revival of normative and applied ethics, and provided a context within which the philosophy of international relations could once again be a viable project. Indeed, many of the most important recent studies of applied ethics have had international dimensions – such matters as nuclear deterrence, world hunger and population policy and human rights have been subjects to which moral philosophers have devoted much attention. After a period in which such matters were generally seen as no part of the brief of the philosopher, a reversal of attitudes has taken place. The next section of this chapter will examine the evolution of the discipline of international relations since its formation in the inter-war years, leading up to the point at which the international interest of the moral philosopher and the philosophical interests of the international theorist begin to emerge.

INTERNATIONAL RELATIONS AND INTERNATIONAL THEORY

In the introduction to this book it is suggested that the 'international theory' of the English school has directed attention away from the most fruitful real sources of the theory of international relations – the work of Kant, Hegel, Bentham and others discussed in chapters 2 and 3 above. Although there is no reason to revise this judgement, it is, in one crucial respect, somewhat harsh. What needs to be said on the other side of the argument is that the 'English school' of international theorists – of which the key figures were Martin Wight, Hedley Bull and C.A.W. Manning – did at least try to keep alive the idea that international relations was an academic discipline that ought to be looking at how 'things hang together'. Even if, as is argued above, these writers attempted this task with, as it were, one hand tied behind their back because of their dependence upon a restrictive notion of political philosophy, none the less their achievements were considerable. Most other schools of international relations were simply unconcerned with the issues which the English school did at least try to address, and the widespread acceptance of the legitimacy of these issues did not emerge until the discipline had passed its fiftieth anniversary in the 1970s.

The attempt to create an academic discipline of international relations is conventionally taken to date from the ending of the First World War, with, in the United Kingdom at least, the foundation of the David Davies Chair at Aberystwyth in 1919 as a symbolic point of departure. This is somewhat misleading; although the attempt to discipline international relations did begin in these years, the modern discipline owes its origin to the events of the 1930s and 1940s, and the intellectual reaction to these events, rather than to the impact of the Great War. In a way, this is a pity; on the one hand, the work of interwar theorists such as Zimmern and Stawell, for all its inadequacies, was in closer touch with the necessary philosophical roots of the discipline than was that of their successors;[39] on the other hand, it can be argued that the experiences of the decades leading up to 1919 were of rather more long-run significance than those of the 1930s and 1940s – a point elaborated below. In any event, the founders of the dominant approach to international theory of the contemporary discipline are the writers of the latter period rather than the former: for example, Carr and Wight in the United Kingdom, Spykman and Morgenthau in the United States (and, in a somewhat different context, also in the United States, Quincy Wright).[40]

These are the 'realists' – the school of theorists that dominated international relations until at least the 1970s, the teachers of the teachers of the discipline. Each of these writers contributed to realism and each was more subtle than their creation. The complexities of the thought of Carr and Morgenthau (the two most influential writers) is far greater than their own summary statements would indicate, much less the programmes of their adherents, but, as is always the way, these complexities were for the most part lost in the form in which their work came to be passed on to students. Instead of subtle distinctions, realism came to be characterised by bold programmatic positions, each of which was hostile to the concerns of this book.

These positions can be summarised as statism, amorality and a crude version of the correspondence theory of truth.[41] What is important about the statism of realism is that it is of a particularly narrowly focussed variety; the state is seen as a mechanism for the provision of public goods and the solution of the free-rider problem by a concentration of social power in the hands of decision makers. The state is Weberian, claiming the monopoly of legitimate force, and rationalist, existing solely as a problem-solving mechanism, with no concern as to the source of problems or the possibility that the state itself might shape human existence in a positive way. Domestically, the state is a concentration of power, and states relate to each other as concentrations of power. States are assumed to be hard-shelled entities relating to each other through their governments and via the medium of political power.[42]

In this competition for power, morals and ethics have no, or very little, part to play. Some realists dismiss the role of morals in politics at all levels, others are amoralist only in international relations. The characteristic position is that to be concerned with morals is likely to lead to a 'moralising' attitude to international affairs and this in turn is likely to lead to disaster.[43] Prudence is the only virtue of the statesman.[44] The important point here is the assumption that the alternative to the prudentialism of the realist is a universalist code in which principles of conduct appropriate to private life are applied inappropriately to international affairs. Such a position is rejected as 'utopian' or 'idealist' – and much of the international relations theory of the past is rejected under these labels.

Realism validates itself by its claim to correspond to reality. International politics, like all politics, is governed by 'laws' which tell us what is or is not possible, what can or cannot be done, and these laws are validated because they correspond to the way things are.[45] The strong and simple, oversimple, response of the realist to criticism is to deny moral responsibility for the course of action advocated or the outcome of an analysis of a situation, because the advice and the outcome are determined by the facts, by the 'reality' of the situation. Realists prescribe courses of action but deny normative intent. Prescription is based on the logic of a situation, the imperatives that emerge out of the 'realm of recurrence and repetition'.

It must be stressed that this conception of realism as statist, amoral and epistemologically simplistic has some of the elements of a caricature. Very few flesh-and-blood realists have all the attributes of the cartoon-character realist. However, it seems reasonable to argue that the further away from these positions any individual writer is to be found, the less convincingly his or her work can be described as realist. Theorists of international society such as Bull and Wight illustrate the point. As was suggested at the outset of chapter 2, some so-called realists are actually best seen as half-hearted, closet or tacit communitarians rather than as realists in the full-blooded sense of the term. In any event, what is crucial for the purpose of this discussion is that the account of realism given above is the account that crystallised in the literature and is widely employed for teaching purposes – even if no particular individual's work fits the bill.

It would be foolish to deny that this set of ideas has points in its favour. The state is, for the moment, the key social actor in international politics, its role as a concentration of power is clearly enormously salient; moralism is a Bad Thing, and prudence is an important virtue; situations do have a logic of their own which it is unwise to ignore. Moreover, these ideas had particular salience in the context within which they were formulated, in the 1930s and 1940s. Statesmen who had to deal with Hitler and Stalin, leaders of the two most appalling political regimes in European history, could be forgiven for adopting a realist perspective on international relations. It is difficult to think of any other period of European history when so much was at stake and the view that victory had to be achieved at all costs was one with which it is easy to sympathise. However, things have changed, and whatever the practical merits of a realist orientation in the 1930s and 1940s, the poverty of this theory is apparent in the subsequent development of the discipline. The abandonment of the philosophical aspirations of the cosmopolitan and communitarian theories that had provided the background to the practical discourses of international relations before the emergence of realism may have been an understandable reaction to the situation in the middle of the century, but it left the resulting discipline unable to come to a reasonable understanding of any state of affairs other than one of total crisis.

After the realist triumph in its contest with what it termed utopianism, the next stage in the general development of the discipline is marked by a concern with method, and by the positivist aspiration to develop a science of international relations on the model of the 'natural' sciences. The 1950s and 1960s saw a number of separate but related attempts to bring to bear on international relations the techniques and aspirations of the sciences – formal theories such as systems analysis and game theory, methods of data generation, such as content analysis, causal modelling, empirical data collection and processing, as in the Correlates of War project, which represented an early computer-age version of Quincy Wright's study of war, and direct theoretical imports from other more 'advanced' social sciences such as economics and psychology.[46] At the time many of the old-style realists resisted this development, but in retrospect it seems clear that the movement for science was not merely compatible with realism, but actually preordained by the realist view of the world. Vasquez and others have demonstrated that the scientists for the most part adopted the concepts of realist theory, but more important is the extent to which realism's claim that its approach corresponds to 'reality' positively invites the development of more systematic methods of exploring that, unproblematic, reality. Methods sanctioned by the successes of the sciences naturally seem preferable to those that are at the mercy of the wisdom of the interpreter.[47] The strongest case against the aspiration to science is precisely the view that the world is not simply there to be studied but is in significant ways constituted by the notions we bring to it, a viewpoint that cannot be accepted by a realism which draws its legitimacy from its claim to be able to discern how things actually are. The affinities between the realist position and the scientific are demonstrated by the success of neo-realism, which restates the old doctrines in language which is compatible with a claim to science.[48]

In the 1960s the grip of realism in both its prescientific and scientific forms began to weaken. Partly, this was a response to a relative decline in the salience of a state-centric view of the world, with the rise in significance of the international economy and of studies based on this phenomenon, along with the development of new forms of relations between the major Western countries, again mainly, but not exclusively, concerned with economic affairs. But it was also a response to the perceived weakness of, especially, the scientific version of realism when it came to the normative dimension of international relations. The 'new revolution' in political science, generally, represented an awareness that the academic study of politics had lost contact with the real world – 'relevance', a key word of the 1960s, required that politics and international relations addressed the big issues of the day, and in American international relations in particular this meant the Vietnam War. The so-called post-behavioural movement was an attempt to move the academic study of international relations away from the aspiration to produce accounts of how the world was, towards accounts of how the world should be.

This task was initially understood as that of bringing back 'values' into the subject, and some early postbehavioural writings seemed to assume that this could be done without a wholesale rethinking of the discipline – that values could be treated as simply one more variable within a scientific model. Gradually, however, it became clear that this would not do, and that a deeper theory of international relations was required. The way became clear for a re-appraisal of the philosophical past of the discipline; this openness in turn coincided with the reawakening of interest in normative and applied ethics amongst moral philosophers, and, of course, fitted in with the perspectives of those theorists of international relations who had never lost the desire to address this agenda. The coming together of these different groups provided the context for the revival of international political philosophy of the last two decades.

CONCLUSION: THE TWO AGENDAS OF CONTEMPORARY INTERNATIONAL POLITICAL PHILOSOPHY

This chapter has attempted to identify the movements in thought that have between them created a space for the revival of normative international theory; part II of this work will examine some of the substantive work that this revival has produced. The final section of this chapter offers a brief overview, not so much of this work itself, but of the agendas to which it is addressed. One of these agendas concerns issues of force and violence in international relations and as such picks up on themes which have always been part of international relations theory; however, in contemporary circumstances these themes have had to be substantially reworked in ways that will be described below. The second agenda has less of a relevant past; it concerns the global distribution of wealth and the appropriateness or inappropriateness of applying to this distribution notions of social justice. Although such concerns are not entirely without precedent, it is certainly the case that they now have a salience which they did not have in the past, partly because of movements in normative ethics, partly because of the changes in the international environment produced by decolonisation and growth of 'Third World' or 'Southern' pressure groups in international organisations.

The role of force and violence in international relations has always been a central concern for theory. For thinkers of a cosmopolitan disposition, war has been the great scandal of international relations, while communitarians who generally have been less willing to condemn out of hand the use of force have, none the less, felt it necessary to address at length the issue of the justification of violence. The international legal tradition, building upon medieval notions of *jus ad bellum* and *jus in bello*, has explored the circumstances in which resort to force is justified, and the just means that may be employed in war. Contemporary theorists of international relations have a rich literature on which to draw for thoughts on these problems. However, there are a number of respects in which contemporary circumstances throw up new problems, or new variations on old problems.

First, the engagement of whole populations in war in the twentieth century has called into question the distinction between combatant and non-combatant upon which traditional considerations of just means in warfare were based. Second, the combination of strategic warfare with weapons of mass destruction has raised a new set of problems concerned with the ethics of deterrence. Is it morally permissible to threaten to carry out an immoral act in order to defend values which, plausibly, would be in danger were no such threat to be made? Consequentialist versus deontological arguments are involved; equally, the nature of the values allegedly under threat will be a key to the discussion, and in particular the value assigned to the preservation of the autonomy of the community will be an important factor in clarifying the issues involved. Third, the contemporary world has seen the rise in significance of what might be termed 'informal' violence and force – guerrilla warfare, state and non-state terrorism, hostage taking and the like. The moral issues raised by these changes again cannot readily be assimilated to the traditional categories within which the ethics of force have been examined.

Finally, and perhaps most fundamentally, the contemporary world has seen a striking divergence between, on the one hand, the erecting of legal barriers to the use of force in international relations, to the point where it is doubtful whether it is any longer possible, legally, to make war, and, on the other, the dismantling of the moral inhibitions on the use of force which once were associated with the existence of a common religion, culture and, within certain broad limits, political heritage. The apparent impotence of legal restraints which do not give an accurate reflection of the plurality of cultures and ideologies in the contemporary world, the absence of a legitimate base for the construction of restraints following on from the de-Europeanisation of the system – these are deep issues which need to be addressed in serious discussion of the ethics of force; indeed, they may make such a discussion impossible, although the elaboration of this thought will be left to the conclusion of this work.

It would be inaccurate to say that global distributive justice is a new topic in international theory. On the contrary, the perceived inequalities of nations has often featured in international theory as a justification for action directed against the international status quo. Carr in the 1930s based his justification of appeasement in terms of the moral hypocrisy of the rich and powerful nations who condemned the use of force by the revisionist powers while forgetting that the status quo they defended was based on their own, successful, use of force in the past.[49] The fact that classical international political philosophy has been so heavily concerned with the control of force has often been taken to reflect the interests of status quo powers, likewise the paucity of thought on the processes of peaceful change – although it should be said that since the rich and powerful are more likely to be effective in the application of force, measures taken to limit its use in international affairs can hardly be described as inimical to the interests of the weak and poor. Be this as it may, there are a number of features of the contemporary system that make current debates on the issue of global distribution justice substantially different from those of the past.

First, the actual disparities that exist in the system have grown steadily wider over the last two centuries to the point where today the rich are richer than the poor by factors of ten or more. Carr's revisionist powers were Germany, Italy, Japan and the Soviet Union; in the 1930s a gap certainly did exist between these countries and Britain and the United States, but even then the real inequalities were within the great empires rather than between them. At the time these disparities were hidden by imperialism, and the belief was that the relief of poverty, in so far as it was accepted as a duty at all, was something that was the exclusive concern of the imperial power. Now, with decolonisation, the real inequalities are laid bare, and the successor states are in a position to press their claims internationally.

Second, the issue of the global distribution of wealth is no longer simply a matter of *ad hoc*, and occasionally *ad hominem*, assertions by realists wishing to deflate the pretensions of international moralisers, but has to be seen in the context of elaborate and well-worked theories of justice. Since at least the time of Plato it has been appreciated that reflective men and women will require that the arrangements of their society be justifiable, but it is, in fact, only within the last two decades that the same requirement has become attached to arrangements that pertain between nations – and even now there are many who, for quite valid reasons, would resist the application of the requirement of justice to international relations.

Even if it be accepted that international relations is not *sui generis* and that international inequalities need to be justified if they are to be morally acceptable, then the process of developing a theory of international justice involves a great many interesting questions. Are the same principles of justice to be applied internationally as in domestic society – and if so, what are these principles? Are states the subject of international justice or are individuals? What weight should be given to the preservation of the autonomy of particular societies as opposed to the welfare of their citizens? The range of issues that a theory of international justice must address is potentially so wide as to make the project itself seem at times virtually impossible, and the traditions of international thought outlined in chapters 2 and 3 above offer only limited help with this task. Although it is possible to construct Kantian or utilitarian positions on the global distribution of wealth and power (or a Hegelian account of why such positions do not work), there are no substantive theories here to help the modern political philosopher; instead, these past theories offer only attitudinal predispositions.

The final point that needs to be made before proceeding to address these agendas is that it is important to realise that the old and the new agendas are quite closely related. Although, for convenience of exposition, it makes sense to separate the issue of force from the issue of distributive justice, it should be realised that this separation can be misleading. It may be that the only way in which justice can be achieved is via the use of force – an unpalatable conclusion, but not one that can be ruled out *ab initio*.

These, then, are the subjects addressed in part II of this book. But before these matters of substance are examined, chapter 5, the introduction to part II, is devoted to the most general of all issues in normative international relations theory – the moral status of state autonomy.

NOTES

1. Obviously, it would be possible to provide an account of political philosophy less closely tied to moral philosophy: in order to forestall a long argument, a symbiotic relationship between the two modes of philosophising is simply asserted here.
2. This threefold classification uses the terminology of Peter Singer in his Introduction to Singer (ed.) *Applied Ethics* (Oxford University Press, Oxford, 1986).
3. Cited from Singer, *ibid.*, p. 2.
4. C.E.M. Joad was a regular member of the BBC's 'Brain's Trust', famous for prefacing all his replies to listeners' questions with 'It depends what you mean by . . . ' Bertrand Russell's opinions on the great issues of half a century were frequently expressed but seem to have been largely divorced from his professional activities.
5. The best short account of these movements is J.O. Urmson, *Philosophical Analysis* (Oxford University Press, Oxford, 1956).
6. An excellent account of Wittgenstein in this period is D. Pears, *The False Prison: A study in the development of Wittgenstein's Philosophy*, vol. 1

(Oxford University Press, Oxford, 1987). vol. 2 of this work (Oxford University Press, Oxford, 1989) covers the later Wittgenstein of *Philosophical Investigations*. A.J. Ayer's *Wittgenstein* (Penguin, Harmondsworth, 1985) is a useful briefer introduction.

7. See A.J. Ayer, *Language, Truth and Logic* (Gollancz, London, 1936).
8. These passages from the *Tractatus* are cited from Urmson, *op. cit.*, p. 104.
9. A good short study, on which this account relies heavily, is G.J. Warnock, *Contemporary Moral Philosophy* (Macmillan, London, 1967). Also very valuable are the relevant collections in the Oxford University Press Oxford Readings in Philosophy series: for example P. Foot (ed.)*Theories of Ethics* (1967); Singer, *op. cit.*; and S. Scheffler, *Consequentialism and Its Critics* (1988).
10. G.E. Moore, *Principia Ethica* (Cambridge University Press, Cambridge, 1903); W.D. Ross, *The Right and the Good* (Oxford University Press, Oxford, 1930).
11. These doctrines are discussed by Stevenson, Moore and Frankena in contributions to Foot, *op. cit.*, and in Warnock, *op. cit.*, ch. II.
12. Yale University Press, New Haven, Conn., 1944: see ch. III of Warnock, *op. cit.*
13. R.M. Hare, Oxford University Press, Oxford, 1952 and 1963 respectively. See ch. IV of Warnock, *op. cit.*
14. See Pears, *op. cit.*, vol. II, and Urmson, *op. cit.*, part III.
15. On 'speech acts' in general, see J.L. Austin, *How To Do Things With Words* (Oxford University Press, Oxford, 1962).
16. A collection of essays by a contemporary philosopher much influenced by these writers is R. Rorty, *Consequences of Pragmatism* (Harvester Wheatsheaf, Hemel Hempstead, 1982). Several of these papers examine James and Dewey: the paper 'Dewey's metaphysics' makes the point that, at least initially, Dewey was heavily influenced by Hegel and the English Idealists.
17. On these matters see C. Brown 'Marxism and international ethics', in T. Nardin and D. Mapel (eds) *Traditions of International Ethics* (Cambridge University Press, Cambridge, 1992).
18. See, for example, the papers by Urmson and Rawls in Foot, *op. cit.*
19. J.J.C. Smart, 'An outline of a system of utilitarian ethics' is published with 'A critique of utilitarianism' in J.J.C. Smart and B. Williams *Utilitarianism: For and Against* (Cambridge University Press, Cambridge, 1973). Singer's work is collected in *Practical Ethics* (Cambridge University Press, Cambridge, 1979). The issue of infanticide is discussed in chapter 6.
20. J. Rawls, *A Theory of Justice* (Oxford University Press, Oxford, 1971), p. 27.
21. See Smart and Williams, *op. cit.*
22. Brian Barry makes this point in 'And who is my neighbour', in his *Democracy, Power and Justice: Essays in political theory* (Clarendon, Oxford, 1989), when he suggests that an emphasis on integrity can become a form of narcissism (p. 340).
23. (Oxford University Press, Oxford, 1984), ch. 11.

24. *ibid.*, ch. 2.
25. See Singer, *op. cit.*, ch. 8, and his 'Famine, affluence and morality', *Philosophy and Public Affairs* vol. 1, no. 1 (1972).
26. See 'Kant's global rationalism' by Thomas Donaldson, in Nardin, *op. cit.*
27. The essays in Scheffler, *op. cit.*, are valuable for this debate.
28. See the discussion of this literature in R.J. Vincent, *Human Rights and International Relations* (Cambridge University Press, Cambridge, 1986).
29. For the moment the following can stand as examples of this work: M. Walzer, *Just and Unjust Wars* (Penguin, Harmondsworth, 1980); T. Nagel, *Mortal Questions* (Cambridge University Press, Cambridge, 1979); J. Finnis, J. Boyle and G. Grisez, *Nuclear Deterrence, Morality and Realism* (Oxford University Press, Oxford, 1987); and two philosophy and public affairs collections, Marshall Cohen *et al.* (eds) *War and Moral Responsibility* (Princeton University Press, Princeton, N.J., 1974) and C.R. Beitz *et al.* (eds) *International Ethics* (Princeton University Press, Princeton, N.J., 1985).
30. O. O'Neill, *Faces of Hunger: An essay on poverty, justice and development* (Allen and Unwin, London, 1986), is a very valuable account of obligation along these lines.
31. See, for example, Finnis, *et al.*, *op. cit.*, for an explicitly Roman Catholic, natural-law-based account of the morality of deterrence.
32. For an account of ethics whose conventionalist leanings are expressed in the sub-title see J.L. Mackie, *Ethics: Inventing right and wrong* (Penguin, Harmondsworth, 1977).
33. D. Hume, *A Treatise on Human Nature* (Penguin, Harmondsworth, 1969), p. 521.
34. Aristotle, *The Nichomachean Ethics* Trans. and Ed. D. Ross (World's Classics; Oxford University Press, London, 1969).
35. W.A. Galston, *Justice and the Human Good* (University of Chicago Press, Chicago, 1980).
36. H. Shue *Basic Rights* (Princeton University Press, Princeton, N.J., 1980); M. Walzer *Spheres of Justice* (Martin Robertson, Oxford, 1983); A. MacIntyre *After Virtue* (University of Notre Dame, Notre Dame, Ind., 1981) and *Whose Justice, which Rationality?* (Duckworth, London, 1988).
37. J. Rawls, *A Theory of Justice*, p. 51.
38. See esp. MacIntyre, *op. cit.*, and Walzer, *op. cit.*
39. See, for example, A. Zimmern, *The League of Nations and the Rule of Law 1918-1935* (Macmillan, London, 1939), but also his *Greek Commonwealth* (Oxford University Press, Oxford, 1931); F. Melian Stawell, *The Growth of International Thought* (Home University Library; Butterworth, London, 1929).
40. E.H. Carr, *The Twenty Years Crisis* (Macmillan, London, 1939); M. Wight, *Power Politics* (RIIA, London, 1946); N. Spykman, *America's Strategy in World Affairs* (Harcourt Brace, New York, 1942); H.J. Morgenthau, *Politics Among Nations* 1st end (Alfred A. Knopf, New York, 1948); Q. Wright, *A Study of War* (Chicago University Press, Chicago, 1942).

41. It should be stressed that this is the characterisation of a composite figure – 'The Realist' – rather than any specific writer.

42. On the, crucial, hard shell of the state, see J. Herz, *International Politics in the Atomic Age* (Columbia University Press, New York, 1959), and A.J. Wolfers, *Discord and Collaboration* (Johns Hopkins University Press, Baltimore, Md., 1962).

43. See, for example, G. Kennan's indictment of the moralising attitude in *American Diplomacy 1900–1950* (Mentor, New York, 1951).

44. The great theorist of the virtue of prudence is R. Aron, *Peace and War* (Weidenfeld and Nicholson, London, 1962).

45. For example, Morgenthau, *op. cit.*, ch. 1.

46. For useful surveys of this kind of material see, for example, J.D. Singer (ed.) *Quantitative International Politics* (Free Press, New York, 1967); D.A. Zinnes, *Contemporary Research in International Relations* (Free Press, New York, 1976); M.P. Sullivan, *International Relations: Theories and evidence* (Prentice Hall, Englewood Cliffs, N.J., 1976).

47. J.A. Vasquez, *The Power of Power-Politics* (Pinter, London, 1982).

48. See, for example, K.N. Waltz, *Theory of International Politics* (Addison-Wesley, Mass., 1979); R. Gilpin, *War and Change in World Politics* (Cambridge University Press, Cambridge, 1981); and R.O. Keohane (ed.) *Neo-Realism and its Critics* (Columbia University Press, New York, 1986).

49. Carr, *op. cit.*

Part II

Contemporary Theory: Force and Justice

Chapter 5

Introduction to Part II: The Moral Basis of State Autonomy

Do states have a right to be left to their own devices? If so, is this an absolute right, or is it conditional on their acceptance of self-imposed limits? Do all states have the same kinds of rights irrespective of their domestic circumstances? If states cannot be said to have a right to be left alone, who has the right to intervene in their affairs? Other states? Or the world community? If the latter, how is this to be put into practice? Looking at the issue from the other end of the telescope, what kind of distinction should individuals make between the rights they claim from and duties they owe to fellow citizens as opposed to people of other nationalities? Is there moral justification for giving priority to the interests and needs of the former as opposed to those of the latter?

These questions lie at the heart of normative international relations theory. They address the most central question that such theory can pose – the moral status of the claim to autonomy made, with varying degrees of success, by all sovereign states – and, although moss-covered with age, they still retain the capacity to resist simplification. There are no easy answers to these questions, which is one reason why they have survived intact the transformations that international relations theory has undergone over the course of this century. Another reason for this survival is that they recur again and again in the realm of public as well as academic discourse – most recently in the debates generated both by the aftermath of the 1991 Gulf War and public awareness of famine in the Horn of Africa.

The moral standing of state autonomy can be examined in two ways: at the macro level by the investigation of general theories which develop position on the nature of the state; and at the micro level by the detailed study of particular circumstances where state autonomy clearly poses moral problems. In chapters 2 and 3 of part I of this book two sets of general theories, the main lines of which were in place nearly two centuries ago – 'cosmopolitanism' and 'communitaria-nism' – were expounded and criticised. In chapters 6 and 7 of part II recent work on two of the most important areas where state autonomy poses particular problems – the ethics of interstate violence and the issue of global distributive justice – will be examined. In this chapter, which introduces part II, the attempt will be made to link these two levels of investigation. After a very brief review of the argument of part I, and an overview of intervention and non-intervention seen from the perspective of 'international theory', the remainder of the chapter will examine a number of recent general studies which, in different ways, link the theories of the past with the thinking of the present.

COSMOPOLITAN AND COMMUNITARIAN POSITIONS

The essential outlines of the cosmopolitan and communitarian positions on the moral standing of state autonomy will be clear from earlier chapters and, indeed, from a common-sense understanding of the meaning of these two terms. Cosmopolitan thought rejects the idea that states have a right to autonomy when this autonomy could involve the violation of universally applicable standards of behaviour, while communitarian thought is unwilling to accept constraints on state behaviour which do not grow out of the community itself. This much is reasonably clear; what is interesting is the extent to which, even as classically formulated by writers such as Kant, Bentham, Hegel and Mill, these principles cease to be quite such clear-cut alternatives once one moves beyond the general and towards the particular. Both sets of general principles are subject to modifications which dilute the purity of the original stance.

In the case of cosmopolitanism, the main dilution is a product of pragmatism: states exist and state authorities claim and will defend to the best of their ability the right to act autonomously – this is a fact about the world that cannot be simply disregarded. Given the absolute claim made by Kant on behalf of the categorical imperative, it may seem strange to suggest that his writings involve a pragmatic acceptance of the status quo, and yet, as the Second Definitive Article of a Perpetual Peace makes clear, the unwillingness of princes to surrender their sovereignty is, to Kant, a fact that must be incorporated in his thought.[1] From a Benthamite perspective the case is even clearer; the greatest-happiness principle precludes assigning any kind of absolute value to the state, but the same principle mandates recognition of the costs involved in challenging state autonomy – which will almost always be quite considerable. The point is that neither from a Kantian nor from a Benthamite perspective can classical cosmopolitan thought be shaped in such a way that it involves some kind of universal duty on all human beings to override state autonomy whenever the latter presents problems and regardless of cost. Such a position would involve the world in unending conflict.

Pragmatism also lies behind some communitarian thinking; it is particularly visible in Mill's justification of a norm of non-intervention, one of his arguments being that however clear-cut a case for intervention may seem in theory, in practice it is not possible for one people to give freedom to another.[2] However, the more important modifier of the communitarian position comes out of the unwillingness of communitarians to admit that any and all communities have an equal right to be left alone. Clearly, nationalist thinkers deny any such right to non- or multi-national states, but it is equally the case that Hegelian thought does not simply endorse the right of all states to autonomy. Hegel's account of the necessity for state sovereignty is based on the role of the state in the constitution of individuality, and it is only the modern, rational, ethical state that can perform this constitutive role. A key issue is the extent to which actual states conform to the structures of the rational state, and whether the degree of conformity of actual and real is such as to pass on to existing states the moral immunity from external interference that only the truly ethical state can claim as of right.[3] This will always be a subject for heated debate. In any event, if the arguments of the English Idealists are followed, the ethical state is itself subject to law – albeit not law enforceable by other states.[4]

The reason for making these points is not to undermine the distinction between cosmopolitan and communitarian thought – which remains basic to the structure of this book – but to guard against caricatures of these positions. In practice, the gap is rather less wide than might at first sight seem to be the case; the conflict between the stony-hearted communitarian indifferent to human suffering unless it be located within the community, and the wild-eyed cosmopolitan determined to right all wrongs wherever they may occur regardless of cost can sometimes be seen in public debates but is not to be found in the classical accounts of these positions.

INTERNATIONAL THEORY, INTERVENTION AND NON-INTERVENTION

The moral standing of the sovereign state is one of the major topics discussed by 'international theory' – identified in chapter 1 as the attempt to create normative international relations theory as a companion to, rather than an aspect of, political theory. The way in which this issue is set up in international theory is in terms of intervention and non-intervention, thus linking a moral issue with a legal issue. International theory identifies a clear distinction between the external activities of a state and its 'domestic jurisdiction' – to use the terminology of Article 2.7 of the United Nations Charter, which precludes UN intervention in 'matters which are essentially within the domestic jurisdiction of any State'. The norm is, thus, non-intervention, but – with the exception of 'realists', who, in any event, are not greatly concerned with normative issues – international theorists generally acknowledge that there will be circumstances in which this norm can and should be breached. The question is, which circumstances? The literature on this subject is extensive and well-surveyed, but a brief overview of the issues may be useful.[5]

As a first element in this overview, it is necessary to draw a distinction between *intervention* and *influence*. To intervene in the affairs of another state is to breach the norm of non-intervention and thus to act in a way that requires justification if it is to be acceptable; to seek to influence another state in the conduct of its affairs, on the other hand, is a legitimate act of diplomacy which requires no special justification. In principle this is clear, but in practice the distinction is anything but. If by influence is meant the marshalling of rational arguments in favour or against a particular course of action then there is no problem, but this is by no means the only way in which influence is exercised in diplomacy. Positive and negative sanctions – threats and promises – are equally part of the repertoire, and here the potential for confusion between intervention and influence is great. Perhaps the most useful distinction rests not on means, but on the degree of control over outcomes; influence can be resisted by states, possibly at a cost, while intervention results in a loss of autonomy, temporary or permanent. This way of drawing the distinction has the added advantage of making it clear that intervention is something that the powerful impose on the weak, whereas influence could, at least in principle, be mutual.

Having tentatively distinguished intervention from other diplomatic tools, the next step is to identify possible circumstances in which intervention might be legitimate. Three categories of legitimate intervention can be identified. First, and uncontroversially, states may intervene in each other's affairs when they have entered into legal arrangements that legitimate such action – by, for example, signing and ratifying the European Convention on Human Rights. Second, state autonomy cannot involve a right to create intolerable difficulties for one's neighbours, who thus have a right to intervene to prevent action which has this effect. The key question here, of course, is what is 'intolerable'. There is no obvious answer to this question, which leaves the 'public nuisance' defence of intervention somewhat in the air.[6] However, the basic principle is clear and may come to have more importance in the future – it is, for example, obviously of considerable relevance to the issue of environmental protection and the international control of pollution.

The most controversial and problematic examples of legitimate intervention concern violations of human dignity so gross as to constitute in themselves a reason for humanitarian intervention. Today such intervention could, perhaps, rest on legal grounds provided by international declarations and treaties on human rights, but the general principle predates such legalities by a matter of centuries. At the very beginning of the modern international system, the Spanish theologian and lawyer Vitoria justified the conquests in the New World partly on the basis that the Aztec custom of human sacrifice constituted so gross a violation of human dignity as to warrant intervention on behalf of the innocent victims against their rulers. Actually, as readily acknowledged elsewhere by Vitoria, it was laughable to suggest that the Spaniards were motivated by a concern to protect the innocent, but, this aside and more to the point, this early justification for humanitarian intervention – in common with most later examples – is based on an account of human dignity that is obviously ethnocentric. For the Spaniards tyranny was ritual human sacrifice and cannibalism rather than the massacres they perpetrated in eradicating this phenomenon.[7]

The general problem here is that humanitarian intervention is always going to be based on the cultural predilections of those with the power to carry it out, whether or not these predilections are enshrined in legal documents or reflect a temporary consensus. This is not to say that such intervention is always illegitimate; on the contrary, there may be many cases where acting on cultural prejudice is, taking all things into consideration, the best thing to do.[8] It is to say that such intervention can never be uncontroversial and ought not to be treated as though it were.[9]

Aside from these and other similarly restrictive cases of legitimate intervention, the basic presupposition of international theory is that non-intervention is the norm. It is intervention that needs to be justified by special arguments; states have a right to be left to their own devices unless there is some good reason to the contrary. In this as in other respects international theory reveals its distant kinship with communitarian approaches to international relations. However, the fact that legitimate reasons for intervention can be found also reflects the thinking behind these approaches – as suggested above, not all states can claim the protection entailed by the idea of community, any more than the norm of non-intervention can be said to cover all circumstances.

The international theory of intervention and non-intervention is thus necessarily indeterminate; it offers a number of categories into which certain kinds of state behaviour can be fitted, but without offering a clear guide as to the moral status of these categories. It offers a vocabulary and a grammar which enable us to talk about these issues and which takes its place alongside the language inherited from the cosmopolitan and communitarian thinkers discussed above. The question for the rest of part II is whether the new normative international relations theory offers either useful refinements of these languages, or, more ambitiously, the beginnings of solutions to the problems raised. In the next two chapters this new work will be examined in the context of specific issues; the rest of this chapter is devoted to a number of studies which elaborate general positions: the neo-cosmopolitanism of Charles R. Beitz, the neo-communitarianism of Mervyn Frost, Terry Nardin's Oakeshottian reconstruction of the norms of international society, and – as an adjunct – Robert H. Jackson's reworking of the notion of sovereignty in the context of the quasi-states of the Third World.

COSMOPOLITANISM AND INTERDEPENDENCE

One of the most basic reasons for accepting that state autonomy is morally defensible rests upon a quasi-empirical proposition about the quality and depth of relationships that exist between citizens of a particular state as opposed to relations between non-citizens. It may simply be a fact about the world that fellow citizens have more interactions with one another than with non-citizens, and it is not necessary to assume that these interactions create 'community' in order to regard their relative frequency as morally significant. Social-contract theory, for example, as formulated by Hobbes or Locke, does not involve the creation of community in any strong sense of the word, but it does involve a clear sense of the different status of relations between those who are parties to the contract and those who are not. Contractors have obligations towards each other which go deeper than the obligations they have towards non-contractors.

The most celebrated recent employer of contract theory is John Rawls.[10] His intent is to produce a theory of justice in society, and 'society' for this purpose is defined as a 'co-operative venture for mutual advantage'.[11] Rawls is clear that the world as a whole is *not* such a venture, and for this reason justice on a world scale is different from social justice. Whereas justice within society involves the legitimation of all social arrangements including inequalities, international justice requires no more (nor less) than the acceptance of legal rules governing relations between autonomous jurisdictions, one such rule being the rule of non-intervention. Two contracts are required, the first between those who regularly interact for mutual advantage, the second – and more limited in scope – between the societies created by the first.[12]

The details of Rawls' argument – especially as it applies to international justice – will be examined in chapter 7 below. What deserves examination here is the first premise of this argument, which is that there is a clear empirical difference between the scope and frequency of interpersonal relations within states as opposed to those which take place across state frontiers. This premise can be challenged, and Charles R. Beitz, in *Political Theory and International Relations*, builds one of the most impressive of modern statements of cosmopolitanism on precisely such a challenge.[13] On his view, state autonomy could only be morally justifiable if it reflected certain empirical contingencies, which, in fact, it does not.

Following the line of argument set out above, Beitz assumes that the strongest defence of the idea of the moral autonomy of the state rests on a contractarian position, and in particular on the view that states are in their relations with one another in a position analogous to the Hobbesian state of nature. If this analogy holds, the 'realist' view that interstate relations are not subject to moral reasoning would be justifiable. However, Beitz suggests that for the analogy to work the international system would have to show certain characteristics mirroring those displayed by individuals in a state of nature. It would be necessary (a) that states be the actors in international relations, (b) that they have relatively equal power, (c) that they be independent of each other 'in the sense that they can order their internal (i.e. nonsecurity) affairs independently of the internal policies of other states' and (d) that 'there are no reliable expectations of reciprocal compliance by the actors with rules of co-operation in the absence of a superior power capable of enforcing these rules.'[14] Only if these conditions hold could the modern international system be said to be analogous to a Hobbesian state of nature.

Beitz argues that these conditions do not hold. Some of the arguments he deploys are not strong – for example, the fact that there are great inequalities of power between states would be significant only if these inequalities resulted in a clear hierarchy of power, which does not appear to be the case – but others are convincing. The most important point is that economic interdependence in the modern world undermines condition (c). Even the most powerful state cannot be truly independent in the way that the Hobbesian state of nature requires. It may be the case that Beitz exaggerates the extent to which this interdependence has progressed, and thus underestimates the degree of freedom possessed by states, but, however conservatively the trend is assessed, there seems little reason to doubt that he is right to see this feature of the modern system as one that has great significance for the morality of state autonomy.

Having established this point in the first part of *Political Theory and International Relations*, Beitz goes on in the second part to present arguments against all the usual positions defending state autonomy. States are not like individuals; they do not have a right to have their 'personalities' respected. The idea of state autonomy brings 'a spurious order to complex and conflicting moral considerations'.[15] It is right and proper to condemn imperialism, colonialism and dependence, not because they constitute external interference in the internal affairs of another country, but because they are in themselves unjust. Again, international 'paternalism' may or may not be undesirable – it is the quality of the act that is crucial not the fact that it involves intervention. The point about all these activities, and about principles such as nationality and self-determination, is that their moral worth cannot be assessed with reference to the alleged value of state autonomy; what is important is whether particular arrangement do or do not promote justice and other, non-spurious, values.

The final section of *Political Theory and International Relations* takes up the issue of international distributive justice and confronts the Rawlsian limitation of this notion. The argument here will be considered at some length in chapter 7; a key issue is whether the notion of interdependence is as helpful in respect to distributive justice as Beitz needs it to be, given that relations between rich and poor states are rather less interdependent than are those amongst the rich. In any event, the earlier parts of Beitz's book provide enough material to allow for a summary assessment of his position. Two aspects of his work are particularly interesting: the nature of his cosmopolitanism by contrast to that of the classic defenders of this position; and his assumption that opponents of his position will be implicitly or explicitly realist.

What is interesting about Beitz's cosmopolitanism is its radicalism. As suggested earlier in this chapter, figures such as Kant and Bentham were prepared to accept that there were genuine real-world constraints which meant that second-best solutions were sometimes unavoidable. Beitz is far less willing to make such a concession, although he accepts the 'kernel of truth' in realism that to make decisions without grasping the complex interaction between normative and empirical knowledge is to ask for trouble. He is concerned to create 'ideal theory', in contrast to Bentham's concern for the practical, and in contrast to Kant, who is also interested in the ideal but places this notion within an essentially theological framework in which such notions as 'original sin' and 'providence' have a role to play.[16] However, as against this concern for ideal theory, and unlike either Kant or Bentham, the framework that Beitz does create relies very heavily on an essentially empirical proposition about the world; namely, that it is today characterised by economic interdependence. Kant's cosmopolitanism emerges from his account of what it is to be a human being, while Bentham's stems from the principle of utility, but Beitz has no such foundations for his work.[17] If the trend towards greater interdependence were to be reversed – implausible but not impossible – the logic of Beitz's position would seem to be that the case for the morality of state autonomy would be strengthened.

Another interesting feature of Beitz's handling of the problem of state autonomy – and one that leads naturally to the next section of this chapter – is his assumption that his most dangerous opponents will be realist in their approach to the subject. Plausibly enough, he takes Hobbes to be the patron saint of realism and by demolishing the analogy between the state of nature and the modern international system he believes, again plausibly enough, that he has produced a telling argument against the realist position. Realism is predicated upon an empirical account of the nature of the international system, and by demonstrating the weakness of this account Beitz has revealed the weakness of realism – and, of course, of any other doctrine which rests on similar empirical foundations.

The problem is that some accounts of the moral basis of state autonomy do not rest on this kind of empirical foundation. Rather than seeing the state as the creation of a network of interpersonal relationships, or as a co-operative venture for mutual advantage created by contract, they see the state as a manifestation of community, and see community as possessing moral value, distinct from the value to be assigned to the individuals who constitute this community. From this perspective empirical facts about the degree of autonomy possessed by state authorities are of little significance. Of course, if interdependence reaches the point at which it no longer makes sense to talk about autonomy at all, then that would make a difference; but what would be at stake then would not be a matter of degree but a qualitative change. Sovereignty is something that states either possess or do not. For the time being, Britain is sovereign in a way that, say,

Wales, is not – and the extent to which British decision making is externally constrained is not to the point.

The Beitzian approach to state autonomy can hardly cope with this sort of position; indeed, it is not designed to do so, probably regarding such thinking as so far out of court as not to be worth while confronting. However, this kind of communitarianism does have strong modern supporters, and it is towards one of the strongest of these that the argument now turns.

'SETTLED NORMS' IN INTERNATIONAL RELATIONS

Mervyn Frost, in *Towards a Normative Theory of International Relations*, approaches the subject at the same high level of generality adopted by Beitz, and – again as with Beitz – the first part of his book is devoted to a defence of normative theory in international relations.[18] Frost sees two sources of opposition to the normative project, the positivist bias in international relations, and the prevalence of sceptical and realist arguments against normative theory. He examines these objections and – predictably – concludes that they are unsatisfactory. Some engagement with normative issues in international relations is unavoidable. The arguments deployed here are, in substance if not in style, much the same as those utilised by Beitz, and indeed most every other work on normative theory, including this one. By now they can, presumably, be taken as read.

Where Frost differs from Beitz and many other modern normative theorists is in the next step in the argument. Beitz, having established that normative international relations theory is necessary and possible, proceeds by interrogating the subject matter of international relations from a political theory perspective, somewhat in the manner of an explorer conducting a well-equipped expedition to an unknown continent. Frost, on the other hand, approaches the subject from within. His strategy is to investigate the normative issues generated by the modern states system, employing in the first instance the traditional language of moral discourse characteristic of that system, and moving to the discourse of political philosophy only when 'hard cases' emerge which cannot be resolved within the traditional framework.[19]

The first step here is to identify the settled body of norms in international relations. Frost defines a norm as settled 'where it is generally recognised that any argument denying the norm (or which appears to override the norm) requires special justification.'[20] His point is not that settled norms are always obeyed, but that when they are flouted it is on the basis of reasoning which points to exceptional circumstances. The existence or non-existence of settled norms is demonstrated by the language that states use to justify their actions. Frost suggests that within the modern system it is possible to identify eighteen settled norms, of varying degrees of generality, ranging from the first and second – that *'the preservation of the society of states itself is a good'* and that 'it is a good for states in the system to be accounted as *sovereign*' – to the fourteenth and eighteenth – that *'human rights are a good which need to be protected by states and the international system'* and that 'some kind of system of *economic co-operation* between states is a good.'[21]

The first two norms have primacy in the sense that 'most of the other settled goods are in some way derivative from them'; combining them, 'it appears that the preservation of a system of sovereign states is the primary good.'[22] From this starting point two questions arise: first, what justification can there by for this position; and second, how can this most basic norm be reconciled with other settled norms which appear to contradict the primacy of state sovereignty – such as the norm concerning human rights referred to above, or the norm that democratic institutions within a state is a good? Simplifying his terminology somewhat, Frost sees the task of normative theory to be that of providing a 'background theory' which can both justify the primacy of sovereignty and reconcile sovereignty with rights.

Frost argues that there are three main background theories which attempt this task, none of which is satisfactory. One argument – which he associates with Hedley Bull's *The Anarchical Society*[23] – justifies the norm on the grounds that they promote *order*. This is not satisfactory: depending on the meaning of order, the argument is circular (order being defined as the preservation of sovereign states) or contentless (order being a feature of any social arrangement) or relies on some other deeper normative position to avoid these two traps. Equally, the *utilitarian* justification for the norms fails; even if maximising aggregate utility is a coherent goal (and Frost thinks it is not), there is no reason to believe that the norms of the current international system promote this goal. Finally, Frost examines *rights-based* and *contractarian* background theories. Again unsympathetic to such approaches, his basic point is that even if it could be said that some version of such theories justify some of the settled norms of the system they cannot reconcile the apparent contradiction between sovereignty and rights. Such a contradiction cannot be understood in terms of any of the currently available background theories.[24]

Before turning to Frost's own solution to this problem, it should be said that the way in which he sets up the problem has much in its favour. Intuition is a dangerous guide, but still it does seem intuitively right to stress that there is a real contradiction between the norm of sovereignty and the norm of rights. Beitz removes this contradiction by regarding the moral case for sovereignty as simply spurious; as he sees it, the task of his theory is to reveal the weakness of those arguments generally offered in support of the norm of sovereignty, by demonstrating that in so far as they stand up to close examination it is because they rest on values other than the value of state autonomy. Seen close up there simply is no contradiction – rights take precedence. Frost, on the other hand, starts from the position that the value that people and states quite clearly do assign to sovereignty cannot simply be dismissed as the product of defective powers of reasoning or some kind of persisting mass hallucination.[25] This seems sensible.

The solution Frost offers to the apparent contradiction between sovereignty and rights follows the lines of the demythologised Hegelianism set out in chapter 3 above – not surprisingly, since the account given there owes much to Frost and to one of his main sources, John Charvet's *A Critique of Freedom and Equality*.[26] The essential point is that individuality – the basis for rights – is constituted by such institutions as the family, civil society and the state, and the latter cannot perform this role unless it be recognised by other states as autonomous. Thus the contradiction between sovereignty and rights disappears since genuine rights can only emerge in sovereign states; the contradiction existed in the first place only because of the force of the view that rights could be possessed by presocial individuals and therefore require protection from states in ways incompatible with the idea of sovereignty. However widely held, this view is mistaken: individuality itself is a constituted and not a pre-given feature of human existence.

The difficulty with this position, as Frost fully appreciates, is that, in order to be recognised as rightfully autonomous, states have to meet specific requirements that are incredibly demanding. 'An autonomous state is one in which the citizens experience the well-being of the state as fundamental to their own well-being'[27] It is a state whose constitution is recognised by the people as the proper way of doing things, as a set of rules in terms of which people constitute each other. Few, if any, actual states fit the bill, but states which do not meet the requirement for autonomy cannot properly claim to be sovereign in their dealings with other states.

In the final chapter of this book, Frost examines unconventional violence in international relations (such as the campaign of the Irish Republican Army in Northern Ireland or of the Palestine Liberation Organisation in the Middle East) as a 'hard case' for normative theory, where sovereignty and rights seem dramatically at odds. He concludes that there are possible circumstances in which such violence might be justified if the state is set up in such a way as to deny to its people the possibility of individuality – although the means employed must be consistent with the desire to establish a constitutional state.[28] The argument here is interesting, but it might be doubted whether this sort of melodramatic situation actually constitutes the best test for Frost's approach. It is not really necessary to go to extreme cases to find examples where the sovereignty of the state can be challenged. Since probably considerably fewer than a quarter of the present members of the United Nations come close to meeting the constitutional requirements for having their autonomy respected, the circumstances in which sovereignty and rights are actually seen to go together are far outnumbered by those in which the contradiction remains unreconciled. Charles Beitz sees the moral case for the autonomy of the state as essentially spurious: Frost wholeheartedly disagrees, but the logic of his position is that the vast majority of claims made by states to have their sovereignty respected are every bit as spurious as Beitz would say all such claims are. The disagreement between these two conceptions of the world is total at the level of theory, marginal at the level of practice.

Part of the problem with Frost's formulation of these issues is a product of his desire to produce normative theory from the starting point of the ways in which normative issues are actually framed in the modern system of states. The first principle of prescriptive international relations, as promulgated by such bodies as the United Nations, is state sovereignty, and this notion is coupled with a refusal to distinguish between different kinds of states. From the UN viewpoint, a state is a state is a state – and any attempt to distinguish between those states that have earned the right to autonomy and those that have not is totally unacceptable. The problem is that from Frost's viewpoint it is essential to make this distinction because, if it is not made, the principles he annunciates become simply rationalisations for the status quo – and this is most certainly not his intention. There is a dislocation between the starting point of his argument and its conclusion.

It may be that it is the starting point that ought to be revised. It may be that it is impossible to defend the morality of state autonomy while accepting the definition of a state that is dominant within the modern state system. This is a conclusion that could be drawn from a major recent study of Third World international relations, Robert H. Jackson's *Quasi-States: Sovereignty, international relations and the Third World*.[29]

QUASI-STATES

Jackson's basic point is that the norms underlying the notion of sovereignty have changed in the post-Second World War era. The old sovereignty regime was based on two dimensions, negative and positive sovereignty. Negative sovereignty refers to the right to be left alone to conduct one's internal affairs without external interference. Positive sovereignty refers to the capacities that states have to act in the world. Negative sovereignty is a formal-legal condition; positive sovereignty is substantive – a positively sovereign government is one that 'possesses the wherewithal to provide political goods for its citizens'.[30] Positive sovereignty is a political, not a legal, status.

In the past, only states that had the capacity to exercise positive sovereignty could claim the rights of non-intervention and other international immunities involved in negative sovereignty. For a short period it was actually explicit that candidates for full membership of international society had to meet the standard of 'civilisation' established by the dominant states – a standard which involved effective government and the existence of the rule of law – but even when implicit some such notion lay behind the idea of sovereignty.[31]

Since the second world war this way of looking at sovereignty has fallen into disrepute. The right to self-determination has taken precedence over all other criteria for membership of international society – decolonisation, promoted by the United Nations, has taken place irrespective of the substantive capabilities of putative postcolonial governments. It is no longer acceptable to argue that a particular colony is not ready for self-government. The dominant norm assumes that all colonies that want independence are entitled to get it – and sooner rather than later. The result of the operation of this norm is the existence of a large number of states claiming the full set of international immunities associated with negative sovereignty, but unable to come close to meeting the substantive requirements of positive sovereignty. Indeed, another norm of the modern system is that those states that do meet these substantive requirements ought, through development assistance, to help these 'quasi-states' to acquire the attributes of positive sovereignty. Jackson, rightly, suggests that the divorce between positive and negative sovereignty is a source of much of the incoherence characteristic of modern debates on topics such as intervention and non-intervention in the Third World. The background theory which lies behind the norm of non-intervention contains assumptions about the nature of states which simply do not apply to a great many members of the modern international system.

The distinction between states and quasi-states may be helpful from the perspective of normative international relations theory, and it may be that it is only plausible to think of a full defence of the notion that state autonomy could be morally justified if this defence is restricted to states which have the attributes of positive as well as negative sovereignty. However, it should be noted that the distinction between states and quasi-states does not tie in with the arguments deployed by either Beitz or Frost. Both of these authors are not concerned with whether states have the substantive attributes of positive sovereignty, but either with the way they use these attributes or with the form taken by these attributes. It is perfectly possible to imagine states having the wherewithal to provide political goods for their citizens but using this capacity in ways that Beitz (and others) would consider unjust and indefensible. A positively sovereign government may not rule the sort of constitutional state that, according to Frost, alone has the right to claim immunity from external interference.

Thus far in this chapter the issue of the moral standing of state autonomy has been approached by means of an investigation of the nature of states themselves. Beitz and Frost ask what, if anything, it is about states that entitles them legitimately to claim a right to be left to their own devices, while Jackson offers a helpful distinction between different kinds of states. Each of these authors clarifies, without resolving, the issues; it may be that this is the most that can be expected and that there are genuinely unresolvable paradoxes associated with the morality of state sovereignty – if so, the study of particular issues and cases may be the only way forward. However, before reaching this conclusion it may be helpful to approach the issue from another direction.

The idea of 'international society' plays a major role in traditional international theory. The proposition is that relations between states do not simply create an international *system* but a *society*, the implication being that there is a normative content to these relationships, a 'morality of states' which may be different from the morality that governs individuals, but which is not simply a cloak for self-interest and instrumental behaviour.[32] International society is not based on member states with common or compatible domestic structures, but on the willingness of its members to behave towards each other in ways that conform to its norms, that is, in accordance with international law and custom. States achieve international legitimacy and the rights of non-intervention by virtue of their conformity to law and custom and not by virtue of their domestic structures – although, as suggested above, there are some limits to acceptable state behaviour such as the ban on gross violations of human dignity.

The key question, of course, is why this form of legitimacy should be accepted. The tradition either more or less assumes that autonomy itself is a good (which begs the question) or raises the sort of points about the order-creating virtues of the system rightly challenged by Frost in his critique of Hedley Bull. What is required if this approach is to make moral sense is a better conceptualisation of the notion of international society than the tradition offers – and the final author examined in this chapter has produced the best modern attempt to carry out this task.

INTERNATIONAL SOCIETY AS A PRACTICAL ASSOCIATION

Terry Nardin, in *Law, Morality and the Relations of States*, defends a traditional notion of international society, but brings to this task ideas on the nature of politics and society developed by one of the most important of twentieth-century political philosophers, Michael Oakeshott, in his greatest work, *On Human Conduct*.[33] Oakeshott's work is not easy to summarise, but an essential feature is what majority opinion would regard as a very limited and somewhat idiosyncratic conception of what constitutes politics and political action. For Oakeshott, politics is 'civil association', discourse between citizens about the general arrangements of society, particularly discourse oriented towards the rule of law. What it most definitely is not is an activity concerned with the collective pursuit of common ends or purposes. The pursuit of common goals involves 'enterprise association' and has nothing to do with politics. Enterprises pursue goals common to all associates – no such goals exist for all citizens of the modern state, save the goal of living in a society which through the rule of law prevents their free individuality being conscripted into enterprises to which they do not give their consent.

This is a conception of politics that is somewhat too restrictive even for the majority of neo-liberals who in other respects share Oakeshott's belief that contemporary states have taken on too many inappropriate enterprises. However, the civil-association/enterprise-association dichotomy provides Nardin with a way of expounding the nature of international society. First, he renames and changes slightly these two forms of association. Civil association becomes 'practical' association – a practice being 'a set of considerations to be taken into account in deciding and acting, and in evaluating decisions and actions'. Enterprise association becomes 'purposive' association – a change, incidentally, that is a source of some confusion.[34] Purposive associations exist in international relations in the form of alliances, free-trade areas, common markets and the like, but international society as such is not a purposive association. It is a practical association whose members share no common goals other than a desire to co-exist in peace and security. The authoritative practices of international law and diplomacy are at the heart of the practical association that is international society.

The presupposition here is the pluralist nature of international society; states are assumed to have different goals, different purposes internationally, different conceptions of the good life and different notions of what is good and bad. No all-inclusive purposive association could cope with these differences. Only a form of association that does not assume common purposes can be legitimate. It follows that attempts to give a more substantive content to international society are mistaken in principle and unworkable in practice – and much of Nardin's book is given over to an account of the ways in which such attempts in the twentieth century, and especially since the foundation of the United Nations, have simply resulted in an undermining of the rule of law rather than in the creation of substantive goods.

This is a compelling account of the nature of international society, and the distinction between practical and purposive association is illuminating in a number of ways. However, in terms of the questions posed at the outset of this chapter, the idea of international society as a practical association is not particularly helpful. From a normative point of view it rests on two propositions about pluralism in international relations, neither of which is self-evidently true. The first is that the states that make up international society actually embody different conceptions of the good; this may not be so at all – it may be the case that such different conceptions are actually to be found in ideologies and social movements which cut across state boundaries. But second – and more fundamentally – even if different states do embody different conceptions of the good, it is by no means clear that this is a state of affairs that is morally desirable.

The practical conception of international society assumes that pluralism is desirable; but it is precisely this assumption that writers such as Beitz and Frost, from their different perspectives, challenge. If diversity entails that states have the right to mistreat their populations, then it is difficult to see why such diversity is to be valued. Of course, the term 'mistreat' implies a standard of judgement, and in the absence of a 'view from nowhere' such a standard will inevitably reflect one particular position: but unless one is prepared to defend international pluralism by developing a full-blown theory of moral relativism, which Nardin is not, some such standard has to be adopted.[35] It is difficult to see why diversity should be respected *morally* simply because it is a fact about the modern international system, although, in so far as it is a fact, it would indeed be sensible to take it into account in the formation of state policy.

Conclusion

The positions articulated by Beitz, Frost, Jackson and Nardin can be taken as examples of the best modern attempts to make sense of the dilemmas raised by questions concerning the moral standing of state sovereignty. Between them they bring to bear on these dilemmas many of the most powerful tools of contemporary political philosophy – whether from modern contractarianism, neo-Hegelianism or Oakeshottian notions of political association. However, at the end of the day, the questions set out at the beginning of this chapter remain unanswered. Beitz's answers involve regarding as spurious the values that maintain one side of the dilemma, that concerning the good that is autonomy. Frost's approach reconciles sovereignty with rights but only in the most limited circumstances. Nardin's conception of international society explains why autonomy is to be valued but only if the initial judgement that diversity is not simply a fact but also a good is accepted.

The absence of uncontroversial answers to these questions ought not to be surprising. It is of the nature of this sort of question not to be answerable – there is a clash of values involved, each of which is real, and in such circumstances it is unrealistic to expect that a background theory can always be found which will reveal that the clash is more apparent than real. It may be the case that there is a genuine paradox here, and the best that can be expected of philosophical analysis is that it will clarify the terms of the paradox. This, it can be said, has been achieved in the work of these authors.

The next stage in the argument, pursued in the next two chapters, is to move from the macro to the micro level. If no general resolution of the moral dilemmas of state autonomy is available, it may still be the case that progress is possible when specific issues come into focus. Two of the most basic of such issues concern the ethics of international violence and the meaning of social justice in international affairs, the subject matter of the next two chapters. In examining these issues the general positions of Beitz, Frost and Nardin will form a backdrop to the more issue-specific contributions of authors such as Walzer, Nagel, Singer and Barry.

NOTES

1. See 'Perpetual Peace' in H. Reiss (ed.) *Kant's Political Writings*, trans. H.B. Nisbet (Cambridge University Press, Cambridge, 1970), pp. 102ff., and the discussion in ch. 2 above.
2. J.S. Mill, 'A few words on non-intervention', in *Essays on Politics and Culture* ed. G. Himmelfarb (Anchor Doubleday, New York, 1963), pp. 368ff.
3. The answer given to this question is one way of distinguishing between 'left' and 'right' Hegelians, the latter being more willing to give moral endorsement to the status quo than the former.
4. See, for example, B. Bosanquet, *The Philosophical Theory of the State*, 4th edn (Macmillan, London, 1965), p. 304, where it is stated that states guilty of violating law would be judged 'before the tribunal of humanity and of history'.
5. R.J. Vincent, *Nonintervention and International Order* (Princeton University Press, Princeton, N.J., 1974); H. Bull (ed.) *Intervention in World Politics* (Clarendon, Oxford, 1984); R. Little, *Intervention: External involvement in civil wars* (Martin Robertson, London, 1975) are some general studies of the subject.
6. In 1961 the Republic of India invaded Goa on the basis that continued Portuguese rule of this enclave amounted to an intolerable 'public nuisance'; on the whole, the international community accepted this reasoning, which C.A.W. Manning took to be the signal for a return to international lawlessness – see the Preface to the reissue of *The Nature of International Society* (Macmillan/London School of Economics, London, 1975), p. xxv.
7. These issues are brilliantly illuminated by T. Todorov, *The Conquest of America* (Harper Torchbooks, New York, 1987).
8. There are many ways of dramatising this issue: for example, the thought experiment of putting oneself in the position of a British East India Company administrator in the 1840s and 1850s who has the power to abolish the Hindu custom of widow-burning and is concerned whether to use this power or not.
9. The best discussions of humanitarian intervention are R.J. Vincent, *Human Rights and International Relations* (Cambridge University Press, Cambridge, 1986), and J. Donnelly, 'Humanitarian Intervention', *Journal of International Affairs*, vol. 37 (Winter 1984).
10. *A Theory of Justice* (Oxford University Press, Oxford, 1971).
11. *ibid.*, p. 4.
12. *ibid.*, pp. 378ff., is the best source for these points, although Rawls' ideas on international justice are scattered throughout the book.
13. Princeton University Press, Princeton, N.J., 1979.
14. *ibid.*, p. 36.
15. *ibid.*, p. 69.
16. For Beitz on 'ideal theory' see *ibid.*, pp. 169ff.
17. At least not in *Political Theory and International Relations*. His later

'Cosmopolitan ideals and national sentiment', *Journal of Philosophy*, vol. 80 (1983), pp. 591–600, amounts to a wholesale revision of his chain of reasoning, although not his conclusions. In this work he adopts a far more Kantian approach to the case for cosmopolitanism with arguments for the unity of the human race based on rationality and fellow-feeling.

18. Cambridge University Press, Cambridge, 1986.
19. Frost takes the idea of 'hard cases' from the work of R. Dworkin – *Taking Rights Seriously* (Duckworth, London, 1977).
20. *ibid.*, p. 121.
21. *ibid.*, pp. 121–7.
22. *ibid.*, p. 128.
23. *The Anarchical Society: A study of order in world politics* (Macmillan, London, 1977).
24. These justificatory background theories are discussed in ch. 4.2, pp. 128ff.
25. Beitz, in 'Cosmopolitan ideals' (see note 17 above), goes some way towards recognising the reality of national sentiments, but without essentially revising his view that to assign moral priority to the needs of fellow nationals cannot be justified.
26. Cambridge University Press, Cambridge, 1981.
27. Frost, *op. cit.*, p. 179.
28. Frost extended these ideas in a paper 'Just means against apartheid', presented to the Joint Congress of the British International Studies Association and the (American) International Studies Association, London, 1989.
29. Cambridge University Press, Cambridge, 1990.
30. *ibid.*, p. 29.
31. On the 'standard of Civilisation', see G.C. Gong, *The Standard of 'Civilisation' in International Society* (Oxford University Press, Oxford, 1984), and in general see H. Bull and A. Watson (eds) *The Expansion of International Society* (Clarendon, Oxford, 1984).
32. The idea of international society pervades modern international theory, but the work of Hedley Bull and R.J. Vincent on the 'morality of states' is particularly relevant here – see the writings of these authors cited above.
33. Nardin (Princeton University Press, Princeton, N.J., 1983), Oakeshott (Oxford University Press, Oxford, 1975). C. Brown, 'Ethics of co-existence: The international theory of Terry Nardin', *Review of International Studies*, vol. 14, no. 3 (1988), gives a more detailed account of Nardin's contribution to international relations theory.
34. Because practical associations also have a purpose, albeit of a different type, namely the purpose of living together in conditions of peace and justice.
35. Nardin's discussion of these issues in 'The problem of relativism in international ethics' *Journal of International Studies, Millennium*: vol. 18, no. 2 (1989), makes it clear that he is willing to go some way in the direction of relativism, but a relativism that is combined with an explicit moralism not usually associated with this approach.

Chapter 6
The Ethics of Force

INTRODUCTION: PEACE, VIOLENCE AND WAR, SOME PRELIMINARY OBSERVATIONS

It is a major premise of virtually all international relations theory that 'peace' is a desirable state of affairs; interstate violence is identified by most theorists of international relations as something close to the supreme evil – to the understanding, and ultimate elimination, of which international thought is dedicated. There is a high level of consensus in support of the view that resort to force – 'aggression' – is to be avoided at almost all costs, and that only in self-defence or the defence of others can violence be employed without moral sanction. The consensus here is so extensive that it includes the majority of realists, who defend their refusal to accept a moral account of international relations on the basis that moralism undermines a prudential approach to war prevention. Only the relatively few consistent amoralists who refuse to apply the terms 'good' or 'bad' to any (international) political situation stand outside the consensus for peace, and of modern political movements only fascism purports to regard war as desirable in its own terms – and, perhaps, this is one of the reasons why fascism is commonly seen as even more appalling than its totalitarian twin, communism, which, whatever its practice, is, at least in principle, committed to peace. The strength of the consensus for peace is such that any willingness to see positive elements in war is widely condemned as a step on the slippery slope towards actual approval – the experience of Hegel and the English Idealists is relevant here. Although it is clear from the *Philosophy of Right* that Hegel regards peace as a norm, his account of the potential side-benefits of war has resulted in his being classified as a militarist by many liberal thinkers, while the unwillingness of the English Idealists to accept that war could be a crime against *other states* – while insisting that it could be an offence against *common morality* – was also misinterpreted.[1]

Clearly, war and peace is, at least in the twentieth century, one of those issues where decent opinion is all on one side of an argument that, as a result, never actually takes place. There seems to be no great difficulty in accounting for the existence of this anti-war consensus. Obviously, war is destructive of people, property and civilised social relations, to an extent that no putative side-benefits in the form of communal solidarity could begin to compensate for. This is especially true in the modern era; the development of weapons of mass destruction poses a threat which goes beyond the destructive capacities of past armaments, and as a result the imperative of peace seems more compelling today than ever before. All this seems obvious, barely worth stating.

While in the end the imperative of peace may indeed be compelling, a degree of suspicion ought to be attached to any position which attracts the degree of consensual support that seems to exist in this case. One of the first principles of critical thought is that arguments that seem so obvious that opposition to them appears perverse are quite likely to be carrying along in their wake ideas or positions that are less obviously compelling. The view that war is the ultimate evil in international relations and that the elimination of war is a key practical task for international theory may be precisely such a common-sense position that, once investigated, proves to be covering other, more contestable, stances.

The basic argument in favour of a close questioning of common sense in this case is that by giving so much attention to the disasters of war, international relations theory is in danger of underestimating the oppressions of peace. More precisely, the privileged position within international relations of theories which focus on interstate war reflects and reinforces an interpretation of the relationship between peoples and their governments that is, at best, highly contentious. The key point here is that 'war-centricity' is a major support to the classical doctrine of the two dimensions of sovereignty, a doctrine crucial to the intellectual formation of the modern international system.[2] The two dimensions in question are the domestic, in which the sovereign is the source of order, and the international, in which the effect of multiple sovereignties is anarchy. The image is of a social world where the primary threat to the life, liberty and happiness of the individual comes from the outside, where a well-regulated society needs to be protected from external incursions by the power of the sovereign, where order and justice are sustained internally in a moral community, but threatened externally by alien violence. Sovereignty in this case is a legal notion; to a lesser extent, the moral case for state autonomy, examined in the previous chapter, rests on similar oppositions.

This is an image of great power and durability. It appears in all sorts of unlikely places; hidden not very deeply, for example, in much radical criticism of the activities of multi-national capital in the modern world economy, where the external nature of the alleged threat implicitly promotes an image of internal harmony.[3] It is an image that is consonant with communitarian international theory, although neither classical nor contemporary communitarians would make the key assumption that moral communities and legal communities necessarily coincide in the clear-cut way that the doctrine of sovereignty requires – a point elaborated in chapter 5 above. However, the key point that needs to be made about this image of the world is that the vision of domestic society as a haven of order where the threat to the security of peoples comes from beyond the city walls simply does not stand up to critical examination. For most people, in most societies, most of the time, the most important obstacles to the good life come from within the walls, the most serious threats to life and liberty come either from those allegedly providing 'protection' or, at the very least, with the acquiescence of these guardians of security. In so far as international relations allows itself to become a war-centred discourse, it is in danger of forgetting that this is so. Just as within domestic society 'moral panics' about muggers and crime on the streets can mask the fact that most violence is perpetrated by men on women and children within the home, so a focus on the disastrous effects of war can serve to mask the routine oppressions of peace.[4] In each case, those designated by convention as protectors of the innocent and powerless are as likely as not to function in practice as oppressors and exploiters; indeed, the very fact that they are so designated makes their oppression more difficult to resist.[5] The doctrine of sovereignty can act to hide one form of oppression while bringing to the fore and, allegedly, erecting barriers to another.

It is important that this point should not be misunderstood. Domestic violence may be statistically more serious than street crime but this does not mean that street crime is unimportant or that resources should not be devoted to its eradication. The political role of war-centric international theory may be to give credence to an image of the social world that cannot survive critical scrutiny, but this does not mean that war is not a serious problem. The destructiveness of war is incontestable, even if the delights of peace are sometimes overstated. The destructiveness of contemporary warfare is potentially of an order of magnitude such as to reduce to insignificance all other threats to humanity and, even if the phenomenon of war in general were less serious than it is, this feature of modern warfare would demand attention. The point of these preliminary considerations is not to suggest that war is unimportant, but to underline the point that a concern with war to the exclusion of other social problems is not as innocent a priority as it may at first glance seem to be. In certain circumstances the problems of justice may be more important than the problem of peace – a line of thought that will be pursued in the next chapter.

One of the features of the 'war-centricity' of international thought is that contemporary writers on war and international theory have an extensive literary and theoretical inheritance upon which to draw. This inheritance and the debates it generates will be the subject of the next section of this chapter. To anticipate the argument somewhat, one of the features of this work to be examined is the extent to which the established principles of international law on war and violence have proved resistant to contemporary challenges, and it is to these principles that we now turn.

THE JUST WAR AND THE ETHICS OF FORCE

The ethics of international violence is a subject dominated by a single notion, that of the 'just war'; this must be one of the only areas of contemporary moral philosophy where an essentially medieval theoretical construction still has common currency. The idea of just war has two components: *ius ad bellum* (the circumstances under which it is just to resort to war) and *ius in bello* (means it is just to employ in war). In each case the ideas concerned can be applied to violent conflict in general and not simply the legal category of war. The origins of the notion are to be found in attempts by Christian theologians to come to terms with the implications of the dispersed nature of political power in medieval Christendom and, at a less theoretical level, in attempts by the Church as an institution to control the civil authorities by promulgating codes of conduct which restricted the tactics available and defined quite narrowly which such authorities were, in any event, entitled to make war.[6] To these religious considerations should be added, in the case of *ius in bello*, the – albeit somewhat tenuous – impact of the medieval codes of chivalry, which, at least in principle, addressed such matters as the status of combatants and non-combatants, and the means that might properly be employed in war.[7]

This medieval inheritance was accepted in an adapted form by the founders of the Law of Nations – the Spanish theologians Vitoria and Suarez, and the seventeenth- and eighteenth-century writers Grotius, Pufendorf, Vattel and Wolff.[8] In the case of *ius ad bellum* the effect of their adaptations of the medieval doctrine was to lessen its discriminatory impact by a gradual and initially grudging acceptance of the modern doctrine of sovereignty, with the implication that the sovereign state itself can alone judge the justice of its own actions – although the trend towards accepting this position has been reversed in the twentieth century as states have accepted the legal restraints on their war-making powers implied in the Covenant of the League of Nations, the Treaty of Paris of 1928 and the Charter of the United Nations. On the other hand, in the case of *ius in bello* the effect of turning medieval social and religious codes into modern international law has been towards greater restrictiveness. The Geneva Conventions (on the treatment of casualties, prisoners of war and non-combatants) and the Hague Conventions (on the conduct of military operations) supplemented by the Charter of London of 1945, and the subsequent judgements of the International Military Tribunal at Nuremburg, have created, taken together, an impressive body of statutory international law governing these matters.[9]

There is obviously a difference between just war seen as a moral and religious doctrine, on the one hand, and the modern legal rules surrounding the use of force in the international system, on the other; however, in spite of these obvious differences a continuity in terms of principles can be discerned. In any event, the status of international law is such as to make the gap between law and ethics rather narrower in this case than in equivalent domestic circumstances. The modern principles of the just war occupy a grey area between law, ethics and political philosophy, and attempts to make their status less ambiguous seem unfruitful.

What are these principles? In the case of *ius ad bellum* Michael Walzer in his outstanding, if controversial, study, *Just and Unjust Wars*, has provided a useful summary of the current conventional legal wisdom.[10] The modern legal notion of *ius ad bellum* takes the form of a theory of aggression which, in turn, emerges out of an analogy with domestic society and the crimes of robbery and murder. Walzer calls the primary form of this theory of aggression the 'legalist paradigm' which he summarises in six propositions as follows:

1. There exists an international society of independent states.
2. This international society has a law that establishes the rights of its members – above all, the rights of territorial integrity and political sovereignty.
3. Any use of force or imminent threat of force by one state against the political sovereignty or territorial integrity of another constitutes aggression and is a criminal act.
4. Aggression justifies two kinds of violent response: a war of self-defence by the victim and a war of law enforcement by the victim and any other member of international society.

5. Nothing but aggression can justify war.
6. Once the aggressor state has been militarily repulsed it can also be punished.[11]

In setting out this paradigm, Walzer believes that he is simply making explicit the modern conventions that determine the justice of a particular resort to violence. His own version of a defensible paradigm entails a number of revisions – in particular, he would weaken somewhat the case against intervention implied by proposition 2, and he would allow for greater tolerance for preventive war than is implied by propositions 3 and 4.[12] Whether the legalist paradigm, amended or not, is satisfactory will be considered below; for the moment, all that is needful is to recognise that Walzer has indeed correctly summarised the current legal consensus on the *ius ad bellum* doctrine.

In the case of *ius in bello* there is a much greater body of international statute law than in the case of *ius ad bellum*. This law essentially clusters around two questions: 'In the course of war, who may lawfully be killed and by what means?' (this puts the matter rather brutally, but occasionally it is salutary to employ language reflective of the reality under discussion).[13] The first of these questions is traditionally answered in terms of non-combatant immunity, and there is an extensive body of international law which addresses the definition of a non-combatant. In the case of the second question, there is again a body of positive law outlawing certain kinds of weaponry – chemical, biological and so on – but in this case specific restrictions are more difficult to relate to a clear-cut principle, and perhaps for this reason, seem less compelling. Whereas the modern notion of non-combatant immunity relates to the widely held belief that innocence deserves protection, attempts to restrict the means employed in warfare go against the sort of popular beliefs summarised in the saying 'All's fair in love and war'; moreover, they are redolent of such futile attempts to protect a privileged position in warfare as the chivalric ban on cross-bows and later firearms. However, as will be seen below, a good defence of the notion that there should be restraints on the lawful means available to armies can be mounted, and in any event the law in these matters is perfectly clear.

One final point that needs to be examined with respect to the modern conventional understanding of the ethics of force and the notion of just war concerns the matter of individual and state responsibility. In medieval thinking, a war could only be just on one side (or, more likely, on neither side). This is also the contemporary position as a result of legal developments in the twentieth century, and in contradiction to the standard nineteenth-century position that the justice of a war was solely a matter for the sovereign to determine. The Charter of London, which established the law which was to be applied by the International Military Tribunal at Nuremburg, makes it clear that members of governments should be held to be legally responsible for their actions in making war – although the tribunal interpreted this law in a very restrictive way.[14] However, the laws of war (*ius in bello*) apply irrespective of the justice of the war in question, and soldiers on both sides are legally responsible for their conduct; as the judgement at Nuremburg famously declared, obedience to the orders of superiors is no defence in the case of crimes against the laws of war.

In the last three paragraphs an attempt has been made to summarise the current 'authorised version' of the just-war inheritance with an account which is reasonably neutral and descriptive; the rest of this chapter will be devoted to literature that challenges, re-interprets or reinforces this inheritance. Three clusters of questions have been posed with some frequency and will be considered here – two substantive and one meta-ethical. The first set of questions concerns the 'legalist paradigm' and the privileged position it accords to state autonomy; this legal notion has been criticised from a number of perspectives and is, in interesting ways, at variance with the traditional thinking on the just war.

Another set of questions concerns *ius in bello*; here what is particularly at stake is the question of the current force of non-combatant immunity, and other rules, given the involvement of whole populations in warfare, given the prevalence of informal violence in wars of national liberation and given the existence of weapons of mass destruction and strategies for their use which involve assaults on whole populations.

Underlying both these sets of questions is the meta-ethical matter of the status of the notion of a just war and its concomitant codes. Clearly, the original foundation for the notion of a just war was theological; restraints on war were the product of reason underwritten by God. For some modern writers this remains an acceptable basis; others have argued that a new foundation must be found. Debates between consequentialists and deontologists have been fierce – the laws of war have been one of the battlefields upon which these ethical positions have exchanged fire, important as much for their exemplary value as for their intrinsic significance. These meta-ethical issues will be treated here largely in instrumental terms, raised only when necessary to clarify a particular position, but it needs to be kept in mind that major issues of moral philosophy are at stake in some of these discussions.

FOR AND AGAINST THE LEGALIST PARADIGM

Walzer's 'legalist paradigm' accurately summarises the current legal position on the nature of aggression, and this legal position is reflected in the political and diplomatic stances of states evinced in public arenas such as the United Nations. However, it remains to be demonstrated that this set of legal norms is morally defensible. Walzer thinks it is, largely because he places a high moral value on the right of states to autonomy, but critics of Walzer, such as Charles Beitz, Gerald Doppelt and David Luban, have argued that such value is wrongly assigned – that Walzer has been seduced by, in Luban's evocative phrase, the 'romance of the nation–state', failing thereby to see that state autonomy is the source of much of the world's suffering rather than a positive feature of contemporary world politics.[15] As was demonstrated in chapter 5 above, the moral standing of states is the most basic and controversial of issues in normative international relations theory, and the debate generated by *Just and Unjust Wars* is one of the best introductions to this controversy available in the literature – the American debate, that is; with the honourable exception of Michael Donelan's review of Walzer, the British international relations establishment's reaction to *Just and Unjust Wars* was patronising in the extreme, the gist of the critique being that Walzer's philosophical grasp is shallow and his notion of morality platitudinous.[16] This is nonsense: whether one approves of his position or not, in *Just and Unjust Wars* Walzer has produced the best book on the subject currently available.

Walzer's approach is legalist, secular and communitarian – although he rejects the latter term as self-description, in the context of this book it is unavoidable.[17] To get a fix on the subject of just war it may be helpful to outline a view of the subject from another direction altogether, namely the perspective of current Christian theology, drawing on the Catholic tradition, whose most notable forefather was Aquinas.[18] In part, this perspective coincides with Walzer's legalist paradigm. A just war may be declared only by the proper authorities and in a just cause – self-defence and the restoration of peace and justice being the paradigms of such a just cause. It is, of course, debatable whether all states have this right of self-defence, and the Christian tradition is perhaps slightly less favourable to the claims of the powers that be than is the case with the legalist paradigm, but this is a matter of degree. Other principles, however, are less easily assimilable to the legalist position.

Right intention is an important part of Christian thinking on just war: the only motive that justifies war is the righting of a wrong.[19]

Right intention is made manifest by a concern for other, connected, principles. War must be a last resort when all other means have failed; it may only be entered into if there is a reasonable expectation of success, and action taken must be proportional to the offence. While it might be argued that these requirements are actually implicit in the legalist paradigm, they are central to Christian thinking of just war. The key point is that, from the legalist angle, just-war thinking revolves around the rights and duties of states, whereas from the Christian viewpoint it is the behaviour of individual human beings that is crucial; inevitably, intentionality and its ramifications play different roles in the two schemes.

It should be noted – because it is often overlooked – that different kinds of reasoning, and different sorts of knowledge, are melded together in the Christian approach to just war. Whether a cause is 'just' may be a matter upon which the views of a moral philosopher or theologian may carry particular weight, but whether all opportunities for the peaceful settlement of a dispute are exhausted is a matter for diplomats and other secular specialists rather than the theologians. Whether an action is proportional to an offence is a matter for common sense, but whether in any particular circumstances there is a reasonable chance that military action will be successful is a matter upon which the views of the military will, and should, carry the most weight.

Putting the matter differently, Christian just-war thinking is con-sequentialist as well as deontological.[20] Indeed, in some respects, it is rather more consequentialist than the legalist paradigm – at least as the latter is relayed in Walzer's summary statements; in diplomatic practice consequences always loom large. This feature of the tradition is often disregarded, with at times comical, at times unedifying, results – a recent example being the speculations of learned doctors of theology and senior churchmen on the likelihood of Saddam Hussein's Iraq being forced to quit Kuwait as a result of economic sanctions or other non-military pressures. This, of course, is a subject upon which the views of moral philosophers, churchmen and theo-logians are of no greater significance than those of the man or woman in the street, and of considerably less significance than those of regional specialists, diplomats and military men. Any philosopher or theologian who wishes to employ the just-war tradition is obliged at some stage of the argument, after the principles of the matter have been expounded, to step down in favour of different kinds of expertise – an abdication some find uncongenial.

The Christian emphasis on intentionality necessarily brings in issues such as the prospects of success in a war, and this opens up the possibility of linking the justice of a war to the political wisdom of a decision to wage it – even if the theologians and philosophers have little of interest to say on the latter. In contrast Walzer's approach is the view that the political wisdom of war is a separate matter from its justice. The justice of a war is determined by reference to the legalist paradigm (perhaps suitably amended) but its wisdom can only be determined by reference to wider issues including the dangers involved.[21] Thus it might well be the case that in certain circumstances it would be wise not to fight a just war if by so doing intolerable dangers would be faced. Christian thinking might reach the same conclusion but – perhaps confusingly – factors the consequentialist weighing of the political wisdom of a war into the process of determining its justice.

However, the fact that both of these approaches incorporate consequentialist reasoning at some stage places them jointly in opposition to some of the cosmopolitan critics of Walzer mentioned above. These critics concentrate on Walzer's willingness to license wars of national self-defence, and propose alternative criteria which focus on less statist accounts of a just peace, emphasising, for example, the promotion of human rights and justice rather than simply national survival. But, as Walzer rightly replies, the effect of such principles would be to license far more wars than could be justified under the terms of the legalist paradigm. Although his critics nod in the direction of proportionality, the effect of the criteria they propose is to undermine limits rather than strengthen them.

Just-war arguments often, it seems, go in directions that are unpredictable, to the point of turning against the intentions of those who use them. The reason for this seems clear: just-war thinking involves both the licensing and the limiting of warfare, while users of the theory more commonly are concerned simply with limitations. Just-war theory is not for pacifists. The first premise of just-war thinking is that there are circumstances in which war might be morally justifiable – indeed morally required. At least some of those who purport to think in just-war terms seem unwilling to accept that this could be so in practice, rather in the manner of the (apocryphal?) conscientious objector who argued that while he accepted his church's teaching that there could be a just war, he did not believe that any actual war had ever been just. Such a position is logically unassailable but lacks common sense. Preferable would be the out-and-out pacifism of a Tolstoy or a Gandhi (or a Jesus of Nazareth?), which is at least consistent in its refusal to make the sort of discriminations upon which the theory of the just war is necessarily based.

Whether in its Walzerian legalist form, or in the shape of Christian ethics, just-war thinking poses a great many problems, but it has none the less survived over the centuries, at least in part because the idea of distinguishing just from unjust causes of war does seem to be in line with general moral intuitions. Few are actually willing to put aside altogether the possibility of discriminating in this way, however difficult in practice it may be to specify the relevant criteria. Similar thinking underlies the survival of *ius in bello* - restrictions on the means that may justly be used in warfare - and similar problems are associated with this idea. To these we now turn.

THE WAR CONVENTION

War and massacre

Walzer - an indefatigable coiner of useful phrases - uses the term 'the war convention' to refer to the set of laws, principles, norms and codes of conduct that have emerged around the issue of just means in warfare.[22] The 'war convention' is the modern code governing *ius in bello*. In one respect at least, the notion of a war convention is less controversial than the legalist paradigm: whereas the latter involves the difficult task of determining guilt and innocence on the part of states on the basis of general principles that are always difficult to apply, the war convention applies to all participants in a war – irrespective of the issue of just cause – and its content is embodied, albeit imperfectly, in international treaties and conventions.

Moreover, whereas a substantial body of opinion rejects the notion of a just war - either on the grounds that no war is just, or on the basis that justice is irrelevant in the circumstances of international relations - very few would reject the notion that there should be some kind of war convention. The controversies here are usually about the content of this convention rather than its existence. The strongest case against the idea of a war convention is based on an elaboration of General Sherman's doctrine that 'war is cruelty and you cannot refine it.' Sherman's March to the Sea through Georgia was designed to inflict maximum damage on the Confederacy and thereby hasten the end of the war, and he rejected criticism of his tactics on straightforward consequentialist grounds - his way created less suffering overall.[23] Sir Arthur Harris of Bomber Command appears to have held the same view in the Second World War in defence of the area bombing of German cities.[24] However, neither Sherman nor Harris actually seem to have been fully consistent in their opposition to the idea of rules. Both directed the commission of acts which breached the rules of war as currently understood, but neither abandoned all notion of rules, in spite of their rhetorics. Sherman burnt and destroyed but he did not authorise the murder of civilians; Harris did authorise the murder of civilians, but still saw some part of the war convention as operative, believing, for example, that his airmen should be accorded prisoner-of-war status.

To find genuine examples of a refusal to accept any kind of war convention it is necessary to move away from war that takes place between members of the international system to 'extra-systemic' wars – such as the wars of conquest fought by the conquistadors in Latin America, or, with less system, by other imperial aggressors in Africa, Asia and (especially) Australia. This kind of war of extermination occurs when the enemy is the Other – a strange, barely comprehensible being not inhabiting the same moral universe, not governed by the same rules as the nations of 'civilisation'.[25] This effect can also be a matter of place. Again, in the seventeenth century the rules governing conflicts between European nations were widely considered not to apply 'beyond the line', in the waters and on the coastlines of the newly 'discovered' territories; indeed, fighting could take place in these outlands even when the relevant nations were, in principle, at peace at home in Europe. Lest it should be thought that rejection of the idea of a war convention is an exclusively European reaction to contact with outsiders, the examples of the careers of Genghis Khan or Timur would dispel this illusion; something much more basic than a specifically European cast of mind is in operation here, and the prevalence in recent history of European crimes is simply a function of the power differential in favour of Europeans in the modern system.

As well as committing atrocities, Europeans have eloquently condemned them; the conquistadors were matched by defenders of the Indians such as Las Casas – although, as Todorov demonstrates, such humanitarianism only rarely rose to the level of defending Otherness in its own terms – the Indians were to be protected not as actual aliens but as potential Christians.[26] However, even given this limitation the struggle for justice in warfare has been as much a feature of European thought on extra-systemic war as violation of the demands of justice has been part of its practice. Both features have been in evidence in recent debates on the war convention. One body of recent work on the war convention has been generated by the new technologies which have produced strategic bombing and nuclear deterrence – this will be discussed in the next section of this chapter – but a great deal of recent work has emerged out of situations which parallel, or mirror in reverse, the circumstances of the sixteenth century: namely, the vicious wars of decolonisation (or, national liberation) fought by Europeans and their allies against Third World nationalists.

There have been many such wars in the years since 1945, of varying degrees of savagery, but the war that has created the greatest literature is the Vietnam War and, in particular (since so much of this literature has been American), that part of the Vietnam War between, say, 1963 and 1973, when the United States was directly involved. What was distinctive about Vietnam was partly a matter of scale – this was, indeed, the most destructive of colonial wars – but also the fact that the scholars who became engaged for or (mostly) against American involvement brought to the subject of the war convention a degree of freshness that reflected the relatively low involvement of the United States in the colonial wars of the last few centuries – or at least the perceived low involvement in colonialism: overcoming America's collective amnesia on the subject of the massacres of the Indian Wars was one of the by-products of Vietnam.[27] This freshness might be seen as the producer of naïvety, but it did have the effect of leading a number of American philosophers to attempt to think the war convention through from first principles, and the debates this generated are most instructive. Two important works, taken as the best examples of their kind – Thomas Nagel's much anthologised and discussed article of 1972, 'War and massacre', and the later, 'postwar', survey work already referred to of Michael Walzer, *Just and Unjust Wars*, first published in 1977 – will be considered here.[28]

In 'War and massacre', Nagel sets up his argument in such a way as to accept the first premise of the war convention, namely that while by its very nature war involves the commission of acts of brutality in support of strategic goals, some of these acts are morally acceptable and others not. Nagel's concern is not so much to decide what acts fall into which category, but to explore the moral basis of the distinction in question. He sees two ways through which such a distinction can be reached, calling these disparate categories of moral reasoning *utilitarian* and *absolutist*. The distinction here he summarises as follows: 'Utilitarianism gives primacy to a concern with what will *happen*. Absolutism gives primacy to a concern with what one is *doing*' (p. 54). Clearly, this is a renaming of the consequentialist and deontological positions identified in chapter 4 of this book. Nagel sees utilitarianism as lying behind much thinking about the war convention. The idea that rules should reflect the desire to maximise the good, and that in a conflict of evils the lesser should be chosen seems to reflect a common moral intuition; some such reasoning seems to lie behind the reciprocal acceptance of such codes as the Geneva and Hague Conventions. Nagel does not wish to reject utilitarian reasoning entirely, but he is concerned that utilitarian intuitions be balanced by the – he argues – equally common view that some actions are unconditionally wrong.

These absolutist intuitions 'are often the only barrier before the abyss of utilitarian apologetics for large-scale murder' (p. 56).

There are two main components of the war convention, concerning those to whom violence may or may not be directed, and the form of violence that, in any event, is allowable. Nagel believes these components can be combined in one principle:

> that hostile treatment of any person must be justified in terms of something *about that person* which makes the treatment appropriate. [Thus extremely] hostile behaviour towards another is compatible with treating him as a person – even perhaps as an end in himself. (p. 64).

This principle allows us to see the basis for non-combatant immunity. A common critique of the latter makes the point that many non-combatants may have greater moral responsibility for evil than many combatants – contrast, for example, a civilian Nazi party member with a conscripted, politically apathetic, German soldier. However, Nagel points out that the feature of the non-combatant that precludes the offering of violence is not moral innocence but practical harmlessness. What should matter to the soldier is not the moral guilt of an enemy – a matter for conscience or court – but whether or not the enemy poses a threat (p. 70).

Equally, the 'appropriateness' criterion applies to those rules which distinguish between types of weapon. Certain kinds of weapon – poison gas, napalm, dum-dum bullets – inflict pain and suffering of such a nature as to preclude treating the combatant as a human being, in a way that is not necessarily the case with other methods of killing (p. 72). This may seem to be a difficult argument in so far as it relies on the notion that one may kill without depriving of self-respect, but in support of Nagel the testimony of soldiers seems to bear out the distinction.[29]

To reiterate, the absolutist position outlined by Nagel is about what one should do, whereas a utilitarian position focusses on what should happen. While supporting the former stance, Nagel recognises that there are moral dilemmas here which remain:

> when an absolutist knows or believes that the utilitarian cost of refusing to adopt a prohibited course will be very high, he may hold to his refusal to adopt it, but he will find it difficult to feel that a moral dilemma has been satisfactorily resolved. (p. 73)

He is prepared to admit that in certain circumstances we exist in a 'moral blind alley', with no satisfactory answer. In this respect he parts company from Anscombe, whose anti-consequentialism in these matters is otherwise a major source for him and who takes the absolutist position without acknowledging the dilemma to which this might lead.[30] Possibly, this parting of the ways reflects Nagel's lack of Anscombe's religious convictions; a case can be made for the view that a total rejection of consequences can only be defended by a belief in some kind of divine justice.

Nagel's central principle – that combatants should be treated as persons and respected as human beings – is in many respects Kantian, and the sort of distinctions he is reaching for can be found in another form in Kant's Preliminary Articles of Perpetual Peace (see, especially, Article 6, which deals with those methods in war which make mutual confidence impossible during a future time of peace). However, in this respect anticipating Anscombe rather than Nagel, Kant does not believe that moral duties could be in conflict with one another: thus Nagel's moral dilemma could not arise for him.

It is also noteworthy that although Nagel is uneasy at the notion of endorsing a conventional account of the laws of war, in practice his ideas are compatible with the traditional position. Brandt and Hare, two of Nagel's utilitarian critics, point out that if the US army in Vietnam had abided by the rules incorporated in its own Army Field Manual – the American equivalent of the British 'Queen's Regulations' – it would not have committed any acts prohibited by Nagel's absolutism.[31] Their argument is that there is practical convergence between the different justifications for the war convention, and that 'rule-utilitarians' have no difficulty acknowledging some absolute prohibitions, such as those incorporated in the Army Manual. The point is that, from their perspective, such prohibitions are absolute because it is in the general interest that they should be; no better defence of absolutism exists or could exist. Although Nagel would not accept this last point, his acceptance that, in the last resort, there may be an insoluble moral dilemma when undesirable consequences follow from the maintenance of absolutist principles does put him in the position of accepting at least part of the consequentialism argument. It also leaves his analysis indeterminate, unable to decide between two sets of intuitions.

Although referring to Nagel at one point only in a long text, Michael Walzer's *Just and Unjust Wars* can be seen as an attempt to hang on to both sets of intuitions identified by Nagel, while removing at least some of the indeterminacy. *Just and Unjust Wars* is subtitled *A moral argument with historical illustrations*, and the wealth of the latter is one of the major attractions of this wide-ranging study.[32] One of the features of Nagel's work is the limited range of historical examples drawn on and the limited knowledge of past thought on the war convention displayed. By contrast, Walzer is aware of the record and the tradition. He is also more willing to accept that there may actually be just wars that it is important to win and that, as he puts it, 'fighting well' may thus be an imperative (p. 127); although Nagel rejects absolute pacifism and thus acknowledges the possibility of a just war, the tenor of his argument is such as to lead one to suspect that this acceptance is more a matter of theory than of practice. Nagel can see the possibility of a clash between absolutism and utilitarianism; Walzer sees this clash as a *reality*, something that has happened in the past and may again in the future. His communitarian sympathies – seen here and in the later *Spheres of Justice* – lead him to be prepared to give rather more leeway to the state than either Nagel or, indeed, the international legal tradition would countenance, which is particularly noticeable in his treatment of preventive war and his justification of the Israeli first-strike in the Six Days War of 1967.[33]

One of the most interesting and controversial sections of *Just and Unjust Wars* is part IV, 'Dilemmas of war', and, in particular, chapter 16, entitled 'Supreme emergency' (pp. 251ff.). In this section and chapter he explores the dilemma identified by Nagel. Suppose, he suggests plausibly, we see nazism as an ultimate threat to

> everything decent in our lives, an ideology and a practice of domination so murderous, so degrading even to those who might survive, that the consequences of its final victory were literally beyond calculation, immeasurably awful. We see it [as] evil objectified in the world. (p. 253)

Supposing this supreme evil threatened to enslave or exterminate a nation. Would not this nation be entitled to breach the rules of war if this were the only way to guarantee its survival?

> For the survival and freedom of political communities – whose members share a way of life, developed by their ancestors to be passed on to their children – are the highest values of international society. Nazism challenged these values on a grand scale, but challenges more narrowly conceived, *if they are of the same kind*, have similar moral consequences. They bring us under the rule of necessity (and necessity knows no rules). (p. 254)

The last, parenthetical, point seems not actually to be what Walzer is arguing, unless he wants to argue that utilitarianism is not a moral theory and thus involves no 'rules'. His actual point is that in situations of extreme emergency the state would be justified in overriding limitations which it normally would be obliged to support

– and he examines the strategic bombing campaign of the RAF in the Second World War in this light, along with such issues as nuclear deterrence. His conclusion in the case of strategic bombing in the Second World War is not supportive of its morality because the supreme emergency which might have provided its justification had passed before the campaign reached its height (p. 262); however, the important point of principle is that in some circumstances Walzer believes it would be possible to justify the commission of acts directed against the innocent, if absolutely necessary for victory.

There are a number of empirical difficulties with Walzer's argument: determining when a 'supreme emergency' exists will never be easy, and determining whether particular means are actually necessary to bring about the defeat of evil will be even more difficult. Walzer's communitarianism – his willingness to see threats to the survival and freedom not just of peoples but of political communities – is highly controversial. However, his espousal and defence of a kind of 'last-ditch' consequentialism is in many respects rather more satisfactory than either the fundamentalism of the extreme deontologist, or the indeterminacy of a less extreme absolutist such as Nagel. Whether Walzer's position should be described as a 'moral' position is another matter, as his own point that necessity knows no rules would suggest. Nardin, in *Law, Morality and the Relations of States*, is highly critical of Walzer's position, but his own deontological approach is combined with the view that in certain circumstances, the morally correct action may not, all things considered, be the right thing to do.[34] At times, Walzer seems to be saying much the same thing, and it may be the case that this is a situation where apparently diverse positions converge.

It would be a mistake to suggest that recent literature on the war convention has introduced a great many new ideas or principles to the traditional account of *ius in bello*. As in the case of *ius ad bellum*, we are dealing here with a set of problems which have a very long pedigree, and the best we can hope for from modern authors is not so much substantive innovation as a recasting of old arguments in new clothes – in itself, a valuable exercise. However, there is one area where there might be reason to expect innovation because of the nature of the issue: the impact on the war convention of weapons of mass destruction and, in particular, nuclear weapons. This will now be addressed.

Nuclear weapons

The experience of the Second World War initially seemed to give credence to the view that the development of nuclear weapons posed no new issues of principles. So-called 'conventional' strategic bombing of cities such as Hamburg, Cologne, Berlin, Dresden and Tokyo inflicted more casualties than the nuclear bombing of Hiroshima and Nagasaki, and although nuclear weapons could deliver death more quickly and with less effort than a thousand-bomber raid, this appeared to be a change in degree rather than kind. However, such attitudes soon changed. At the strategic level it was already the case by the late 1940s that writers such as Brodie and Blackett were recognising that the existence of nuclear weapons changed forever the nature of the military relations between those who possessed them, with the role of military forces coming to be war prevention rather than war fighting, an insight summarised with customary skill by Churchill with his observation that peace might be the product of a 'balance of terror'.[35] Although the possibility of a war-fighting strategy was present for much of the 1950s, and was briefly revived in the early 1980s, for most of the postwar period the political morality of the nuclear issue has focussed on the theory of deterrence, which purports to show how, by a judicious use of threats, nuclear war can be avoided.

The shift to deterrence was a response to a growing awareness of the potential for destruction possessed by nuclear weapons, a potential already apparent in the era of the atom bomb. The development of hydrogen bombs, which, because they involved fusion rather than fission, were, in theory, virtually unlimited in destructive power, combined with the policy of stock-piling adopted by both super-powers, has, once more, changed the potential nature of the problem. What is at stake now is no longer the survival of a particular nation, or even a civilisation, but, to adopt the title of a quasi-popular study of the early 1980s, *The Fate of the Earth*.[36]

Because of the destructiveness of nuclear weapons, virtually no-one would argue that they could be justly employed in actual warfare, save under circumstances of great implausibility.[37] This fact distinguishes the nuclear issue from other matters concerning the war convention. Whereas usually controversy takes the form of consideration of the circumstances under which the rules of war might be set aside on the grounds of supreme emergency, in the case of nuclear weapons the debate is very different. It is about the circumstances under which it is proper to threaten to do something that it would be wrong actually to do, bearing in mind that for a threat to be credible preparations have to be made to carry it out. Can the behaviour of those who make these threats, and therefore need to carry out these preparations, be justified?

Nuclear weapons do, therefore, raise issues rather different from those which normally occur in discussions of the war convention.

However, the lines or argument deployed in the debate on these issues are much as might be expected from the debate on conventional arms. Thus, the contrast between deontological and consequentialist reasoning is, predictably, important, as is the controversy over the value to be attached to the independence of political communities. Given the degree of continuity, the strategy adopted here for examining the debate over nuclear deterrence will be, as before, to focus on a relatively small number of key contributions which, taken together, represent the best of modern thought on the subject.

None of these contributions comes from professional strategists, who, taken as a class, seem wedded to an oversimple consequentialist defence of nuclear weapons along the lines that the supreme evil of our days would be nuclear war, and that the best way to prevent such a war is to preserve the balance of terror that has existed since the 1950s. Apart from the tendentiousness of the empirical base of this defence – how can we know that superpower peace is a product of deterrence? – such an argument assumes rather too readily that, in the words of the editors of a special issue of *Ethics* devoted to the subject, 'we may do – or threaten – evil that good may come'. Such a position may be defensible as the end point of an argument, but, as the editors of *Ethics* remark, many strategists seem unaware that it is in any way controversial.[38]

An exact mirror image of the strategists' view of the world is to be found in some of the more extreme formulations of the Peace Movement, whose publicists distort the strategists' position by refusing to acknowledge that the latter do have peace as a goal.[39] A more intellectually interesting reversal of the moral world of the strategist is to be found in Finnis, Boyle and Grisez's *Nuclear Deterrence, Morality and Realism*.[40] Unlike most critics of deterrence theory, these authors accept that the consequence of unilateral nuclear disarmament might well be conventional war and the Soviet domination of the West – this was, of course, written before the break-up of the Soviet empire in eastern Europe and of the Soviet Union itself – but they reject the notion that moral choice could be based on consequentialist reasoning. Instead, working from what they term – following Alan Donagan – the precepts of the 'common morality' of Judaeo-Christian civilisation and the notion of human goods, they derive an absolute ban on the intentional killing of innocents.[41] Any strategy which involves such an intention, as deterrence strategies must, is wrong and should be abandoned, whatever the consequences.

The problem with this kind of reasoning – which is, of course, elaborated at great length in a book which should be read by anyone interested in the subject – is that it appears to imply using Nagel's terms, that what one is *doing* is far more important than what *happens*; when what happens might be the destruction of a way of life or the destruction of the world, this seems difficult to accept. Such a position may make sense within a religious framework, where death and suffering are not the end of the story, but it is difficult to see why secularists should accept that the problem of nuclear war should be set up in this way – a general point acknowledged by Alan Donagan in response to his critics.[42] The Christian – indeed, specifically Roman Catholic natural law – background of the authors of *Nuclear Deterrence, Morality and Realism* seems an essential feature of the work, and thus limits its general appeal.

This criticism should not be taken to suggest that consequentialist/utilitarian thinking on the subject of nuclear war is necessarily going to provide the best framework for analysis:

> [Utilitarians] weigh gains and losses that result from specific actions and then choose that action or policy that can be expected to produce the greatest net good. They do not judge kinds of action to be inherently bad independently of such a weighting. But it is a peculiarity of nuclear deterrence that the enormity of what it threatens forces even utilitarians to worry about this question to some extent because it challenges them to see how far they are willing to push their utilitarian principles.[43]

In this, of all issues, an *exclusive* concern either with what one is *doing* or with what will *happen* seems inappropriate.

None the less, the utilitarian method of setting up the problem does seem to have advantages. Essentially, this method consists of an examination and evaluation of the risks associated with particular courses of action. Thus, in comparing the continuation of a strategy of nuclear deterrence with the adoption of a strategy of nuclear disarmament, a common approach is to associate the former with a small risk of a great disaster (i.e. that full-scale nuclear war will break out) and the latter with a larger risk of a smaller disaster (i.e. a one-sided nuclear strike, or loss of independence on the part of the disarmer).[44] Analysis is then in part a matter of assigning probabilities (just how likely is it that in the absence of Western nuclear weapons the Soviet Union would attempt to assert dominance?) and in part a matter of the importance to be attached to particular values (how important is it that the independence of political communities be preserved?).

Consequentialists such as Gauthier and Kavka carry out these calculations and reach the conclusion that deterrence is a justifiable strategy, while from similar methodological positions writers such as Hardin and Lackey come to the opposite conclusion;[45] each of these writers employs different arguments but in the last resort their positions rely on assignments of probabilities that can only be described as the product of guesswork of varying degrees of plausibility. One attempt to break out of this impasse deserves particular note: Robert Goodin's 'Disarmament as a moral certainty'.[46] Goodin argues that even if the notion of probability could be attached to any situation where reflective human agents rather than random processes are concerned, a point he doubts, it is certainly of little use in this case where there is neither reliable statistical evidence nor well-validated scientific theories upon which to rely. He argues that 'the most that can be claimed for deterrence is that it will probably work to prevent war'.[47] On the other hand, the outbreak of all-out nuclear war could result in the extinction of human life, an infinite and unqualifiable bad. His basic point is that it is not rational to allow even a very small chance of a disaster that would be infinitely bad – and we have no way of knowing if the chance is indeed very small. His conclusion is that the risk must be removed. Obviously, mutual disarmament would remove this risk, but if this strategy is not available it would be right for one superpower to disarm unilaterally – assuming that the other superpower is minimally rational, this would remove the possibility of an all-out nuclear war, although not of nuclear exchanges at some level below that of total disaster. However, Goodin, optimistically, thinks this latter an unlikely outcome.

This way of setting up the problem seems compelling, but two provisos seem to be worth making. First, it would seem that a similar effect of making all-out war in practice impossible could be achieved by massive force reductions which, none the less, at the end of the day, would leave a small, well-protected arsenal in place. Goodin makes the point that low levels of third-party nuclear weapons do not affect the logic of his argument, and it is difficult to see why a low-level superpower force should. Such a force would be politically more acceptable than total disarmament, and this leads to the second point to be made: namely, that the political aspects of a strategy being adopted cannot be factored out of a utilitarian argument in the way that Goodin seems to suppose. He criticises Hardin for allowing political impossibility to rule out a strategy that he (Hardin) believes to be required for moral reasons, but from a utilitarian perspective a sub-optimal strategy that is politically viable and superior to the status quo ought, surely, to be judged to be superior to a strategy that is best, but unobtainable. Of course, Goodin can justly respond that what is politically viable at any one time is a matter for debate, and subject to political action by concerned citizens, at least in pluralist political systems.

A more general point follows from these considerations. A great deal of the debate on nuclear weapons seems to assume that the effective choice is between the status quo or unilateral nuclear disarmament. Many proposals do exist for changing force structures and reducing force levels, but these proposals largely come from the community of strategists rather than from those moral and political philosophers who have addressed the issue. Possibly, the relatively low level of awareness of moral issues on the part of the strategists – adversely commented on above – may in this instance be to their advantage. One final point should be made about these debates. The course of events in eastern Europe in 1989, and the changes taking place in the former Soviet Union may be producing a situation where the deterrence debate has been overtaken by events. The decision of the US government to end its thirty-year long practice of keeping a continuous airborne strategic control post on patrol can serve as a symbol of the changing environment; at a more practical level, the obvious reluctance of the US Congress to spend money on a new generation of nuclear weapons – and similar reluctance in the former Soviet Union – may, in the medium run, lead to the withering away of nuclear arsenals, reinforcing the effect of any cuts mandated by arms-control agreements made possible in the new climate. It may be, in short, that this is an issue that is resolving itself in a satisfactory manner.

CONCLUSION

Even if a not excessively optimistic perspective on the future can envisage the effective disappearance of nuclear weapons and the particular problems associated with their terrifying effects, no such optimism with respect to conventional war is possible – at least outside of the 'zone of peace' that seems to be coming into existence in Europe. Wars are being fought in the rest of the world and, moreover, with great barbarity. Recent years have seen, for example, a return to the use of chemical weapons, banned since the 1920s, a ban that, largely, survived the Second World War. The mounting volume of international law that rules out the resort to war seems singularly ineffective, save in ensuring that those wars that do take place are not so termed. Thus the 'official' name of the Falklands War in British government pronouncements is the South Atlantic Conflict, the legal difficulties involved in actually declaring and fighting a *war* being beyond the wit of man to resolve.

All this would seem to indicate that the old notion of *ius ad bellum* and *ius in bello* will continue to be required if some kind of moral order is to be achieved in this area. The last decades have seen frequent attempts to amend, reform, abolish or justify the legalist paradigm and the war convention; a legitimate question would be to ask whether, in fact, much progress has been made in this area, whether the moderns have succeeded in displacing the centuries-long legal tradition of discourse on these matters. The answer has to be that in matters of substance they have not. For the most part the value of modern work on the ethics of force has been to translate into the terms of current philospical discourse the traditional distinctions which theologians and lawyers developed over the centuries. This is a valuable exercise, in so far as the old terminology was available only to a very few, but it does not lead to any major conceptual breakthrough. This is in contrast to the recent literature on international distributive justice, to which the next chapter is devoted.

NOTES

1. On this see ch. 3, above.
2. The best short account of this doctrine is F.H. Hinsley, *Sovereignty* (Watts, London, 1966). For some critical studies of the notion see R.B.J. Walker and S.H. Mendlovitz (eds) *Contending Sovereignties: Redefining political community* (Lynn Reimer, Boulder, Colo., 1990).
3. This argument is well expressed in B. Warren, *Imperialism: Pioneer of capitalism* (Verso, London, 1980).
4. For 'moral panics' and related phenomena see S. Hall *et al.*, *Policing the Crisis* (Macmillan, London, 1978) and I. Taylor *et al.*, (eds) *Critical Criminology* (Routledge and Kegan Paul, London, 1975).
5. The subject of terrorism is not addressed in this chapter, but similar points could be made about the way in which this term has been employed so as to mask state terror; see on this R. Falk, *Revolutionaries and Functionaries: The dual face of terrorism* (Dutton, New York, 1988).
6. Two volumes by J. Turner Johnson *Ideology, Reason and the Limitation of War: Religious and secular concepts 1200-1740* (Princeton University Press, Princeton, N.J., 1975), and *Just War Tradition and the Restraint of War* (Princeton University Press, Princeton, N.J., 1981) are seminal on this subject. For a modern statement, P. Ramsey, *The Just War* (Charles Scribner's Sons, New York, 1968), and for an overview text looking at the tradition and modern law, S.D. Bailey, *Prohibitions and Restraints in War* (Oxford University Press/RIIA, Oxford, 1972).
7. A point stressed in Johnson, *Ideology*.
8. On this see texts by Gentili, Grotius and Vattel collected in M.G. Forsyth *et al.* (eds) *The Theory of International Relations* (Allen and Unwin, London, 1970), and A. Linklater, *Men and Citizens in the Theory of International Relations* (Macmillan, London, 1982).

9. See Bailey, *op. cit.*, chs 3 and 4.
10. *Just and Unjust Wars: A moral argument with historical illustrations* (Penguin, Harmondsworth, 1977).
11. pp. 61–3.
12. See Walzer, *op. cit.*, part 2 *passim*.
13. See Bailey, *op. cit.*, for an outline of the current law.
14. See S. Levinson, 'Responsibilities for crimes of war', and R. Wasserstrom, 'The relevance of Nuremburg' both in M. Cohen *et at.* (eds) *War and Moral Responsibility* (Princeton University Press, Princeton, N.J., 1974).
15. C.R. Beitz, 'Bounded morality: justice and the state in world politics', *International Organisation*, vol. 33, no. 3 (1979); G. Doppelt, 'Walzer's theory of morality in international relations', *Philosophy and Public Affairs*, vol. 8, no. 1 (1979); D. Luban, 'Just War and human rights' and 'The romance of the nation–state', *Philosophy and Public Affairs*, vol. 9, nos 2 and 4 respectively (1980). The two essays by Luban, along with extracts from *Just and Unjust Wars* and a general reply from Walzer, 'The moral standing of states: a reply to four critics', *Philosphy and Public Affairs*, vol. 9, no. 3 (1980), are reprinted in C.R. Beitz *et al.* (eds) *International Ethics* (Princeton University Press, Princeton, N.J., 1985).
16. For two reviews from senior figures which, at best, damn with faint praise, see H. Bull, 'Recapturing the just war for political theory', *World Politics*, vol. 31, no. 4 (1979), and W.B. Gallie, 'Wanted: a philosophy of international relations', *Political Studies*, vol. 27, no. 3 (1979). M. Donelan, 'Reason in war', *Review of International Studies*, vol. 8, no. 1 (1982), examines both Walzer and his critics: while, rightly, critical of some aspects of *Just and Unjust Wars*, he does give this remarkable book its due, while rightly castigating some of its critics.
17. Walzer's rejection of the description of himself as a communitarian is explicit in 'The communitarian critique of liberalism', *Political Theory*, vol. 8, no. 1 (1990). Perhaps the aim of this denial is to stress that there is less of a gap between liberalism and communitarianism than is sometimes believed to be the case – a point made also by the anti-communitarian W. Kymlicka in *Liberalism, Community and Culture* (Clarendon, Oxford, 1989); however, Kymlicka certainly takes Walzer to be arguing a communitarian position.
18. What follows is a composite picture of just-war thinking, drawing on the works referred to in note 6 above, along with studies such as B. Paskins and M. Dockrill, *The Ethics of War* (Duckworth, London, 1979); G. Best, *Humanity in Warfare* (Weidenfeld and Nicholson, London, 1980); and J. Finnis, J. Boyle and G. Grisez, *Nuclear Deterrence, Morality and Realism* (Clarendon, Oxford, 1987). Also instructive has been the recent public debate in Britain on the morality of the Gulf Crisis and War of 1990/1. For short statements of the opposing cases, R. Harries (Bishop of Oxford), 'The path to a just war', *The Independent*, 31 October 1990, and R. Williams (Professor of Divinity at Oxford), 'Onward Christian Soldiers?', *The Guardian* 1 November 1990, will serve. The theology is helpfully

summarised by the religious correspondent of *The Times* in 'Going by the Aquinas book', *The Times*, 3 November 1990. When the shooting war began, Bishop Harries gave the best account of why this was a war 'morally worth fighting' in 'A just war not a crusade', *The Observer*, 20 January 1991.

19. It should be said that although this and the following principle historically emerge from the Christian tradition, they do not rely on revelation. The Catholic natural lawyers would stress that their conclusions are reachable simply by the exercise of reason.

20. See ch. 4 for definitions of these terms.

21. Michael Walzer discusses the justice and wisdom of the Gulf War in these terms in 'Perplexed', *The New Republic*, 28 January 1991.

22. *Just and Unjust Wars*, p. 44.

23. The case is discussed in Walzer, *ibid.*, pp. 29ff.

24. On Harris and the campaign against German cities see M. Hastings, *Bomber Command* (Pan, London, 1981), and J. Terraine, *The Right of the Line* (Hodder, London, 1985).

25. T. Todorov, *The Conquest of America* (Harper Torchbooks, New York, 1984), is excellent on this topic.

26. *ibid.*, p. 90 Todorov makes the point that Las Casas came close to recognising that the indians have a valid perspective (p. 190).

27. See, for example, D. Brown, *Bury My Heart at Wounded Knee* (Barrie and Jenkins, London, 1970).

28. 'War and massacre' was first published in *Philosophy and Public Affairs*, vol. 1, no. 2 (Winter 1972). It is collected in Cohen *et al.* (eds), *op. cit.*, and Beitz *et al.* (eds), *op. cit.*, and in T. Nagel, *Mortal Questions* (Cambridge University Press, Cambridge, 1979); page references in the text are to this latter source.

29. Soldier's codes in these matters are discussed in J. Keegan, *The Face of Battle* (Cape, London, 1976).

30. Anscombe's essays, 'War and murder', 'Mr Truman's degree' and 'The justice of the present war examined', are in *The Collected Philosophical Papers of G.E.M. Anscombe; Vol. 3: Ethics, Religion and Politics* (Blackwell, Oxford, 1981).

31. R.B. Brandt, 'Utilitarianism and the rules of war', and R.M. Hare, 'The rules of war and moral reasoning', *Philsophy and Public Affairs* vol. 1, no. 2 (1972); also collected in Cohen *et al.* (eds), *op. cit.*

32. Walzer, *op. cit.*

33. See ch. 5. Some might argue that Walzer's sympathies for Israel have led him astray in this case.

34. Nardin, *op. cit.*, p. 300. For his elaboration of the position that morality need not be the supreme guide to conduct see 'The problem of relativism in international ethics', *Millennium: Journal of International Studies*, vol. 18, no. 2 (Summer 1989).

35. For the various stages of awareness of the dilemmas of nuclear weapons see

L. Freedman, *The Evolution of Nuclear Strategy* (Macmillan, London, 1981).

36. J. Schell, *The Fate of the Earth* (Knopf, New York, 1982).
37. Such as those discussed by C. Gray in 'Nuclear strategy: the case for a theory for victory', *International Security*, vol. 4 (1979).
38. R. Hardin and J.J. Mearsheimer, Introduction to Special Issue on Nuclear Deterrence and Disarmament, *Ethics*, Vol. 95, no. 3 (1985).
39. The classic example of this tendency is E.P. Thomson and D. Smith (eds) *Protest and Survive* (Penguin, Harmondsworth, 1980), best seen as an (unsuccessful) political intervention rather than a serious attempt to develop a moral argument.
40. Clarendon Press, Oxford, 1987.
41. A. Donagan, *The Theory of Morality* (University of Chicago Press, Chicago, 1977).
42. See A. Donagan, 'Comments on Dan Brock and Terence Reynolds', *Ethics*, vol. 95, no. 4 (1985).
43. Hardin and Mearsheimer, *op. cit.*, p. 412.
44. This is the way the issue is set up by the Harvard Nuclear Study Group among other interested scholars; S.D. Sagan *et al.*, *Living with Nuclear Weapons* (Harvard University Press, Cambridge, Mass., 1983).
45. D. Gauthier, 'Deterrence, maximisation and rationality', *Ethics*, vol. 94, no. 3 (1984); G. Kavka, *Moral Paradoxes of Nuclear Deterrence* (Cambridge University Press, Cambridge, 1987); R. Hardin, 'Unilateral vs. mutal disarmament', *Philosophy and Public Affairs*, vol. 11, no. 3 (1982).
46. *Ethics*, vol. 95, no. 3 (1985).
47. *ibid.*, p. 644.

Chapter 7

International Justice

INTRODUCTION: INEQUALITY AND THE THEORY OF INTERNATIONAL RELATIONS

Consider the following selection of facts, drawn from the authoritative statistical tables contained in the World Bank's *World Development Report* for 1991:[1]

In 1989, 21 countries had Gross National Products (GNP) per capita in excess of $10,000, while 34 had GNPs per capita of less than $500 (table 1).

The GNP per capita for the 772.6 million inhabitants of the Organisation for Economic Co-operation and Development (OECD) countries was $19,090, while for the 4,052.8 million inhabitants of low- and middle-income countries it was $800, and for the 480.4 million inhabitants of sub-Saharan Africa it was $340 (table 1).

Income figures can be misleading; an alternative approach is to look at social indicators. In 1989 the life expectancy at birth in the OECD countries was 76, in low- and middle-income countries 63 and in sub-Saharan Africa 51 (table 1).

Infant mortality per 1,000 live births in 1989 was 8 in the OECD countries, 65 in low- and middle-income countries and 107 in sub-Saharan Africa (table 28).

Daily calorie supply per capita was 3,417 in the OECD countries, 2,468 in low- and middle-income countries and 2,011 in sub-Saharan Africa (table 28).

Population per physician and nurse in 1984 was 450 and 130 respectively in the OECD countries, 4,990 and 1,880 in low- and middle-income countries and 26,640 and 2,170 in sub-Saharan Africa (table 28).

In relative terms, most of these figures have actually improved since the 1960s, but looking to the future, the 1990 Report of the UN Population Fund is somewhat pessimistic.[2] The current world population of 5.3 billion is predicted to stabilise in about a century at 11 billion, assuming that growth rates fall; if they continue at or near present rates the final stable total could be 14 billion. Already around 512 million people are undernourished, and on realistic assumptions this total will grow.

Now clearly, these figures describe a serious situation and an unsatisfactory state of affairs. What is less clear is how this problem is to be characterised and, in particular, whether it can or should be seen as a problem that falls within the scope of normative international relations theory. Whose problem is this? Obviously, world proverty is a problem for the poor, but is it, or should it be, a problem for the rich? And if so, for rich countries or rich people? A problem demanding charity or justice?

The simple answer to these rhetorical questions is that international relations theory as conventionally understood has refused to accept that issues of international wealth and poverty could be its concern. The notion of state autonomy, promoted as a good in its own terms by communitarian thinkers and largely accepted on pragmatic grounds by cosmopolitans, seemed to rule out the idea that a rich state had any *obligation* to provide assistance to a poor state – although it would not, of course preclude charitable donations to relieve poverty, or the use of 'aid' as an instrument of foreign policy. Even those classical cosmopolitan thinkers who attacked the notion of state sovereignty and proposed institutional arrangements which would limit autonomy did so from the perspective of restricting war-making powers rather than of subverting 'domestic jurisdiction'. The settled norms of the international system – to employ again Frost's notion – simply do not recognise the existence or significance of the dramatic inequalities outlined above and offer no conceptual framework within which these inequalities can be turned into a problem for international relations theory.

That this should be so is not surprising, because the situation described by the above statistics is, quite literally, unprecedented. The inequalities that currently characterise the international system are the product of the last two hundred years, while the emergence of sovereign states of such unequal socio-economic positions is the product of the decolonisation of the last forty years. It may be helpful to dwell on these points for a little while, since an awareness of how new the problem of international inequality actually is may help to explain why existing international theory is so poorly equipped to deal with it.

It was suggested in chapters 2 and 3 above that Kant and Hegel were the two most important international theorists, their late/post-Enlightenment thought laying down the basis for much later cosmopolitan and communitarian thought. Each writer was certainly conscious of the role of the economy in determining state policy and in setting the context of international theory, although neither saw this role as dominant; in the case of Kant, some early signs of a theory of economic interdependence can be weakly discerned, while rather stronger indication of economic nationalism and a theory of economic imperialism can be found in Hegel.[3] However, in neither case is the issue of international economic inequality formulated or addressed. The reason is quite clear; although in this period, at the end of the eighteenth, beginning of the nineteenth centuries, there probably were some differences in GNP per capita between different parts of the world and indeed different countries in Europe, these differences were difficult to measure accurately, probably were not very great and certainly were considerably less obvious than those differences that existed *within* particular societies.

Accuracy of measurement of real standards of living was at that time a problem even in those European societies which were the most 'advanced' – witness the continuing controversy as to the degree of immiseration of the English proletariat in this period. It was only with the development of bureaucratic systems capable of collecting accurate statistics that comparative time-series become available. However, anecdotal evidence of the early nineteenth century does not suggest a great difference in real living standards across frontiers. Obviously, some peasantries were better off than others, and the emerging proletariats of north-west Europe were rather worse off than the artisans of land-rich, underpopulated North America, but it seems likely that it was only towards the middle of the last century that the sort of differences documented in the *World Development Report* began to emerge. It was only then that industrial capitalism began to deliver to its ordinary workers a standard of living higher by any measure than that enjoyed by their forefathers, while the spread of Western and medical and sanitary technologies began to cut death rates in the non-industrial world without, at the same time, increasing proportionately food production or slowing birth rates. The emergence of a qualitative difference in the meaning of poverty as between, say, the poor in Britain and the poor in India is a product of the last 150 years.[4]

Moreover, for the first two-thirds of this period, the qualitative differences that were emerging were to be found within single jurisdictions as much as between them. The industrial worker in England, the villager in West Africa and the slum dweller in Calcutta were all subjects of the one British Empire, and although the political equality this seemed to offer was, of course, illusory, the existence of a single jurisdiction did have considerable effect on the ways in which poverty was seen as an international issue. Effectively, it ensured that emerging radical inequality would be seen as a matter for imperial rather than international politics. After 1919 most imperial powers accepted that, in principle, their colonies were held in some kind of trust, and most instituted programmes designed to develop the poor areas of their empire, but such programmes were not international as such. The moral basis of support in the metropolitan countries for development was the idea that political control brought with it responsibilities; this was clearly not a principle that applied generally to rich–poor relations in the world at large, nor a principle that would survive the ending of formal political control after decolonisation.

Adding these points together, it becomes clear that the combination of radical inequality and separate political jurisdictions within one international system is a relatively recent development. The absence of a tradition of thought on this matter is unsurprising; the fact that the classical theorists did not see international inequality as an issue does not reflect a conscious decision on their part to exclude this agenda. It is all the more depressing to note that while over the last two decades quite a substantial theoretical literature has emerged on this subject, only a part of it has come from international theorists as such; far more extensive and interesting has been that work which has spilled over from debates and controversies about the meaning of distributive justice in *domestic* society.

The aim of this chapter is to examine ways in which international inequality might come to be seen as an issue in international relations theory. The aim is not to analyse the causes of international inequality, or potential solutions to the problem, but to examine the different ways in which the obligations of the rich to the poor can be understood, and in particular to ask whether these obligations can be seen as deriving from the requirements of justice, or whether benevolence and charity are more appropriate terms.

Although causes and remedies are in general outside the scope of this discussion, the next step in the argument will be to examine two approaches to international inequality which rely heavily on particular accounts of the causes and consequences of international poverty: one arguing that the guilt of the rich for the poverty of the poor in itself establishes an obligation; the other, by contrast, that obligations to approach this problem cannot exist in the absence of effective remedies. Clearly, both of these positions derive moral obligations or lack of them from empirical propositions; if acceptable, they will shape the rest of the discussion – or make it irrelevant. It will be argued, in fact, that they are not acceptable in extreme form, and the discussion will then move on to an account of the obligations of the rich to the poor which, while very radical in its implications, is interpersonal rather than intersocietal in scope – the radical utilitarianism of Peter Singer. The final sections of the chapter will look at theorists of international distributive justice in the full sense of these terms.

POVERTY, GUILT AND IMPOTENCE

While there are, no doubt, interesting things to say about the relationship between guilt and impotence in general terms, these notions are linked together in this context because they share the property of simplifying what threatens otherwise to be a rather complex argument. If it is the case that the poverty of poor countries/ peoples is the result of actions by rich countries/peoples, then there would seem to be quite a strong *prima facie* case for saying that the latter have a clear responsibility to act in such a way as to make reparations; the notion of state autonomy would clearly be an inappropriate basis upon which to refuse to accept international inequality as a fit subject for international relations theory. If, on the other hand, it were to be established that there is, in practice, nothing that the people of the more fortunate areas of the world can actually do to assist the impoverished, then again the situation would be fairly clear; if no remedy is available then no action can be required, and international inequality could not be a suitable subject for international relations theory. Since both these hypothetical positions have their supporters they need to be considered at the outset of this chapter.

The argument from the guilt of the rich takes two forms, one of which is reasonably clear but not convincing, the other much less easy either to pin down or to come to a firm decision upon. The first argument points simply to the record of imperial rule over the last four centuries, and the exploitation in this period of those countries that are poor today by many of those that are today rich. The gold and silver of the New World forcibly extracted by the conquistadors, the labour of millions of Africans transported by slave traders across the Atlantic, the pillaging of the wealth of India by Clive and his successors in the eighteenth century, the damage wrought by the drug traffickers of the China coast in the period of the Opium Wars, the unfree labour systems established on all continents by the imperialists and continuing into the twentieth century – the list of such crimes could be extended almost indefinitely. Few would wish to deny that great wrongs have been done, and that many of today's poorest peoples have been grievously afflicted in the past.[5]

However, there are several reasons why this line of argument is not a sound basis upon which to construct contemporary rich-poor relations. First, the full balance sheet of empire is less one-sided. This is not simply a matter of listing the crimes of empire on one side of the balance and its alleged benefits on the other; such attempts to find a moral calculus which allows one to measure, say, the destruction of a local economy against the introduction of an effective transport system are distasteful and unsuccessful.[6] More to the point is the fact that the successor states of imperialism are themselves the product of empire. Imperialism destroyed the old cultures of the non-European world and even if some of the old names are resurrected ('Ghana', 'Zimbabwe') the new societies cannot simply return to the *status quo ante*. The victims of imperialism died; even the poorest of modern postcolonial states are in some sense its beneficiaries. Whether the new societies created by imperialism are or are not superior to their predecessors is a moot point – although it should be said that there is a remarkable consensus around the view that they are superior, encompassing liberal defenders of capitalism, Marxist opponents and, more to the point, for the time being at least, most of the postcolonial elites. What is difficult to deny is that these societies are radically different from those discovered in the first place by the imperialists. The continuity required by the 'reparations' argument is difficult to establish.[7]

A second reason to suspect the simple reparations argument is that, as with any position based on past events, its force lessens with the passage of time and with changes in the circumstances of those involved. Exactly what responsibilities contemporary liberal-democratic Britain has for the crimes of the pre-Reform Act oligarchy is by no means clear. In general, although it need not be thought that decolonisation wiped the slate clean of past debts, it surely has to be the case that the more time passes the less plausible it is to suggest that current miseries can be traced back to past wrongs.

A more difficult argument relates not to simple acts of oppression and violence, but to the alleged existence of a systematic relationship of exploitation built into the fabric of economic exchanges between rich and poor – and thus unaffected by decolonisation, a movement which, in any event has brought no real freedom of manoeuvre to its alleged beneficiaries. On this 'structuralist', 'dependency' account of the world the poor of the world are not simply undeveloped: they have been 'underdeveloped' by the rich. A chain of exploitation linking 'satellite' and 'metropolitan' countries has been in existence as a structure since the sixteenth century. Individual acts of plunder have taken place but have been less significant than the more invidious, because less visible, processes of exploitation based on trade relations between 'centres' and 'peripheries'. The capitalist centres of the world economy have integrated the whole of the rest of the world into one structure which works to funnel wealth in their direction. The rich of today are rich because of this process and the poor have been impoverished by it. The radical inequality revealed by the World Bank's figures is not a contingent feature of the modern world, it is a necessary facet of the operation of the modern world system.[8]

This is a difficult argument to evaluate, for three reasons: it is not clear what the mechanism of exploitation is, nor what would count as evidence of exploitation, nor what action would be appropriate were the structuralist position to be well founded.

Why exactly does international trade between rich and poor countries *necessarily* involve the exploitation of the latter? It is easy to see that manifestly unfair bargains sometimes follow from the exploitation of political inequalities, but, as Marx argues in *Capital*, it is not possible to base a systematic theory of exploitation on acts of plunder and piracy, which is why he assumes in his political economy that commodities exchange at their average values. Some structuralists simply dodge this point – Galtung, for example, simply asserts that if exchanges take place between rich and poor it is axiomatic that the poor are being exploited.[9] The best, indeed only, attempt to come up with a theoretically sophisticated account of unequal exchange – that of Arrighi Emmanuel – suggests that wages are the key independent variable.[10] In the processes of exchange high-wage countries exploit low-wage countries because the prices at which goods trade reflect *historically determined* subsistence wages. Even if this were a widely accepted argument, which it is not, it could hardly explain how the structure of exploitation came into being in a period *before* wide differentials in wages existed.

Does the existence of a chain of exploitation imply that the development of the 'underdeveloped' countries is impossible? The logic of the argument would seem to suggest that this is so, but the problem then is that of defining 'development'. In simple statistical terms real living conditions in most of the poorer areas of the world have improved over the last quarter of a century. Growth has taken place, even in per capita terms, infant mortality rates have fallen and so on – although in some countries (not necessarily those with the closest relationship to the metropolitan centres) things have got worse. Possibly, the development that has taken place could be described as 'dependent development' – but what, under contemporary conditions, would '*in*dependent development' look like?[11]

If the structuralist model is correct, what are the implications for action in both rich and poor countries? The implication would seem to be that since the problems of underdevelopment are externally generated, individual poor countries can do nothing for themselves short of completely breaking ties with the metropolitan centres. But, again, the statistical evidence suggests that local policies matter a great deal, that even if poor countries are unable to 'pull themselves up by their bootstraps', as the rhetoric of the New Right has it, they certainly have the ability to make a real difference to the standard of living of their peoples. When one notes that the life expectancy at birth in Sri Lanka (71) is five years higher than that of Brazil even though Brazilian GNP per capita ($2,540) is over five times greater, it is difficult to avoid thinking that this reflects the different priorities of the elites of these countries, and hard to see how these priorities could reasonably be attributed to the influence of the structure of the world economy.[12]

Similarly, from the dependency perspective all that rich countries can do about world poverty is have a revolution and break the chain of exploitation – simply to change policies towards the poor solves nothing, a point that seems to have escaped the Brandt Commission, whose liberal reformist policies were encased in a fair amount of structuralist rhetoric.[13]

These arguments will continue; but to sum up, it seems doubtful that any attempt to understand rich–poor relations on the principle that the rich are exclusively or even mainly responsible for the poverty of the poor will succeed – which is not to say that there are not practices which have in the past contributed to poverty, or that many of the things done today by rich countries are not still making things worse. Such factors are clearly highly relevant to a moral understanding of rich–poor relations, but not determinant. The implanting of such relations in international relations theory cannot be based predominantly on the notion of the guilt of the rich.

The argument that the rich are, in practice, unable to help the poor also comes in two versions, one simple and almost certainly wrong, the other more complex and difficult to assess. The simple argument here is the neo-Malthusian position most famously expressed recently by Garrett Hardin in an article entitled 'Lifeboat ethics: the case against helping the poor'.[14] The argument is that foreign aid simply allows more people to survive than would otherwise be the case without bringing about an equivalent increase in the food supply for the society in question; this in turn increases dependence on foreign aid, which in turn allows further population growth until eventually the system crashes with mass starvation. Now, although this is a theoretically possible model, there is no reason to believe that this sort of Malthusian crisis necessarily would follow from successful aid programmes. On the experience of the developed world one would expect that birth rates would begin to fall with increased wealth, and there is certainly no warrant for assuming that population growth must outstrip the growth of resources. The best that can be said of this argument is that, unsurprisingly, the possibility exists that in certain circumstances effective aid could be counterproductive.

The neo-Malthusian position assumes that aid can be effective in the short-term but suggests that if it is, it will be self-defeating. A more serious point is that many economists doubt whether foreign aid has ever been effective. The ineffectiveness of Official Development Assistance (ODA) has been a long-standing position of radical right economists such as P. T. Bauer and Deepak Lal, but is now acknowledged from many points of the political compass, for instance in the work of Paul Moseley, Ian Little and Graham Hancock.[15] The argument takes a number of different forms. For the right, the issue is the need to develop markets in the poorer countries of the world and for the factors of production to be priced in accordance with market forces; aid flows distort the operation of markets and actually interfere with development. Even if managed growth via planning was a sensible strategy in general – and obviously, these writers think it is not – poor countries lack the bureaucratic structures that would allow them to adopt this route to the modern world. Instead, planning simply provides opportunities for corruption.

The social–democratic and radical critique of ODA is less likely to be impressed with the powers of the market, more likely to stress that most aid is tied to the products of the 'donor', that it is almost invariably based on external and wrong assessments of what is actually required, that it is exploited by local elites to perpetuate themselves in power in circumstances where often the power of local elites is precisely the problem, and – this from Hancock's swingeing polemic – that it largely serves to keep in business the 'lords of poverty', the international civil servants whose (very affluent) livelihood is dependent upon ODA programmes. Whereas a writer such as Moseley argues in favour of redesigned aid programmes, Hancock is opposed to ODA root and branch:

> Aid is not bad, however, because it is sometimes misused, corrupt, or crass: rather, it is *inherently* bad, bad to the bone and utterly beyond reform. As a welfare dole to buy the repulsive loyalty of whining, idle and malevolent governments, or as a hidden, inefficient and inadequately regulated subsidy for Western business, it is possibly the most formidable obstacle to the productive endeavours of the poor.[16]

This is strong meat, and if we follow this argument to its obvious conclusion, it is clear that those international theorists who refuse to see international inequality as an issue in international theory will receive strong support from this quarter – although Hancock does see a continuing role for private aid agencies and individual donations. Indeed, he also anticipates the possibility that in the future, once poor countries have sorted out their domestic problems and are strong enough to define their own needs, there may again be a role for ODA – of a very different kind, needless to say.

It may be that Hancock is right and that aid is inherently bad, or it may be that Moseley and others are right in assuming that, whatever past failures, there is no necessary reason why an adequate aid system could not be produced. We have to choose one of these positions now, on inadequate evidence, and it seems that in the circumstances the safe choice is the less radical position. Unless an absolutely compelling argument to the contrary is produced, it seems best to assume that a rational and effective aid programme could be devised and thus that international inequality is not a matter over which states can have no control. The alternative assumption of helplessness in the face of appalling poverty is surely to be rejected if there is any doubt in the matter at all. However, this discussion has not been without point, for it will need to be borne constantly in mind that relieving poverty, even with the best will in the world, is not a simple task – a point to which some of the authors now to be examined sometimes seem to give too little attention.

FAMINE, AFFLUENCE AND PERSONAL MORALITY

Had it been possible to establish either guilt or impotence in the previous section, the task of establishing the basis for rich–poor relations in the modern system would have been radically simplified. Either there would be simply nothing the rich could do for the poor, or the rich would have been directly responsible for the poverty of the poor, in which case a moral requirement to do something about this state of affairs would have been easy to establish. However, both of these simplifying positions must be rejected, albeit with some hesitation. It has to be assumed that rich countries/people could, if they wished, do something about the poverty of the poor, even though this will not be an easy task; it cannot be assumed that the rich are obliged to take up this task because of their guilt for past oppressions – even though the fact that wrongs were committed cannot be regarded as morally irrelevant.

How, then, should radical international inequality be handled as an issue of international relations theory, given that these possible simplifiers must be rejected? The most dramatic answers to this question are those which require us to rethink the meaning of international 'society' by accepting that the peoples of the world are in such a relationship one with another as to require that the social arrangements which distribute advantages and disadvantages must be defended as justified. Within domestic society the demand that social arrangements be defensible is a demand for 'justice', and it may be that this notion must now be extended to the world scene; certainly, if it be the case that the demand for justice follows naturally from awareness that inequalities appear not to have a rational basis, then it is clear that international justice is already on the agenda.

The very notion of *international* justice immediately raises a crucial point that may make the analogy with domestic justice hard to sustain. The inequalities that exist in the international system exist between – as well as within – states; that is to say, between separate political territorial jurisdictions which *may* enclose separate communities (whether they do or not being a moot point, as the discussion of the moral basis for state autonomy in chapter 5 revealed). It would seem that the notion of international justice implies that this separatedness be recognised in one way or another. The potential difficulty here is easy to see; the difficulties of comprehending the requirements of justice are great enough as it is, without the added complication of a requirement to respect the autonomy of the state. However, it may be that state autonomy ought not to be respected and at least some of the theorists whose work will be examined in the following sections take this position. These theorists do, however, at least acknowledge that there is a difficulty here; by contrast, the rest of this section is devoted to an author who cuts through these issues by giving attention not to the proper relationship between *societies* rich and poor, but to what ought to be right conduct for *individual* men and women whether decision makers or not. It will be argued that this attempt does not succeed, but, as is usually the case, is instructive in its failure.

The radical utilitarian Peter Singer has produced one of the strongest cases for cutting through all the complexities of international relations theory in favour of a direct appeal to individual action in his paper of 1972, 'Famine, affluence and morality'.[17] The strength of his argument lies in its simplicity. After outlining an emerging famine situation – in Bengal – and the inadequate reactions of governments to this horror – for example, Australia giving a sum amounting to one-twelfth of the cost of the Sydney Opera House – Singer states an assumption, outlines a principle and gives an illustration; the rest of the argument follows from these three moves.

The assumption is that suffering and death from lack of food, shelter and medical care are bad. The principle is 'if it is in our power to prevent something bad from happening, without thereby sacrificing anything of comparable moral importance, we ought, morally, to do it'.

A weaker version of this principle refers to 'anything morally significant' rather than to 'anything of comparable moral significance'. In most of the rest of his argument Singer uses this weaker version, although his own adherence is to the stronger principle. The illustration is meant to show what this means.

> If I am walking past a shallow pond and see a child drowning in it, I ought to wade in and pull the child out. This will mean getting my clothes muddy, but this is insignificant, while the death of the child would presumably be a very bad thing. (p. 249)

Singer rightly points out that the uncontroversial appearance of this principle is deceptive. The reason is simple: it takes no account of distance (whether the suffering is in front of one or half-way around the world) or of the number of other people who are similarly obligated (whether it is I alone or millions of others who are obliged to act). Singer's simple principle abolishes the distinction between 'duty' and 'charity'. As a utilitarian, he invites his readers simply to compare states of affairs and act so as to bring about the better of whatever alternatives are on offer. The obligation to act in accordance with this principle is not in any respect lessened by the fact that the states of affairs in question occur in Bengal, or by the fact that others – including governement leaders – are faced with the same obligation.

What level of sacrifice is required of individuals in pursuit of this principle? On the strong version of the principle, which refers to something of 'comparable moral importance', one ought to give up to the point of marginal utility, where to give more would weaken one's own or one's dependants' position below that of the victims of famine. The weaker version of Singer's principle would still require that one gives 'up to the point at which by giving more one would begin to cause serious suffering for one's self and one's dependants' (p. 252). Singer prefers the strong version of his principle – although he acknowledges that it could lead to the 'absurd' consequence that more was given than could be used, and thus that some of the sacrifice was pointless. Irrespective of the details here, the basic point is that even the weakest version of Singer's principle requires more from us than is generally thought necessary. For example, to forgo a new car in order to give the money to famine relief would normally be thought to be something that should attract special praise as a 'supererogatory' act – an act that it would be good to do, but not wrong not to do. For Singer no such argument holds; on the contrary, it would be wrong to use money so obviously surplus to the requirements of necessity in any other way.

Singer is aware that some would argue that to require the level of sacrifice built into even the weaker version of his principle might be counterproductive. A less extreme requirement might produce better results – see the end of the previous chapter for a similar argument *vis-à-vis* nuclear disarmament. His response is that extreme situations require extreme remedies and that the role of the moral philosopher is not always to work within the prevailing set of norms but sometimes to work to change them. He regards the priorities revealed by our present consumption patterns as simply wrong. We should change these priorities.

In the final section of this short paper, Singer considers some of the practical points about relieving poverty: the argument that this should be a government activity, not one for private persons, that famine relief might be counterproductive, preparing the ground for a greater famine later, and the point that too great a level of transfer of resources could hurt the capacity of rich societies to reproduce themselves, and thus be counter to the long-run goals of the programme. Singer takes these points seriously but his response – surely justified – is that, given that at the moment transfers of as little as 1 per cent of GNP from rich to poor are considered generous, discussions which assume that excessive generosity might be a problem are academic in the worse sense of the term.

How is Singer's argument to be assessed? To some extent it is subject to the sort of critiques that utilitarianism usually attracts, as set out, for example, in Williams' reply to Smart in *Utilitarianism: For and against,* and summarised crisply by Rawls' point that utilitarians do not take sufficiently seriously the distinction between persons. The essential argument here is that individuals have their own projects for their lives and that utilitarians do not offer sufficient reasons why we should accept a general obligation to promote the greatest happiness. Unless we are wrong to think of ourselves as essentially separate individual beings – a possibility that Parfit takes seriously – it is difficult to see why we should assess states of affairs from an impersonal perspective.[18] Such debates are, of course, of long standing; an interesting point here, from the perspective of international relations is different in direction, but similar in form – namely, whether Singer (to adapt Rawls' dictum) takes sufficiently seriously the distinctions between *states.*

Consider Singer's illustration: it is a child who is drowning in the shallow pond. Why? Why not an adult? Presumably, because it avoids the complication that the person drowning might be doing so deliberately – we would probably refuse to accept that by preventing a child from committing suicide we were interfering with his or her autonomy, a thought that might occur were the drowning person an adult attempting to commit suicide. Suppose, having been rescued, the child returns immediately to the water? We dive in again, of course, but this time, we apply some physical restraint to prevent a recurrence – again behaviour acceptable because the person is not to be considered fully responsible for his or her actions. By now the difficulty of moving from this simple illustration to the problem of famine and poverty ought to be apparent. Are we empowered by Singer's principle to treat poor countries as though they were irresponsible children? Of course, the facts may not warrant such a general assessment, but sometimes they will. The fact that Ethopia is the poorest country in the world today surely has something to do with the priorities of the recently expelled Ethiopian elite, whose desire to resist secession on the part of Eritrea, and to impose its own version of Marxism–Leninism, must bear great responsibility for the plight of its people.

Suppose – not implausibly – that in this case the best way to prevent death and suffering would have been to intervene and overthrow the Ethiopian government, perhaps instituting a period of direct colonial rule. Presumably, from a utilitarian point of view there could be no objection to this course of action if it really were the case that this would be the most effective way of preventing suffering; much of the time, of course, it would not be, but the possibility is there.[19] It is, I think, fairly clear that even if Singer would accept that this would be the right thing to do, none of the actual governments of the poor countries would agree with him – more to the point, it does not seem likely that the peoples of these countries would agree either. Certainly, the white South African argument that blacks are materially better off in the republic than they are in independent Africa, while obviously true, appears to cut no ice in the townships.

The key point here is that while freedom from want is something that people place a high value on, it is not the only thing that is similarly valued. Self-government as an expression of autonomy is also highly valued, as witness the refusal of the British government to make peace in 1940 even though that was clearly the 'rational' thing to do. Obviously, people would prefer to be well fed *and* free, but the assumption that the former is always the most basic desire seems not to be borne out by the choices people actually make. Now, of course, the victims of famine are not usually victims by their own choice, and not always by virtue of the policies of their governments, but, given the way in which Singer sets up his position, they will always be passive figures, having things done for them. The rich are obliged to help the poor; the poor are there to be helped. They are children, waiting to be saved by external intervention.

Perhaps in the case of actual famine – a dire emergency – there is something to be said for this perspective, although the sort of evidence marshalled by Hancock does not lead one to be very confident that even with a good will emergency aid is easy to deliver. What is less plausible is that this could be the basis for a long-term relationship between rich and poor countries. The Singer principle, with its disregard for values other than the relief of suffering, sanctions behaviour that is incompatible with the autonomy of states. Perhaps this autonomy should be jettisoned, but, if so, this should surely be on the basis of a wider discussion of the problem that Singer provides.

The problem with Singer's approach is that it assumes that people do not have irreconcilable desires and therefore that there cannot be genuine moral dilemmas associated with international inequality. Doing the right thing may be difficult and painful but what the right thing to do is need not be in doubt – the principle of utility will reveal the right answer. The presupposition that this is so cannot be shown conclusively to be either right or wrong, but there seems to be at least some reason to be dubious about its application in this case. People clearly do not want to be malnourished, let alone to starve, but equally they seem to want to run their own affairs even in circumstances where loss of autonomy might improve their calorific intake. Any adequate account of rich–poor relations ought to take this into account.

One way of doing so might be via an explicitly Kantian cos-mopolitanism – in contrast to Singer's neo-Benthamite approach. Onora O'Neill provides just such a route in her recent work, *Faces of Hunger: An essay on poverty, justice and development.*[20] O'Neill shares with Singer a sense of outrage at the terms in which the debate about world poverty and hunger is conducted, but rejects the view that Singer's consequentialism can provide a way of moralising the debate. Consequentialist calculations of the sort upon which utilitarians such as Singer ultimately rely are simply too difficult to make, and this difficulty is not simply a practical matter – the way in which the problem is set up in the first place cannot be value-neutral because of the very nature of the social sciences.

However, unlike the writers to be examined in subsequent sections of this chapter, O'Neill rejects the possibility of developing an alternative to consequentialism based on the *rights* of the poor. The ontological status of 'rights' is just too problematic, and O'Neill rejects the idea that such a fundamental difficulty can be overcome by contractarian fictions. Instead, she proposes a duty-based approach. Her position is that as moral agents, all human beings have general obligations towards each other entailed by our common humanity, and that Kantian assumptions about generalisability and human equality are the best starting point for an examination of these obligations. We are obliged to act on maxims that can be acted upon by all – such as truth-telling and non-coercion in social relations. But if everyone is to act on these maxims, they must be provided with the capacity to do so; our obligations as moral agents require us to help others to be moral agents. Her point is that if the peoples of the privileged world were to take such obligations seriously, the result would be a transformation in relations between rich and poor countries every bit as radical as that which would result from the application of Singer's simple principle.

The advantage of O'Neill's Kantianism over and against Singer's utilitarianism is that it does allow space for arguments based on political justifications of state autonomy, albeit limiting such arguments quite severely, and it does allow for the application of selective beneficence. Put differently, we cannot meet all needs now unmet and we cannot disregard the possibilities of existing political structures, and a doctrine such as utilitarianism that regards an unmet need as a sign of failure, and normal political activity as a necessarily inadequate response to abnormal circumstances is creating obstacles for itself.[21] However, O'Neill's approach shares with Singer an emphasis on individuals and individual action; even though her principles can be used to assess the justice of social institutions, this is not their primary focus. It could be argued that an adequate theory of international justice needs to be more closely focussed on institutions, and in the following sections approaches meeting this requirement will be examined.

INTERNATIONAL JUSTICE: RAWLS AND BEITZ

It has been argued above that international inequality is not simply the product of wrongdoing on the part of the rich, nor is it simply a fact of nature about which nothing can be done. The moral of the last section is that international inequality is not something that can be understood by the application of simple and unambiguous principles of personal morality; any account of the problem that forgets that international inequality is *international* and not simply interpersonal cannot be sensitive to the genuine dilemmas posed by the coexistence in the world today not just of rich and poor people but of rich and poor communities. It may be that the principle of international autonomy ought to be abandoned – that those who value autonomy ought to be persuaded not to – but in order to arrive at this result this principle needs to be taken seriously.

In domestic society, social justice is precisely about taking differences seriously and attempting to cope with irreconcilable desires. A society in which roles are not differentiated – or in which differentiation is seen as part of the natural order and not a human creation – is a society that has no experience of justice. The demand for justice emerges once social arrangements are perceived to involve differences which are of human creation; the demand for justice is the demand that these differences be *justified*. In principle, it would seem that international relations has now reached the point where this domestic analogy – if not all others – holds. In principle, we ought to be able to put to the test of reasoned argument the differences that exist between states; the assumption being not that such differences are necessarily illegitimate, but that they need to be reflectively justified. A theory of international justice ought to allow us to place relations between rich and poor countries on a footing that recognises diversity yet meets the obligations people have towards one another – or, at least, tries to perform the same sort of role that notions of justice try to perform in domestic society.

The most important modern theorist of justice is certainly John Rawls, whose *A Theory of Justice* has overshadowed thinking on the subject since its publication in 1971.[22] In view of this dominance, it is interesting to note that although Rawls does generate principles of international justice, these are radically different from the principles of social justice for which he is most renowned. In effect, he rejects the analogy set out in the preceding paragraph. However, the first major study of international distributive justice, Charles Beitz's *Political Theory and International Relations*, adopts a Rawlsian perspective on the subject, arguing that Rawls has misconceived the implications of his own work.[23] The rest of this section will examine the work of these two authors.

A Theory of Justice is an enormously complex work; only those themes that are needful for this discussion will be examined here. The most appropriate place to start is with Rawls' definition of society as a 'co-operative venture for mutual advantage';[24] individuals who, in principle, pre-exist society (Rawls is in this respect a Kantian liberal) join together and co-operate in society because it is to their advantage to do so in that the 'goods' (in the broad sense) produced by co-operation are greater than could be produced by a collection of non-co-operating individuals. However, this social product, made possible by the contributions of all, is distributed unevenly. How can such a distribution be justified? Rawls is not unambiguous on this point, but his basic position seems to be that what makes a particular distribution just is that it is based on principles that would be freely chosen by individuals prior to their coming together in society in the first place.

Rawls proposes a 'thought experiment'. We are to imagine an 'original position' (somewhat similar to the 'state of nature' of classical contract theorists) where individuals meet under 'the veil of ignorance'.[25] The veil of ignorance means that these individuals know nothing about their personal circumstances, age, sex, skin colour, level of intelligence and so on; they only know that there are certain 'primary goods' that all people desire – such as liberty, wealth, self-respect – which can be met more abundantly through co-operation than outside society.[26] The participants in the original position realise that to achieve the benefits of social co-operation it is necessary to determine principles for the distribution of these benefits – the principles of social justice. The question is, what principles would the contractors agree on in these circumstances?

Rawls assumes that in political terms, contractors would choose the principle that 'each person is to have an equal right to the most extensive total system of equal basic liberties compatible with a similar system of liberty for all'; moreover, this principle of liberty has priority over other principles.[27] More difficult is the derivation of principles for distributive justice. How might social and economic inequalities be justified? One answer might be via a legal notion of equality of opportunity, with all posts and positions in principle open to all; however, the advantages of inherited wealth and superior education make it unlikely that his would be regarded as fair. A 'fair meritocracy' looks more promising: equality of opportunity in circumstances where everyone has the ability to develop to the full their talents. But why should talent be rewarded? If contractors would be unwilling to allow advantage on the basis of family position, why would they be willing to allow the lottery of genetic endowment to determine rewards in society? Many talents are no more deserved than are parents. Perhaps inequalities should be arranged on the principle of utility – whatever system produces the greatest total happiness; but utilitarianism does not treat seriously the distinction between person, and contractors would not risk disadvantage solely for the good of greater utility. Perhaps there should be no social or economic inequalities at all? The problem here is that, quite plausibly, to rule out inequality is to eliminate a great many of the potential gains of social co-operation. It seems likely that without some inequality co-operation would be ineffective; for example, talents that might be to the benefit of society might not be developed or deployed unless appropriately rewarded.

Rawls' answer to this conundrum is his 'difference principle':

> Social and economic inequalities are to be arranged so that they are both:
> (a) to the greatest benefit of the least advantaged, consistent with the just savings principle [which concerns obligations to later generations, on which more below] and
> (b) attached to offices and positions open to all under conditions of fair equality of opportunity.[28]

This is one of the most controversial propositions of twentieth-century political philosophy. The enormous literature it has generated will not be discussed directly here, but one or two points need to be made before proceeding to look at the international aspects of *A Theory of Justice*. First, it should be noted that Rawls is not entirely clear whether the difference principle is fair because it is chosen in the original position under a veil of ignorance or whether it is chosen because it is fair – the more Kantian side of his work, recently in evidence, would seem to suggest the latter, but if so, why set up an elaborate thought experiment in the first place if we already know what it will produce?[29] Second, the proposition that this principle would be chosen under the veil of ignorance is not, perhaps, as certain as Rawls would seem to think. His argument is that contractors will adopt a 'mini-max' game strategy – maximising the minimum gain, minimising the maximum loss. Suppose the contractors were less risk-averse than Rawls assumes? Might they not choose principles which gave more to the majority, accepting a risk that they might be losers? More reason, perhaps, for thinking that the 'original position' is not simply a thought experiment, but a smoke screen to allow Rawls to expound his own ideas of justice under the cloak of the impartial choice of contractors, ignorant of their own position.

In any event, Rawls does not believe that his principles of justice can apply on a world scale, for the simple reason that these are principles of social justice, a society is a 'co-operative venture for mutual advantage', and no such co-operative venture exists on a world scale. Rawls assumes that societies can be treated as effectively self-sufficient. World 'society', so-called, is not a society in this sense because it does not co-operatively create a surplus that has to be divided; thus principles of distributive justice are not required on a world scale because there is nothing to distribute. Individual societies do not co-operate but they do have to coexist. International justice is about this co-existence, and the principles are determined by a second 'original position'. This time representatives of societies come together under the veil of ignorance – not knowing whether they represent major powers or small countries or whatever – and decide on the principles that will govern their relations one with another. What they are presumed to come up with is a series of principles which reflect the equal rights of states; self-determination, non-intervention, a right of self-defence, *ius ad bellum, ius in bello* and so on – in other words, the familiar principles of international law. By contrast with his apparent radicalism *vis-à-vis* domestic justice, Rawls' account of international justice produces, as he admits, no surprises.[30]

For a writer whose roots are so clearly in the cosmopolitan camp, whose main influences are Hume and Kant, so formal a sense of international justice seems surprising. For example, although Kant endorsed the content of the law of nations in his Preliminary Articles, the Definitive Articles for a Perpetual Peace assumed that the law of nations could gradually be transcended.[31] Kant does not propose a system of international distributive justice, but none the less most thinkers with Rawls' Kantian roots would be critical of his notion of the relationship between social and international justice. Indeed, the general reaction to this account of the relationship has been critical. Modern communitarians such as Sandel might accept his conclusions *vis-à-vis* international justice, but not the way in which he reaches them; whereas the inadequacies of Rawls' handling of international justice is for a critic such as Barry a symptom of the general problems with his approach. These criticisms will be examined below in the next section, which will follow analysis of a more sympathetic critic, Charles Beitz. However, since so much of the reaction to Rawls on international justice is critical, it may be worth making the point that although his conclusions are unsurprising and conventional, this does not mean either that they are wrong or that they are not acutely reasoned. Although the international sections of *A Theory of Justice* are scattered widely through the text, the argument is developed with great skill and amounts to the most impressive recent defence of the traditional notion of an international legal order to be found within the liberal framework – only Nardin's Oakeshottian account approaches the standard of sophistication to be found here.[32] The disappointment is that one does not expect Rawls to defend the traditional international legal order; there need be no disappointment with the quality of the reasoning.

Charles Beitz's *Political Theory and International Relations* has been discussed already in connection with the arguments surrounding the moral status of state autonomy. Beitz is one of the strongest modern critics of the idea of the autonomy of states; he rejects the notion both as an empirical account of the world and as the basis for a morality of states. On the other hand, Beitz broadly accepts Rawls' account of social justice – the liberty principle and the difference principle.[33] His argument is that Rawls misapplies these notions when it comes to international justice. Beitz is more royalist than the king; his aim is to demonstrate that Rawls makes both theoretical and empirical errors when he applies his principles internationally.

Beitz deploys two separate arguments, the first of which accepts that Rawls is right to regard national societies as self-contained and self-sufficient but wrong to think that the international version of the original position would lead to a set of purely formal rules. Instead, he suggests that the representatives of states operating under the veil of ignorance would propose as one of their principles a redistribution of natural resources, such that each society would have 'a fair chance to develop just political institutions and an economy capable of satisfying its members' basic needs'.[34]

His reasoning here is by analogy with the way in which Rawls treats equality of opportunity. Rawls' central point is that outcomes ought not to be affected by factors that are, from a moral point of view, arbitrary, such as accidents of birth, differences in talent and so on. This is a view that has been criticised – is talent really arbitrary? – but Beitz makes the point that if anything is to be regarded as morally arbitrary, the different resource endowments of states must fit the bill. There is no way that states could be regarded as *deserving* deposits of oil, coal or whatever.[35] Why should they benefit from such undeserved riches? The answer Rawls gives to this is that since societies are to be regarded as self-sufficient and self-contained, they are not to be treated as though engaged in a collective co-operative venture; it follows, therefore, that the analogy with the equality of opportunity does not apply. Beitz replies by arguing that although the lack of a co-operative framework would rule out the application of an international 'difference principle', what is at stake here is not the gains of co-operation but the initial endowment, and contributors might well agree a fair redistribution.

If the fiction of choice in the original position under the veil of ignorance is to be taken seriously, then Beitz surely has a point. Obviously, in the absence of co-operation the representatives of states would have no co-operative surplus to redistribute, but it seems quite plausible that they would want to insure against the risk of being bereft of resources by producing a rule to ensure that the initial distribution was fair. The strongest point against Beitz's position is actually empirical; it is by no means clear that, except in very extreme cases, political/economic success or failure is closely related to initial resource endowments. An equal division of the world's resources on a per capita basis would involve giving mineral rights to Japan and taking them away from Namibia. One could make a good case for saying that at least some of the oil-rich Middle Eastern countries would be better off with more (unredistributable) rainfall and less oil. It is by no means clear that justice would necessarily be served by a redistribution of resources.

In any event, Beitz offers a second objection to Rawls' handling of international justice, which, if accepted, would make his first point redundant. It will be recalled that for Rawls a society is a 'co-operative venture for mutual advantage' and that it is because the world as a whole does not meet this description that the difference principle does not apply. Beitz argues that this is simply incorrect; global interdependence has reached the point at which the assumption that societies are essentially self-sufficient and self-contained can no longer be justified. Instead, the same sort of reasoning that leads Rawls to the difference principle for domestic society applies internationally. Rawls is wrong to limit the scope of the principle to national societies.

As Beitz now concedes, this is a difficult argument to sustain.[36] At what point does the intensity of international interdependence reach a level which would justify the description of international society as a 'co-operative venture'? Even more to the point, what level of mutuality is needed if this co-operative venture is to be seen as being for 'mutual advantage'? Many would argue that in rich–poor relations generally the level of mutuality is very low; the poor are dependent on the rich in a way that the rich are not, on the whole, dependent on the poor, *pace* a great deal of 'One World' rhetoric. The irony of Beitz's position is that it works best where it is least needed and most irrelevant. It could very easily be argued that the developed economies of the OECD do form a society in the Rawlsian sense, and thus that the difference principle should operate over this whole area – but, of course, although there are differences in wealth within OECD, as people in Britain are well aware, these are of little moral significance as compared to the gap between the OECD as a whole and the poorest three-quarters of the countries of the world.

Beitz still favours the application of an international difference principle, but in response to his critics he now grounds the principle on the explicitly Kantian perspective that the criterion for membership in the original position is simply 'possession of the two essential powers of moral personality – a capacity for an effective sense of justice and a capacity to form, revise and pursue a conception of the good', this definition of moral personality being drawn from a later statement of his position by Rawls.[37] Differences between members of national societies are morally irrelevant even if there is no common co-operative venture, and the awarding of priority to one's own fellow nationals is morally unjustified. This is a very strong cosmopolitan position, and Beitz regards much of the opposition to it as self-interested and non-moral. However, rather confusingly, he also acknowledges that there are some reasons for supporting patriotic sentiments that, although non-moral, are also non-self-interested: notions of shared loyalty and the like.[38] Once this is accepted, Beitz seems to be backing away from his own cosmopolitanism without developing an alternative. It is difficult to see why shared loyalty, the capacity of a nation to develop its own projects and so on should be valued by Beitz, given his Kantian account of moral personality.

Beitz wishes to hang on to Rawls' difference principle while rejecting the notion of mutual advantage which underlies the latter's account of society. This would seem to be an unstable position since the point of the difference principle is that it represents a just distribution of the benefits of mutual co-operation. A better approach to problems of international justice might be to subject the basic Rawlsian concepts to critique in a way that Beitz is unwilling to do. The next section will examine a number of attempts, from different perspectives, to develop such a critique.

THE CIRCUMSTANCES OF INTERNATIONAL JUSTICE: SANDEL AND BARRY

The publication of *A Theory of Justice* both marked and stimulated a revival of normative ethics. The last twenty years have seen the publication of a mountain of literature on justice in society, some explicitly in response to Rawls, some developing different lines.[39] Fortunately, from the point of view of the length of this work, only a portion of this material is actually relevant to international theory. Writers such as Nozick, Gauthier and Ackerman have interesting things to say in general but either nothing to say about international justice, or nothing that advances the matter beyond the point at which Rawls and Beitz left it.[40] However, there are two philosophers, critics of Rawls with their own substantive positions, whose work is highly relevant to international theory, either implicitly, as with Michael Sandel, or explicitly, as with Brian Barry. These authors have different positions but both see the weakness in Rawls as a product of the mix of Humean and Kantian features of his work; a brief return to Rawls will be valuable here, to explain what is meant by this point.

The Kantian side of Rawls is caught by his insistence that 'justice is the first virtue of social institutions'.[41] Unlike a rule-utilitarian such as J. S. Mill, but following from Kant's deontology, Rawls insists that the autonomy of individuals on which their moral status rests cannot be overriden by considerations of the common good. Justice is about a system of rights which are primary – utilitarianism does not take seriously the distinction between persons, and it is thus unacceptable to regard rights as supported in the last instance by considerations of general utility.

Kant's moral philosophy was developed in opposition to Hume, and a novel aspect of Rawls is the way in which he combines Kantian moral individualism with an account of the original position, which is based on the Humean notion of the 'circumstances of justice'.[42] The idea here is that the possibility of justice depends upon certain assumptions about human nature and the human condition, summarised by Rawls as moderate scarcity, moderate selfishness and relative equality.[43] In conditions of abundance there will be no problem of distributive justice because everyone can have what they want; in conditions of absolute scarcity necessity will rule, and it is unrealistic to expect distribution to follow rules of justice – thus moderate scarcity is a 'circumstance of justice'. If everyone were always totally unselfish, human benevolence would make a system of rights unnecessary; if everyone were totally selfish, such a system would be unworkable – hence 'moderate selfishness'. If one group in society was totally helpless in the face of another there would again be no possibility that the former could assert rights against the latter – they would have to rely on their benevolence, as does, for example, the animal kingdom. Thus justice is the primary virtue of social institutions when the human condition is neither so favourable to co-operation as to make it unnecessary nor so hostile to co-operation as to make it unworkable. The principles of justice chosen in the original position under the veil of ignorance are such as will work in a world characterised in this way.

Sandel's critique of Rawls is based upon a rejection of the Kant/ Rawls account of a morally autonomous presocial individual.[44] His point is that what we know about the human self and personality simply does not allow for the possibility of a presocial individual; social institutions are not simply places where pre-existing individuals exercise their rights, they are actually constitutive of individuality. Sandel is a communitarian, restating the sort of objections to Kant outlined in chapter 3 above. Because individuals are constituted by community, Sandel rejects the notion that justice has primacy over the general good. Mill was correct to see rights as ultimately based on general utility. The role of community also makes it possible to argue that in certain circumstances the assumption of limited benevolence built into the circumstance of justice will not apply – whereas presocial individuals might not be prepared to make extensive sacrifices to gain the benefits of co-operation, individuals who know themselves to be members of a community with which they identify their own interests will not see things in these terms in the first place. The title of Sandel's book, with its stress on the *limits* of justice, makes his point; for Rawls justice is required because community is eliminated from the original position by assumption – but given the presence of community, justice becomes a limited virtue.

Sandel acknowledges that not all societies are communities; perhaps none are in the strong sense, in which 'community must be constitutive of the shared self understandings of the participants, and embodied in their institutional arrangements, not simply an attribute of certain of the participant's plans of life', but such a community is a worthwhile goal.[45] What Sandel is doing here is making explicit and comprehensible the non-self-interested notions of patriotism that somewhat puzzled Beitz when the latter attempted to understand why we might sometimes give priority to our fellow citizens. Although Sandel does not discuss international justice in *Liberalism and the Limits of Justice* it would seem to follow from his position that unless we can see the world as a whole as a community in the strong sense the possibilities of seeing international relations as based on anything much stronger than the procedural rules outlined by Rawls are limited. While Sandel resists the view that justice as opposed to the general good is the prime virtue of domestic society, his argument would seem to lead to the conclusion that at the international level this position would make more sense. This mix of a communitarian account of domestic society with a proceduralist account of international society seems to occur quite naturally. If communities are envisaged as having their own distinctive projects, it is reasonable to expect that the international arena will be a location of coexistence rather than co-operation.

Barry's critique of Rawls shares some features with Sandel – including opposition to deontological accounts of moral obligation – but is formed very differently, and leads to a radically different view on international justice.[46] His essential point is that Rawls' notion of 'justice as fairness' is simply the most recent and elaborate version of a long line of accounts of justice which stress that this virtue must be based in reciprocity, mutual advantage and enlightened self-interest. This basis is reflected in the 'circumstances of justice' adopted by Rawls from Hume.

For Barry there are a number of problems with 'justice as

reciprocity'. The basic point is that justice is most needed in circumstances where reciprocity and mutual advantage are most difficult to find. The idea that the powerless have no rights because they have no power follows from the idea of justice as reciprocity but is simply perverse. Conditions of extreme scarcity are precisely those in which the claims of justice should be heard, even though it is impossible to help the have-nots without hurting the haves. Barry acknowledges that justice as mutual advantage must be part of any theory of justice; his point is that it cannot be the whole. Rawls wishes to use the choice of participants in the original position as a legitimising device, but this simply raises other questions. Participants only get into the original position in the first place if they are already destined to be part of a society based on reciprocity and thus entitled to a share of the benefits of co-operation. Barry's point is that the exclusion of those who do not fit the bill is morally arbitrary – in much the same way as it can be morally arbitrary to distinguish between co-operators on the basis of factors such as birth or intelligence.

The implications of this for international justice are clearly considerable. Barry argues that the poor of the world are for the most part not engaged in a co-operative venture with the rich, and that it is clearly not to the advantage of the rich nations to assist the poor. Any view of justice as reciprocity or mutual advantage must exclude international distributive justice; in this respect Rawls was right to think in terms of two original positions, the second, for states, producing purely procedural justice, and Beitz was wrong to regard this as inconsistent with Rawls' general approach. However, Barry argues that this objection tells against Rawls' original approach rather than against international distributive justice. The greatest inequalities are international, international arrangements are those most in need of reflective justification – a theory of justice that excludes them is inadequate.

What would be adequate? Barry's substantive programme is as yet incomplete, but the main lines of his alternative (or rather supplementary) notion of justice – 'justice as impartiality' – can be discerned. Rawls produces a construction which throws a veil of ignorance over self-interested choice. Barry removes both features. Participants in the debate over justice are assumed to have interests, some of which clash, but to be motivated by the desire to reach an agreement on terms that nobody could reasonably reject – as part of the 'arsenal of persuasion', parties may employ veil-of-ignorance arguments, but these are neither of the essence nor compelling. The key question is 'What is reasonable?', not 'What principles would I agree to not knowing my own identity?' In this formulation, the assumption of a desire to reach agreement takes the place of an assumption of mutual advantage as the underlying premise upon which the construction is based. Barry's argument is that this assumption cannot be avoided. If individuals do not want to reach reasonable agreement it is impossible to persuade them to come round the table on the basis of notions of self-interest and reciprocity which, in key cases such as international justice, are simply false. The role of moral philosophy is not to systematise self-interest but to promote a willingness to submit to reasoned judgement – but it is political action rather than moral philosophy that will be crucial here.[47]

What kinds of principles would pass the test of impartiality with respect to international relations? Barry acknowledges that these might be different from those which governed domestic society – just as an individual might have obligations to family stronger than those to society – but would not see this 'priority' principle as justifying an 'anything goes' approach to international justice, any more than obligations to one's family legitimise murder or theft on their behalf.[48] However, the actual content of the principles of international justice are less clear. Barry's main account of this subject is yet to appear. In studies already published the idea of equal access to the world's resources plays a major role, and Barry envisages a large-scale transfer system to ensure that each country as a collectivity has a fair share of these resources. Such a transfer would be made via international taxation and to countries irrespective of their internal justice – although Barry would regard as legitimate international interventions designed to improve the internal justice of a society.[49]

These principles are close to those of Beitz, although the chain of reasoning that produces this result is different in the two cases. Beitz emphasises resources in the first part of his argument because he asserts this is what contractors under the veil of ignorance would choose. Barry's point is that whether they would choose it or not it would be 'reasonable' – even though it would clearly not be costless for many countries. Barry has the advantage of a greater realism than Beitz; his approach acknowledges that redistribution would hurt and the pain cannot be covered by rhetoric about this being simply a matter of distributing the gains of co-operation. As between the United States and Bangladesh, there can be no reciprocity – for the foreseeable future the relationship will be one-way. The United States should aid Bangladesh not because it is in the United States' interest to do so but because justice as impartiality suggests that the case for such aid cannot be reasonably denied.[50]

In summary, the great benefit of this approach to international justice is that it does not require dubious assumptions about rational self-interest. Instead, critics would no doubt argue, it requires a dubious assumption about the willingness of the 'haves' to be swayed by reasoned argument. There is a general point here about the whole notion of international justice which will be addressed in the next section, but as a criticism of Barry this point misses the mark. His position is not that the rich and powerful will always subject themselves to the dictates of reason, but that if they are not prepared to be swayed by a reasoned argument about the demands of impartiality there is little that moral philosophers can do about the matter. Arguments about mutual advantage may bring the rich and powerful part of the way but not to the point of dealing with hard cases such as the case of international redistribution. The aim must be the construction of political community locally, and, doubtlessly on a somewhat different basis, on a world scale. Normative ethics should contribute to this task of community building rather than to working through the implictions of self-interest – and thus, implicitly or explicitly, accepting the limits to the scope of justice.

This concern with community links Barry to Sandel's communitarianism, although they arrive at similar positions by a different chain of reasoning – and the constitutive theory of individuality espoused by Sandel would seem to be less conducive to the idea of international community than Barry's underlying notion of impartial reasoning. Like Sandel, Barry rejects the extreme cosmopolitanism of the Beitz of *Political Theory and International Relations*; he is willing to accord some kind of priority to fellow citizens, but without seeing this priority as interfering crucially with the requirements of justice *vis-à-vis* other countries. If international justice is to enter international relations theory as a way of conceptualising rich–poor relations, this seems to be, to date, the most promising point of entry. The next, and final, section of this chapter will review the argument so far and ask whether any real progress has been made.

CONCLUSION: HUMANITY, JUSTICE AND POWER

In the course of this chapter a number of themes have emerged, many of which were prefigured in chapters 5 and 6 and, indeed, part I of this work. These themes focus on such matters as the moral worth of state autonomy in circumstances where such autonomy may seem to prevent the relief of suffering, the relative claims on our sentiments of benevolence of fellow citizens as opposed to the world at large, the extent to which countries can be said to have rights to be treated in certain ways and whether such rights can extend beyond the purely procedural and so on.

None of these issues are new, but their application to the problem of internation inequality is novel, and the work of theorists of justice such as Rawls, Beitz and Barry has undoubtedly heightened the general level of sophistication with which contemporary international theory attempts to grasp the world, as indeed has the differently based work of Singer. It is, to put it mildly, surprising that the mainstream of international theory has been so little concerned with this body of work. It is now around twenty years since the problem of rich-poor relations first came to be defined as such, both by the political promoters of the New International Economic Order (NIEO) and by pioneering moral philosophers such as Rawls and Singer. In the course of those two decades the degree of philosophical progress has been quite impressive. Clearly, the major problems listed above have not been 'solved', whatever that would mean, but they have been clarified to the point at which it seems fair to say that disagreements now reflect not confusion but differences of values and priorities. It is still the case that there is no fully specified theory of international justice that would command even majority, let alone unanimous, consent, but the sort of problems with which such a theory would have to cope have been elucidated quite extensively and with a level of sophistication not present in the theory of international relations since the late eighteenth, early nineteenth centuries.

What does all this theoretical sophistication amount to? It is sobering to note that two decades of genuine philosophical progress have also been two decades of substantive political failure. The overall level of world poverty has fallen over the last two decades, but more because of technological changes such as the 'Green Revolution' and general growth in production than because of international transfers. Nearly twenty years after Singer was stimulated by the threat of famine in Bangladesh, only the site of the disaster - now more likely to be in Africa - has moved. Moreover, the intellectual and ideological framework of world politics has moved against the philosophical trend represented by the writers discussed in the last three sections. The rhetoric of interdependence of the 1970s has been replaced in the 1980s by an approach to politics in the rich world which has been systematically unsympathetic to collective efforts to relieve world poverty. The Brandt Reports of 1980 and 1983 now look to have been the last words from a collapsing international Keynesian social-democratic consensus: more characteristic of the last decade has been Reaganomics, whose main impact on the world economy was to create, or at least deepen, the problem of sovereign debt by increasing interest rates

in the United States. Whatever the merits of the proposal for an NIEO
– and there is much debate on this – politically, there can be no doubt
that this initiative has failed.[51] Possibly the 1990s may be a kinder,
gentler decade – to quote out of context President Bush's Inaugural
address – but the move to democratisation in eastern Europe and
elsewhere, although welcome both in its own terms and as something
that will contribute to economic growth in the long run, does not seem
likely to be accompanied by a revival of an agenda of aid and assistance
to the poorest areas of the world. If anything, concentration on the
problems of the newly free may take attention away from those who
continued to subsist in grinding poverty. In short, there has been over
the last two decades a situation in which the philosophical agenda and
the political agenda have moved in different directions – the former
towards an increasing recognition that the poor have rights as against
the rich, the latter towards a refusal to entertain the political implications of such a perspective.

One group of writers would find this unsurprising. Realists, including for the purpose of this discussion some 'Marxist–realists', would
see the events of the last two decades as nothing more than a reflection
of the power of the rich and the lack of power of the poor.[52] Poor
countries simply do not have the capacity to force structural change
against the interests of the rich. Some countries may, as a result of
windfall gains such as the oil-price rise of 1973, gain a degree of power
and wealth, but such changes do nothing to alter the basic structure of
world power; indeed, commodity-price rises tend to hurt other poor
countries more than the rich, the latter generally having the capacity
to adapt to change relatively painlessly. International inequality is
simply a fact about the world and, given the realist premise that states
will be unwilling to act against their interests, a fact that cannot be
changed; the Marxist variant of this argument would be that uneven
development is a built-in feature of the operation of the capitalist
mode of production and unavoidable so long as accumulation on a
world scale continues, that is until the revolutionary overthrow of the
capitalist class.[53] In these circumstances attempts to moralise rich–
poor relations are futile – indeed, may be harmful in so far as they
mislead the poor into thinking that some solution to their problems
can be found via an external mechanism. Again, the Marxist version of
this point would be that talk of international justice – like talk of
social justice domestically – simply promotes false consciousness,
acting as a smokescreen to cover the unwillingness of ruling classes to
envisage real change.[54]

It would be foolish to deny that there is an element of truth in these
charges. Those with power can indeed refuse to engage in just

relations with those without power. This is not a new thought; it is captured in Hume's 'circumstances of justice', where the requirement of relative equality precisely reflects the view that as between the powerful and the powerless no talk of justice needs to be compelling. It is also reflected in the shape of Plato's dialogues of justice. It is worth remembering that Thrasymachus, who puts forward the view that justice is simply the interest of the stronger, is not convinced by Socrates' attack on his position – in *The Republic* he simply leaves the dialogue which is pursued by those who want to take part in it, such as Glaucon with his early contractarian position. Socrates has no way of forcing Thrasymachus to participate any more than the powerful in the world today can be forced to justify their power. In this sense the realist position contains an element of truth and is particularly telling as a critique of those, relatively few, modern writers who argue that a consistent amoralism is impossible.[55] Clearly, those who have power can simply refuse to share it without involving themselves in any logical contradiction.

However, if the realist position be accepted, what normative consequences follow? What then must we do? Some writers in this vein seem content simply to cherish a position of power and to provide support for a refusal to consider the claims of justice.[56] It is difficult to see this as an admirable position. Others argue that the poor can best mitigate the effects of their weakness by lessening their links with the rich – a disengagement would, at least, have the merit of producing a space within which the poor could try to find their own solutions to their problems.[57] Although as a solution this would be strictly 'second-best' to a serious attempt to tackle world poverty as a global problem, it should not be lightly dismissed as an option. The best should not be allowed to be the enemy of the better.

There is less to be said in favour of the Marxist–realist position that invites poor countries to empower themselves to overthrow the capitalist system and regards such a revolutionary upheaval as the only solution to the problem of world poverty. Apart from the obvious point that the economic failures of eastern Europe and the former Soviet Union must cast considerable doubt upon the ability of any kind of planned economy to replace capitalist market relations as a route to a stable economic system capable of removing basic poverty, to invite the poor of the world to take power into their own hands is to misunderstand fatally the nature of the problem. Here, the domestic analogy misleads. The domestic politics of industrial capitalism were indeed conditioned by the fact that the potential power of the working class was not harnessed to the struggle against capitalism. The role of revolutionaries was, in the classic terminology, to develop a situation where the class 'in itself' became a class 'for itself'; that is to say, developed a consciousness of its common interests and potential power, overcoming those ideological constraints which led the working class to see its position as, in some sense, natural.[58]

The poor of the world today are not in an analogous position. Certainly, they are divided, and plagued with corrupt and malevolent leaders, but they are not, on the whole, in thrall to false consciousness. They are not poor because they are divided and badly led; they are badly led and divided because they are poor. Talk of 'justice' and 'morality' in nineteenth-century Britain may well have served the purpose of legitimising class rule, and Marx's well-established contempt for this form of discourse may have been justified. But in late-twentieth-century international society the idea that poor countries could have power were they but to exercise it is devoid of reality. The poorest have no realistic possibility of overthrowing the world economy and attempts to act as if they did are more likely to lead to self-inflicted wounds than to do real damage to the rich.

The poor cannot force the rich to grant them justice but they can try to exercise persuasion. Part of this will be a matter of developing situations of mutual advantage – even a critic of justice as reciprocity such as Barry would accept that reciprocity is always going to be a big part of any notion of justice, and the more poor countries are able to appeal to common concerns the better. But another aspect of persuasion involves an attempt to enlarge the sense of community to persuade the rich that they should identify with the fate of the poor, even if this identification is not as strong as the ties that hold together national communites. It is not necessary that community means the same thing at local, national and international level; one of the drawbacks of cosmopolitan theory is that it is uneasy with the idea that there can be different levels of communal fellow-feeling. So-called common-sense morality which suggests that we have primary obligations towards concentric circles of family, friends and fellow citizens is only damaging if it is used to suggest that we have no obligations to others, or that we may help our nearest and dearest by any means available. Those communitarian theories that assume the communities are a given are equally unhelpful when it comes to the attempt to enlarge the sense of community. It may be that individuals are constituted by their communities – and indeed, this notion of individualism seems more plausible than the presocial, free-floating morally autonomous figure of Kantian theory – but this constitutive function need not be exclusive and exclusionary. Individuals may be constituted in different degrees by different communal contexts, including the context of an international community.

What might the attempt to enlarge the sphere of reference of community involve? The most important feature of such an attempt would be the promotion of an international norm of impartiality. Poor countries demand the right to be treated in such a way that morally irrelevant differences between rich and poor do not count, on the principle that a norm to this effect could be extended to legitimate extensive transfers; the establishment of such a norm ought to be a primary goal of poor-country strategy. The key point here is that the promotion of such a norm may require the abandonment of some of the characteristic weapons of the poor – such as informal violence – and may involve a willingness to allow scrutiny of domestic affairs beyond what would normally be accepted. Corrupt elites who oppress their own people will not persuade the rich of the virtues of justice. Those who intervene will not promote successfully a norm of non-intervention. Those who wish to downplay the role of power in world affairs will not succeed if they use what little power they have in irresponsible ways.

All this could easily be twisted into an imperative to give the rich and powerful an easier time than they have already – were this possible – but this would be a distortion of the point, which is that condemnation of the frequent misuses of power by the rich will have no effect if accompanied by policies which suggest that the only moral difference between the powerful and the powerless is that, to adapt Ernest Hemingway, the powerful have more power. Those who would be dealt with justly must themselves be just; this is a necessary, although not, of course, sufficient condition for the emergence of a just world order.[59]

What obligations such a world might involve is a matter for a political dialogue rather than for theory, although certainly the theorists of justice and benevolence examined in this chapter will have provided some of the materials for this dialogue when, or if, it eventually does get under way. Whether it will take place is partly a matter of political will, partly a matter of political strategy, but also involves the somewhat wider issue of the nature of international relations in the future, in a world no longer dominated by European power, and, possibly, no longer dominated by the Western mind-set that has been sovereign for the last few centuries. This in turn raises a still wider issue, which is whether the sort of social theory examined in this book, which has dominated the mind of the West for longer than that, is not now in crisis. It is now time to re-examine the terms 'modern' and 'contemporary' which have been employed in a fairly unsophisticated way in this text. The next and final chapter will examine the international theory of, if not 'post-'modernity, at least 'late' modernity. This will involve an examination of critical international theory, post-structuralist approaches, and post modernist international theory – the explosive mix of new ideas which over the last decade have been taking international theory away not just from its conventional agenda but from the agenda of political philosophy discussed in this chapter.

NOTES

1. World Bank/Oxford University Press, New York, 1991. References in the text are to the tables between 204 and 269.
2. Cited from *The Independent*, 15 May 1990.
3. See ch. 2, pages 37–40, and ch. 3, pages 66–70.
4. It is difficult to find a point of comparison that enables generalisation on these matters. For an overview of economic history see, for example, A. K. Kenwood and A. L. Lougheed, *The Growth of the International Economy 1820–1980* (Allen and Unwin, London, 1983). Fernand Braudel – a historian prepared to generalise – speaks of a biological *ancien régime* with 'very high infant mortality, famine, chronic undernourishment and virulent epidemics', from which in the eighteenth century 'part of Europe, not even all Western Europe' began to break free. See *Capitalism and Material Life 1400–1800* (Fontana, London, 1973). Anyone tempted to place too early in the nineteenth century the improvement in living conditions that did come later might well examine Engels, *The Condition of the Working Class in England* (Grafton, London, 1969).
5. Accounts of the crimes of empire are legion – see, for example, W. Rodney, *How Europe Underdeveloped Africa* (Tanzania Publishing House, Dar es Salaam, 1971); D. Goulet, *The Cruel Choice* (Atheneum, London, 1973); A. G. Frank, *Capitalism and Underdevelopment in Latin America* (Penguin, Harmondsworth, 1971).
6. The definitive discussion of the balance sheet of empire occurs in the film *Monty Python's 'The Life of Brian'* (screenplay published Eyre Methuen, London, 1979). It is AD 33 (Saturday afternoon, about tea-time). Reg, Chairperson of the Peoples' Front of Judea, rhetorically but unwisely asks a party meeting what, in return for 'bleeding us white', the Romans have given us? A few minutes later he summarises the result of the discussion.

   > All right . . . All right . . . but apart from better sanitation and medicine and education and irrigation and public health and roads and a freshwater system and baths and public order . . . what *have* the Romans done for *us* . . . ?
   > XERXES: Brought Peace!
   > REG: What!? Oh . . . Peace, Yes . . . Shut up! (p. 20)

7. This point is similar to that which arises in utilitarian moral philosophy when the comparison of different end states is made problematic by the

fact that the identity of the persons involved will differ according to the policy choice made. See, for example, D. Parfit, *Reasons and Persons* (Clarendon, Oxford, 1984), ch. 16.

8. See Frank, *op. cit.*; I. Wallerstein, *The Modern World System*, vols I and II (Academic Press, New York, 1974 and 1980), and commentary in C. Brown, 'Development and dependency', in M. Light and A. J. R. Groom (eds) *International Relations: A handbook of current theory* (Frances Pinter, London, 1985).

9. J. Galtung, 'A structural theory of imperialism', *Journal of Peace Research*, vol. 13, no. 2 (1971).

10. A. Emmanuel, *Unequal Exchange* (New Left Books, London, 1982). See D. Evans, 'A critical assessment of some neo-Marxist trade theories', *Journal of Development Studies*, vol. 20, no. 2 (1984), for a critique of this position.

11. P. Evans, *Dependent Development* (Princeton University Press, Princeton, N.J., 1979). For a stringent critique of the whole dependency argument from a classical Marxist perspective see B. Warren, *Imperialsim: Pioneer of capitalism* (Verso, London, 1980).

12. *World Development Report*, *op. cit.*, table 1. Sadly, the civil war in Sri Lanka may cause this relationship to change.

13. Reports of the Independent Commission on International Development Issues (the 'Brandt Reports') *North – South: A programme for survival* (Pan, London, 1980) and *Common Crisis* (Pan, London, 1983).

14. *Psychology Today*, vol. 8 (1974).

15. See, for example, P. T. Bauer, *Equality, The Third World and Economic Delusion* (Weidenfeld and Nicholson, London, 1981); D. Lal, *The Poverty of 'Development Economics'* (Hobart Paperback No. 16; Institute of Economic Affairs, London, 1983); P. Mosley, *Overseas Aid* (Harvester Wheatsheaf, Hemel Hempstead, 1987); I. Little, *Economic Development* (Basic Books, New York, 1982); G. Hancock *Lords of Poverty* (Atlantic Monthly Press, New York, 1989).

16. Hancock, *op. cit.*, p. 183.

17. *Philosophy and Public Affairs*, vol. 1, no. 3 (1972). The argument is repeated in *Practical Ethics* (Cambridge University Press, Cambridge, 1979), and the original paper anthologised in C. R. Beitz et al. (eds) *International Ethics* (Princeton University Press, Princeton, N.J., 1985) – page references in the text are to this last source.

18. On these matters see ch. 4 above.

19. Famines can usually be avoided if the problem is identified early enough, and the best way to achieve this is a free press and a responsive, representative government. It is when local problems are kept quiet that disasters happen – the colonial record on these matters is better than some independent governments, but worse than others.

20. Allen and Unwin, London, 1986. This is a tightly argued text, and for non-philosophers the basic ideas may be more easily approached via O'Neill 'Hunger, needs, and rights', in S. Luper-Foy (ed.) *Problems of International Justice* (Westview Press, Boulder, Colo., 1988), pp. 67–83.

The same collection contains a critique of the argument by W. Aitken, 'World hunger, benevolence, and justice', pp. 84-96.

21. This is a very highly condensed account of the complex argument of ch. 8 of *Faces of Hunger*, and interested readers are urged to refer to the original.

22. Oxford University Press, Oxford, 1971. See also the later thoughts of 'Kantian constructivism in moral theory', *Journal of Philosophy*, vol. 27 (1980) pp. 515-72.

23. Princeton University Press, Princeton, N.J. 1979. Beitz's argument on international distributive justice occurs in part III of this work, which is effectively a reprint of 'Justice and international relations', *Philosophy and Public Affairs*, vol. 4, no. 4 (1975) – in turn reprinted in Beitz *et al.* (eds) *op. cit.*, while part III of *Political Theory* is extracted in Luper-Foy (ed.) *op. cit.* Beitz has revised his arguments, but not his conclusions, in 'Cosmopolitan ideals and national sentiment', *Journal of Philosophy*, vol. 80 (1983), pp. 591-600.

24. *A Theory of Justice*, p. 4.

25. *ibid.*, ch. III.

26. *idid.*, ch. II, section 15.

27. The final version of Rawls' two principles is in section 46 at p. 302. Equal liberty is discussed at length in ch. IV.

28. *ibid.*, p. 302. The difference principle is discussed at a great many points in the text.

29. See 'Kantian constructivism', *passim*.

30. *A Theory of Justice*, pp. 378ff., is the best source for these points, even though this section is allegedly devoted to the justification of conscientious refusal – at no point in the text does Rawls draw together all his ideas on international justice.

31. See chapter 2 of this book.

32. T. Nardin, *Law, Morality and the Relations of States* (Princeton University Press, Princeton, N.J. 1983).

33. *Political Theory* pp. 129ff.

34. *ibid.*, p. 141.

35. *ibid.*, p. 140.

36. See 'Cosmopolitan ideals', p. 595. Beitz is responding here to criticisms of B. Barry, 'Humanity and justice in global perspective', and D. Richards 'International distributive justice', both in J. Roland Pennock and J. W. Chapman (eds) *Nomos XXIL Ethics, Economics and the Law* (New York University Press, New York, 1982). It is interesting that although Beitz responds to these criticisms by adopting a different line of argument in support of his cosmopolitan conclusions, Thomas Pogge, in a recent study of Rawls which devotes much attention to global justice, still argues in favour of a global 'difference principle' arguing that international interaction is at a level that justifies such a criterion. See *Realising Rawls* (Cornell University Press, Ithaca, N.Y., 1989), especially part 3, 'Globalising the Rawlsian conception of justice'.

37. 'Cosmopolitan ideals', p. 595, from Rawls 'Kantian constructivism'.

38. *ibid.*, p. 599.
39. For some immediate reactions see N. Daniels (ed.) *Reading Rawls: Critical studies of 'A Theory of Justice'* (Blackwells, Oxford, 1975).
40. R. Nozick, *Anarchy State and Utopia* (Basic Books, New York, 1974); D. Gauthier, *Morals by Agreement* (Clarendon, Oxford, 1986); B. Ackerman, *Social Justice and the Liberal State* (Yale University Press, New Haven, Conn., 1980). Of these studies Ackerman contains most of interest on international justice. An interesting study of several of these writers is B. Barker, *The Conquest of Politics: Liberal philosophy in democratic times* (Princeton University Press, Princeton, N.J., 1988).
41. *A Theory of Justice*, p. 3.
42. See D. Hume, *A Treatise on Human Nature* (Penguin, Harmondsworth, 1969), book III, part II, section (ii), p. 536. 'Circumstances of justice' is a Rawlsian phrase not taken directly from Hume. The following discussion owes much to the work of Brian Barry, especially his 'Circumstances of justice and future generations', in R. Sikora and B. Barry (eds) *Obligations to Future Generations* (Temple University Press, Philadephia, 1978).
43. *A Theory of Justice*, section 22, pp. 126ff.
44. M. J. Sandel, *Liberalism and the Limits of Justice* (Cambridge University Press, Cambridge, 1982). See also 'The procedural republic and the unencumbered self', *Political Theory*, vol. 12, no. 1 (1984).
45. *Liberalism and the Limits of Justice*, p. 173. W. Kymlicka, in *Liberalism, Community and Culture* (Clarendon,Oxford, 1989), is critical of Sandel's view that the virtues of communities necessarily are in conflict with the premises of liberal social theory.
46. Brian Barry's first response to Rawls was *The Liberal Theory of Justice: A critical examination of the principal doctrines in 'A Theory of Justice' by John Rawls* (Clarendon, Oxford, 1973). Later papers of special interest on the subject of international justice include 'Humanity and justice in global perspective' (see note 37), 'Justice as reciprocity', in E. Kamenka and A. Ehr-Soon Tay (eds) *Justice* (Edward Arnold, London, 1979), and 'Can states be moral? International morality and the compliance problem', in A. Ellis (ed.) *Ethics and International Relations* (Manchester University Press, Manchester, 1986). These papers are collected in *Democracy, Power and Justice: Essays in political theory* (Clarendon, Oxford, 1989), and are referenced here to this latter source. Barry's current project is a three-volume *Treatise on Social Justice*, the first volume of which has been published as *Theories of Justice* (Harvester Wheatsheaf, Hemel Hempstead, 1989).
47. This position will be defended at length in the next volumes of *A Treatise on Social Justice*; the Conclusion to *Theories of Justice* gives a summary of the position.
48. 'Can states be moral?', p. 417.
49. 'Justice as reciprocity', P. 492.
50. *ibid.*, p. 483.
51. For some papers broadly sympathetic to the aims of NIEO see J. N.

Bhagwati and J. G. Ruggie (eds) *Power, Passion and Purpose* (MIT Press, Cambridge, Ma., 1984); for critics see Lal, *op. cit.*, Little, *op. cit.*, and Bauer, *op. cit. ii.*

52. See ch. 4, pp. 97–100 above, for the realist position.
53. See, for example, Frank, *op. cit.*, and Wallerstein, *op. cit. ii.*
54. See on these matters S. Lukes, *Marxism and Morality* (Oxford University Press, Oxford, 1985), and, with specific reference to international relations, C. Brown 'Marxism and international ethics', in T. Nardin (ed.) *Traditions of International Ethics* (Cambridge University Press, Cambridge, 1992).
55. Such as A. Gewirth, *Reason and Morality* (Chicago University Press, Chicago, 1978).
56. It would not be too uncharitable to read R. Tucker, *The Inequality of Nations* (Basic Books, New York, 1979), in this way.
57 See S. Krasner, *Structural Conflict: The Third World against global liberalism* (University of California Press, Berkeley, 1985).
58. The great twentieth-century theorist of 'Hegemony' – ideological domination of one class by another – is Gramsci; see *Selections from the Prison Notebooks of Antonio Gramsci*, ed. and trans. Q. Hoare and G. Nowell Smith (Lawrence and Wishart, London, 1971), esp. part II, section 2, 'State and civil society'.
59. There are, in fact, quite good reasons why internal justice is more difficult to achieve in poor countries; the fact that rich countries have the resources to ease the pains of justice makes their failure to achieve just societies more lamentable. But the point here is that those who must rely on a developing sense of justice if they are to achieve a satisfactory way of life simply have no choice other than to appeal to an impartiality that does not admit of double standards. No other approach will be persuasive.

Part III

New Challenges

Chapter 8

Critical and Postmodern International Relations Theory

INTRODUCTION

The last two chapters have traced the impact on international thought of the revival of normative ethics of the last quarter of a century through a study of some of the major figures who have contributed to this revival and, in particular, to the international dimension of modern moral philosophy. Revival here is a precise term. These figures – Nagel, Walzer, Nardin, Singer, Beitz, Rawls, Sandel and Barry – have quite explicitly returned to an older style of philosophising, eschewing the agenda of mid-century analytical philosophy and meta-ethics in favour of a return to normative theory. The aim has been to theorise in the old way about new problems, for example, international distributive justice or the morality of nuclear deterrence. In some cases new kinds of arguments have been employed – see, for example, Barry's use of rational-choice theory in his discussion of the problems of fair division in *Theories of Justice* – but for the most part the kinds of arguments deployed by, for example, Rawls or Singer, would have been perfectly comprehensible to their explicit models, Hume, Kant and Mill.

One way of characterising these writers is to point out that the work of each can be comfortably situated within the terms of a dialogue between the two major themes of Enlightenment and post-Enlightenment thought: the (Kantian and Benthamite) account of a presocial individual and an ahistorical rationality and morality, and the (Hegelian) historicist account of the emergence of self-conscious individuals and meaning-generating communities. These two themes were discussed in chapters 2 and 3 of this work in their international context as 'cosmopolitanism' and 'communitarianism'. They run through the thought of the last two hundred years and although many of the seminal thinkers of the modern age sit uneasily within either one of these positions, they are for the most part encompassed by the debate between them. Modern social theory works within a space cleared by these philosophies even if it does not directly employ the categories they developed.

Does the fact that the revival of normative international thought has taken place within this space constitute a problem? Obviously, there is no compelling reason why it should be problematic, and, clearly, the authors discussed above are for the most part content to situate themselves within these bounds. However, an ever-increasing body of thought is concerned by what it takes to be the confining, limiting nature of the space defined by the great theorists of modernity. Developing an insight of Max Weber, such thought sees the 'reason' which is central to this space as potentially or actually constituting an 'iron cage', which limits and channels thought into a narrow, confined space.[1] The return of normative ethics responded to a sense that there was something badly wrong with the way in which the positivist–empiricist social science of the 1950s formulated the issues and problems of the day. A key point is whether this insight has been developed in enough depth by the authors discussed in the previous two chapters. Perhaps the terms of the discourse which they revived, although richer by far than that to which this revival was a reaction, none the less constitutes an inadequate response to the problems of developing a viable postpositivist thought? In his collection *The Return of Grand Theory in the Human Sciences* Quentin Skinner includes John Rawls as one of his 'grand theorists', but some of the other subjects of this work – for example, Foucault, Derrida and Habermas – are offering a different kind of grand theory from Rawls, a kind that involves the wholesale restructuring of social and political theory – to adopt another book title – or, indeed, that challenges the received idea of theory altogether.[2]

Many and various are the positions which hold that there is something fundamentally suspect about the thought of modernity. Some genealogies can be discerned. French structuralist linguistics, in particular in the hands of Saussure, led to a more general structuralism (exemplified by, for example, Levi-Strauss, Piaget and Althusser) which produced the (very different) post-structuralist thought of, for example, Foucault, Derrida, Kristeva and, ultimately, in reaction to this, the postmodernism of Lyotard, Baudrillard and Virilio.[3] Classical Marxism via Lukacs, the rediscovery of Marx's Hegelian roots and the work of the Frankfurt School has produced the Critical Theory of Habermas and, indirectly, of the international relations theorists Cox and Linklater.[4] However, as well as these genealogies, more isolated pockets of postpositivist thought can be identified. Michael Oakeshott's critique of rationalism in politics, Richard Rorty's critique of epistemology, Alasdair MacIntyre's neo-Aristotelian critique of the Enlightenment project and Quentin Skinner's radical approach to the history of ideas are examples of work which, if not explicitly postmodernist – of these writers only Rorty would use the term as a self-description – none the less raises the sort of doubts about the 'iron cage' of reason characteristic of postpositivist thought.[5] And to these figures should be added consideration of the aesthetics of postmodernism – a subject of particular importance, perhaps, to architecture, but also to film, music and fiction.[6]

Writing about this work poses peculiar problems. These arise partly because the thinkers listed above are by no means saying the same sort of things, let alone the same thing. Even within the limited area of, say, French post-structuralism, it is clear that Derrida and Foucault are occupying radically different positions – a point frequently missed by both their critics and their adherents in the Anglo-Saxon world. However, there is a more fundamental problem than this which arises from the nature of the project which at least some of these writers have in common – and which is best expressed in negative terms. A common feature of this work is precisely a rejection of the idea that sentences which begin 'postmodernism [or post-structuralism or any variant here] is . . .' can be completed. What it means to say that something 'is' something else 'is' in question. The problem is clear even if the solution is not; because this kind of thought is attempting to bring to the surface the features of discourse which normally are allowed to remain unperceived, it cannot be represented by a linear narrative account. A characteristic technique of this kind of writing involves defamiliarisation – the attempt to turn the familiar into the unfamiliar and (and vice versa) – and such writing is annulled rather than explicated by a narrative that clarifies and familiarises. But, on the other hand, what possibility is there of putting together sentences which do not involve the verb 'to be' in one form or another? Perhaps Derrida is right and some things have to be written 'under erasure' – that is to say, crossed out (because they are inaccurate) but still visible under the deletion (because they are indispensable).[7] But again, as Richard Rorty remarks, Derrida may regard his notion of *différance* as having no clearly defined meaning, but any graduate student in literary studies aspiring to tenure had better have a definition of the term, come what may.[8]

A different approach route to these matters is needed. It may be that these writers can best be understood in the context of the different emphasis they place on their own variety of 'anti-foundationalism'. This requires elaboration. Consider the two great thinkers of modernity, Kant and Hegel – the team leaders of the cosmopolitans and communitarians; each believed, on different grounds, that human knowledge rested on some kind of firm foundation. For Kant, transcendental (universal and necessary) knowledge could be generated by critical reason; for Hegel knowledge comes out of the self-positing of spirit. Each rejects a simple empiricism but each believes that there are foundations for human knowledge – whether created by the human mind itself or by *Geist*. Now, modern members of the Kantian and Hegelian teams, whose work is examined in part II above, do not, on the whole, follow their team captains in this matter. Instead, they 'naturalise' Kant and Hegel; thus, Rawls sees his project as that of providing a theory of 'moral sentiments' rather than an anthropology, and modern communitarians such as Sandel and Walzer, in so far as they explicity employ Hegel, employ a 'demythologised' Hegelianism. Although they may not use this term, the writers discussed in the previous two chapters are 'anti-foundationalists'. They do not believe that firm grounds for human knowledge can be found – and modern understandings of scientific method make this conclusion difficult to avoid.

However, these thinkers are 'pale' anti-foundationalists; they are anti-foundationalists who do not believe that the absence of foundations is a matter of great moment, who believe that life can go on without foundations in much the same way as it did before; the parallel is with the Nietzschean idea of a 'pale' atheist who, while rejecting belief in God, thinks it possible to carry on living in much the same way as before. The writers discussed in this chapter share the important negative characteristic of *not* being pale anti-foundationalists. On the contrary, they experience the lack of foundations for human knowledge in many different ways but with a shared sense that something very important is involved here. Intellectual life cannot simply proceed in the old ways; something profound has happened to Western thought once it becomes clear that the foundations upon which it rests are, ultimately, radically insecure.

If pale anti-foundationalism is an inadequate response to this challenge, what then would be adequate? Here positions differ sharply. Some of the writers to be examined in the following sections seek to establish new foundations of knowledge, rescuing the Enlightenment project rather than undermining it. Others look to live and think without foundations but without developing new substantive ways of seeing the world, aiming for an effect of conscious 'paleness' – typified by Rorty's, perhaps playful, description of his position as that of a 'postmodern bourgeois liberal'.[9] Both of these categories are made up of writers who, in the last resort, can be seen as members of the Kantian or Hegelian teams, writers whose intention is to defend the most important components of Western thought – even if their defences would hardly have been recognised as such by the seminal thinkers of modernity. These thinkers, the subjects of the next two sections, fit without too much difficulty within the cosmopolitan/ communitarian antimony established in the earlier chapters of this text – even if, at times, the rhetorics they employ are unfamiliar.

Other responses to the challenges of late modernity are less easily domesticated. If figures such as Habermas and Rorty can be situated in the Kantian and Hegelian teams, figures such as Derrida and Foucault and their counterparts in international theory cannot be classified in this way. For them we need a third team, led by Captain Nietzsche – or perhaps (in the American fashion) by co-captains Nietzsche and Heidegger – whose aim is not that of finding new ways of constructing the old categories of thought but that of demolishing these old categories more thoroughly.[10] For this third team – who, it must be stressed, are in principle opposed to behaving like a team – the wrong turning that Western thought took did not occur at some point(s) in the last two centuries; the sense of the team meeting is, possibly, that the rot set in with Socrates and Plato, or possibly that there never was a wrong turn because there never was a right turn. In any event, their critique of modernity goes deep and is for this reason difficult to describe and criticise. The final sections of this chapter will return to this matter, after an examination of critical international thought and postmodern communitarianism.

CRITICAL THEORY AND INTERNATIONAL RELATIONS

Marxist thought has not played a major role in this book – a silence that, perhaps, needs to be justified in view of the general intellectual importance of Marxism over the last century. The explanation is simple. Classical Marxists had, on the whole, very little to say about international relations theory. As suggested in chapter 2, Marxist thought is, in priciple, cosmopolitan, resting as it does on the presumptive unity of the proletariat as the universal class whose eventual triumph will annihilate both domestic and international politics. However, the axiom that the real interests of different proletariats cannot diverge makes Marxism less than helpful for an understanding of situations where, to the untutored eye, it is blind-ingly obvious that they do. Moreover, the consequentialist ethics implied by Marxism's materialism – right action being action in accordance with the goal of socialist revolution, a goal predetermined by history – can easily lead to an approach to politics not readily distinguishable from political realism, with the same emphasis on power and interest, the same concern for the constellation of forces.[11] Neither the principles nor the practice of classical Marxism and Marxism–Leninism offer a great deal of interest to the normative international relations theorist, although those whose notion of theory is more positivist may well find Marxist political economy of value.

These comments certainly apply to Engels and the orthodox Marxism of the Second International, as well as to Lenin and Soviet Marxism. Whether they apply to Marx as well is a moot point; certainly, in the interwar years a school of thinkers, most notably based at the Institute of Social Research in Frankfurt, offered a very different account of Marxism, which they believed to be true to the spirit of Marx's work while being highly unorthodox from the perspective of the tradition.[12] The 'Frankfurt School' focussed on political sociology and psychology, culural theory and philosophy rather than political economy; they saw the working class as a non-revolutionary force, integrated into capitalism, and, in reaction to the rise of fascism, developed a position characterised by a deep cultural pessimism. A, probably *the*, key text of the two most important figures of the school – Theodor Adorno and Max Horkheimer's *Dialectic of Enlightenment* – amounts to a root-and-branch assault on the doctrine of progress and the supposedly liberating effects of science and rationality, culminating in an attack on advertising and the 'culture industry' which has made enlightenment a matter of mass deception.[13] What Marx would have made of this is a matter of opinion, but the force of the critique cannot be denied, and this remains one of the key texts of twentieth-century thought.

After 1933, the Institute went into exile – *Dialectic of Enlightenment* was written in 1944 in the United States – and although recreated after 1945, much of its force was dissipated by the experience. The most famous postwar Frankfurt alumnus has been Herbert Marcuse, whose *One Dimensional Man*, an assault on the culture of late capitalism and a plea for the recognition of the revolutionary potential of the groups outside of the proletariat – the *Lumpenproletariat*, blacks and, bizarrely, students – had considerable success in the 1960s.[14] However, the most important intellectual influence to come out of this school in the last quarter of a century has been the philosopher and social theorist Jürgen Habermas, whose critique of positivism and elaboration of the idea of Critical Theory has found many echoes in the Anglo-Saxon as well as German academy, including in departments of international relations.[15]

The key to understanding Habermas' difficult and complex notions is to realise that increasingly he has come to see himself as engaged in a war on two fronts. 'Early' and 'middle' Habermas developed Critical Theory in opposition to positivism and apolitical hermeneutics; 'late' Habermas defends the idea of Critical Theory against postmodernist writers who Habermas takes to be irrationalist and, implicitly, conservative. Habermasian Critical Theory has already had some impact as a substantive position from which a critical international theory can be developed, but in the longer run it may be that Habermas' engagement with postmodernism will prove to be of greater significance.

Positivism is the belief that there is only one kind of knowledge, of which the laws of natural science provide the model; positivist social scientists – including some Marxists – attempt to discern the laws which govern society; such laws are to be seen as operating in much the same way as the laws of physics. There is a long line of criticism of this position, based on the apparent ability of human beings to act so as to frustrate laws said to govern their behaviour. Human subjects, unlike chemical compounds, have the capacity to reflect upon their situation and act in accordance with this reflection. Human conduct can only be understood by interpreting human intentions; hermeneutics – the theory of interpretation – is devoted to this aim, but the same critique of positivist social science has emerged from other traditions – see, for example, Winch's Wittgensteinian *The Idea of a Social Science*.[16] The problem with hermeneutics is that while recognising the reflective nature of human beings, an advance over positivism, it seems to undermine the possibilities of control that science promises. We may want to do more than understand human conduct; we may want to change it. Habermas argues that the natural sciences and hermeneutics both offer valid knowledge, but only in particular contexts and incompletely; they need to be completed by the development of a third kind of knowledge, Critical Theory.

Habermas sees all knowledge as constituted by human interests which develop out of different aspects of human society. There are three 'knowledge-constitutive interests'.[17] The first emerges out of the interactions between society and its material environment which generate an interest in prediction and control, and this is met by the positivist, *empirical–analytical* sciences – which might include some of the social sciences. Societies are also places where human beings communicate with one another in ways which cannot be understood by the empirical–analytical sciences; this generates an interest in the understanding of meaning, met by the *historical–hermeneutic* sciences. So far, so familiar, but Habermas goes on to identify a third aspect of society as the site of power and domination. This generates an interest in freedom, emancipation from domination and the achievement of rational autonomy, an interest which is met by *Critical Theory*.

The idea that all knowledge is constituted by human interests is itself fruitful and liberating, and a number of international theorists have picked up on this notion as the justification for a Critical Theory of international relations. Robert Cox, for example, employs a distinction between 'problem-solving' theory, which takes the world as it is for granted, and 'critical theory', which is self-reflective and devoted to change.[18] This distinction is clearly influenced by Habermas, but makes of his three forms of knowledge merely two. Likewise, Linklater explicitly employs Habermas' notion of knowledge constituting interests in his account of critical international theory.[19] However, the substantive content of Cox's and Linklater's versions of critical international theory are disappointingly conventional – an uneasy mix of Leninist theories of imperialism and neo-Marxist dependency theory. Cox, certainly, is a fairly conventional Marxist (Marxist–Leninist even) and his historical-materialism while explicitly based on a rejection of positivist accounts of Marxism seems much closer to these sources than he is, perhaps, conscious of. While stressing the 'historicism' of Vico and Gramsci in contrast to positivism, he wishes also to include Lenin in his list of anti-positivist forerunners – a much more doubtful proposition.[20] Again, the title of Linklater's major study, *Beyond Realism and Marxism: Critical theory and international relations*, promises more than it delivers – the content of this interesting work is certainly beyond realism, but hardly beyond Marxism. On the contrary, the majority of sources for this study are Marxist of one variant or another.[21]

Habermas' own account of the substantive content of Critical Theory has been much less Marxist – if Marxist at all; his account of the 'legitimation crisis' faced by capitalist states in the final decades of this century – created by the failure of the advanced capitalist economies to provide the sustained growth needed to legitimise the increasingly pragmatic, technical polities which have emerged from out of the old class societies – may have been somewhat premature and pessimistic, but it certainly was not characterised by an overreverent attitude to Marxism.[22] In any event, much of the more recent work of Habermas has taken a different direction, towards developing a theory of truth. Such a theory is required if the idea of Critical Theory is to be rationally defensible. If Critical Theory is constituted by an interest in emancipation; does this mean that any theory that promotes emancipation is 'true'? Habermas sees emancipation as the achievement of rational autonomy of action, and the emphasis on rationality would seem to require that some kind of criterion of validity be appropriate to Critical Theory. But what kind? Truth cannot be 'correspondence to reality' in the case of emancipatory theory since current notions of 'reality' stand in the way of emancipation. Some different notion of truth is required.

This search for foundations results for Habermas in the development of a theory of truth based on rational consensus. What is true is what is agreed by consensus to be true, but Habermas insists that this cannot be simply *any* consensus – such a position would undermine the idea of truth altogether, leaving simply what Habermas would see as the irrationalism of discourses which do not make truth claims. Consensus must be rational consensus, which Habermas describes as the consensus that would be achieved purely on the basis of argument, with no extra-logical or extra-rational considerations being allowed to count; the context where this kind of rational argument would be possible he describes as an 'ideal speech situation'.[23]

The notion of an ideal speech situation bears some relationship to the Rawlsian 'original position', where the 'veil of ignorance' is designed precisely to filter out extraneous factors which might distort principles of justice the participants would choose in Rawls' equivalent of a search for rational consensus. The ideal speech situation is even closer to Barry's idea of impartial reasoning. The difference between Habermas, on the one side, and Rawls and Barry, on the other, is that Habermas believes that the notion of an ideal speech situation is not an artificial construct but something which is built into the nature of language itself. The use of language implies the objective existence of certain kinds of validity claims. Any sentence we utter involves a claim that what is said is meaningful, true, justified and sincere – even an intent to deceive would be meaningless if these validity claims were not normally implicit in speech.[24] Habermas' point is that unless the claim of truth could be validated, at least in principle, human speech would be meaningless. Human speech is not meaningless, therefore there must be the possibility of truth, but the only way truth could be established is via rational consensus in an ideal speech situation. Although it is probably impossible to achieve the conditions for completely free language use in an ideal speech situation, none the less this goal underlies all use of language. Moreover, the ideal speech situation is not simply a description of a context in which truth could be established. It is also a picture of a particular kind of society, one in which individuals would lead free, unconstrained lives, equal and totally open in their communications and relations with one another. Habermas believes that the fully emancipated human society which Critical Theory is designed to bring about is actually built into the very nature of human speech.

This position places Habermas firmly with the spaces of modernity created by Kant and Hegel – perhaps especially the former and certainly, Habermas should be seen as a 'cosmopolitan' thinker, someone who gives a universalist account of mankind. Just as for Kant all rational beings have the capacity to make synthetic *a priori* judgements, so for Habermas all language users by their use of language are testifying to the possibility of free, equal and open societies. Although Habermas believes there are features of Western Society which demonstrate that it has gone farther towards the rule of reason and rationality than other societies – the West has developed a higher level of cognitive adequacy – all societies, peoples and individuals are in the end engaged in the same project. Language use is universal, therefore the ideal speech situation is everywhere implicit in human communication.

These ideas are complex and the account given above barely scratches the surface of the argument. What is interesting in the context of the rest of this chapter is the way in which the nature of the opposition to this position has changed. Critical Theory was first elaborated in opposition to positivist notions of knowledge which either denied the relevance of human liberation, or, in the Marxist variant, saw liberation as a by-product of the working through of the laws of history. The Critical Theorist opposed this view with an account of liberated, equal and open humanity, acting rationally in accordance with a richer notion of truth than that available to the positivist. Things are rather different now, in two respects. In the first place, a great many thinkers, of apparently different political persuasions, are convinced that criteria of validity of the sort that Habermas wants are no longer either available or necessary. Whether it is a matter of Richard Rorty restating Dewean pragmatism (on which see the next section) or the postmodernist endorsement of Nietzsche's 'perspectivism' (on which see the next-but-one section), the main opposition to Habermas' notion of truth is no longer another, less sophisticated notion of truth, but the more subversive notion that truth is something we can – and must – do without in our thinking.

Equally subversive of Habermas' project are critiques of the ideal of a free, equal and open society, characterised by the rational autonomy of its members. The egalitarianism of this ideal has, of course, never been acceptable to the political right; more significant now is the critique of this vision of the good society from the left. Is the openness of the ideal speech society an attainable or desirable goal? The idea that human relations should be based on the assumption that complete transparency as between individuals is possible is expressed in *Capital* and elsewhere by Marx, but nowadays it is not only the political right who deny this ideal and insist upon the essential ambiguity of human relations, the inability of any person ever to understand fully another without the possibility of error. To believe in the possibility of complete transparency is to be committed to an elimination of difference, to deny that the Other could be accepted as Other. Habermas' equality looks like the equality of identity not of difference. And the absence of consensus in social theory, while it may reflect repression, may equally simply reflect the essential ambiguity, the inherent contestability of the theories we generate in the real world of political action. As against this pluralism, it could be argued that in the ideal speech situation 'we have the idealised speech of stoics frozen out of effective participation in public life'.[25]

The ideal speech situation is a restatement of the Enlightenment political ideal, and Habermas represents in an increasingly self-conscious way the values of Enlightenment – rationality and the sovereignty of the human subject. As his extended series of lectures on the subject, *The Philosophical Discourses of Modernity*, demonstrates, he regards the postmodern and post-structuralist critics of this position as inherently conservative and irrationalist, their critiques serving only to reinforce the status quo.[26] The substantive argument here will be referred to again below; for the moment it suffices to note that Habermasian Critical Theory is one of the most important resources available for those who both wish to defend the Enlightenment cosmopolitan ideal and wish to work within a more elaborate and ambitious notion of the role of theory than that provided by Rawls, Beitz, Barry and other more conventional theorists of justice. Whether this is a reasonable ambition is a moot point. As yet, within the field of the theory of international relations it is difficult to see that explicit applications of Critical Theory have significantly advanced the argument.

POSTMODERN COMMUNITARIANISM

Habermas attempts to reconstitute a firm foundation for human knowledge and human values, a guarantee that the Enlightenment project of rational autonomy can be fulfilled. Language use implies the ideal speech situation. A point of reference exists against which truth claims can be judged. In the language of French structuralism a 'transcendental signified' exists after all – discourse is not simply the interplay of signifiers. In terms of the philosophy of science, a neutral framework for enquiry can be constructed. More poetically, there is a still point in an ever-turning world. A foundation exists, knowledge can be grounded. Now, all of the writers to be examined in the rest of this chapter deny that Habermas succeeds in this attempt, or that he could succeed. Rather than looking to recreate foundations, these thinkers are, in different ways, seeking to think and live without foundations. The seriousness with which they take this task leads them out of the theoretical space cleared by Kant, Bentham and Hegel; they are postmodernists rather than modernists, critics rather than defenders of the Enlightenment project although not, necessarily, of Enlightenment politics.

Much of the work produced by these writers will seem strange to social scientists (and indeed, philosophers) whose roots are in the Anglo-American academic tradition. Notions such as the disappearance of the human subject, devices such as deconstruction, writing under erasure and the substitution of genealogy for history are difficult to relate without fatal distortions and it is not always easy to grasp the politics that emerge from these positions; none the less, these matters have to be approached because a substantial body of international relations theory written from one or other of these perspectives is now emerging and deserves to be taken very seriously indeed. Fortunately, there is a way into this material which will be less strange – though no less demanding – for those not steeped in continental philosophy. Richard Rorty is a postmodernist who stands apart from other postmodernists partly because his style of reasoning is non-continental, partly because the political implications of his postmodernism – his postmodern bourgeois liberalism – are much easier to assimilate to older models of politics than is generally the case. These factors make it possible to use his work to introduce some of the ideas of postmodernist (international) politics in a context relatively congenial to the Anglo-American reader.

Rorty sees himself as working within the tradition of American pragmatism as exemplified by William James and John Dewey. James, a Harvard philosopher and psychologist of great prominence in the last decades of the last century, famously defined truth as 'one species of good' and not a category distinct from good. 'The true is the name of whatever proves itself to be good in the way of belief' is the much quoted centre of pragmatist philosophy (less often quoted is the completion of the sentence 'and good, too, for definite assignable reasons').[27] In the twentieth century, John Dewey, a remarkably prolific and long-lived author, elaborated this position in books on epistemology, ethics and politics and was the dominant figure in American philosophy until after the Second World War. Alasdair MacIntyre refers to Dewey's pragmatism as one of the two seminal moral philosophies of the century (the other being that of Moore); in contrast to Moore, who emphasises the gap between 'is' and 'ought', Dewey virtually obliterates this distinction. MacIntyre summarises Dewey's position as follows:

> We only acquired whatever knowledge we have now because we had certain purposes, and the point of that knowledge is for us inseparable from our future purposes. All reason is practical reason. . . . To characterise something as good is to say that it will provide us with satisfaction in our purposes.[28]

MacIntyre also makes the point that Dewey's influence in Britain was less than in the United States precisely because of his refusal to attend explicitly to the issue of the *meaning* of moral predicates – his approach runs contrary to the interest in meta-ethics characteristic of analytical philosophy in the United Kingdom. From this latter perspective pragmatism seemed superficial and uninteresting. It is significant, for example, that in his study of *Pierce and Pragmatism*, W. B. Gallie goes out of his way to distinguish Pierce's notions from the 'anti-intellectual', 'suicidal' misunderstandings of these ideas popularised by James;[29] equally, Gallie suggests that the best work of Dewey stems from Pierce's ultimately foundationalist model of knowledge rather than from James' anti-foundationalism.

One of the interesting features of Rorty's work is that he defends James' (and Dewey's) anti-foundationalist pragmatism with arguments that are formed within the Anglo-American tradition of analytical philosophy. Rorty's major work, *Philosophy and the Mirror of Nature*, employs the rhetorical style of analytical philosophy to launch an all-out assault on 'correspondence' theories of truth and the idea that a neutral framework of enquiry can be constructed.[30] He argues that movements within analytical philosophy, when taken together rather than separately, lead to the inevitable conclusion that no foundations for knowledge can be constructed, and thus that James' much-criticised account of truth is the only one that makes sense.[31] His work is a 'deconstruction' of analytical philosophy; it turns analytical philosophy against itself, revealing the contradictions which are normally suppressed. What is in the end 'deconstructed', however, is more than simply analytical philosophy – Rorty believes that his work undermines the idea of a 'theory of knowledge' as this has been developed at least since Locke, and the idea of the 'mind' as a separate entity, traceable back at least to Descartes. The idea that our knowledge 'mirrors' nature goes very deep and it is this very notion that Rorty believes undermines itself.

The final chapters of *Philosophy and the Mirror of Nature* move from the critique of epistemology to an account of philosophy itself. Rorty contrasts mainstream 'systematic' philosophers who generalise on the basis of some successful line of enquiry, attempting to reshape all knowledge on its model, with 'edifying' philosophers who resemble each other only in so far as they exhibit distrust of these procedures.[32] The edifiers 'kept alive the historicist sense that this century's superstition was the last century's triumph of reason';[33] Their scepticism about philosophical progress is ultimately parasitic on the systematisers (without the work of the latter what would the edifiers be sceptical of?) but the voices of these sceptical, relativist figures is central to the contribution of philosophy to the 'conversation of mankind', an Oakeshottian trope endorsed by Rorty,[34]

These ideas encapsulate many of the themes of postmodernism; radical anti-foundationalism, an emphasis on rhetoric, the importance of dialogue/conversation, the absence of a knowable 'transcendental signified' and so on. Rorty places a remarkable range of thinkers under the same umbrella: Nietzsche's perspectivism is parallel to James' pragmatism; Dewey, the later Wittgenstein and the later Heidegger are taken to be 'edifying' with critiques of foundationalism that point in the same direction, and, in our day Rorty sees himself as offering insights which chime with those of Derrida and Foucault. In a later paper he refers to the difference between Dewey and Foucault as a matter of the 'spin' each puts on *identical* (my emphasis) views; Dewey spins off in the direction of hope, Foucault of despair.[35] It might seem that saying these thinkers were all in some sense saying the same thing is rather like arguing that all nineteenth-century composers before Schoenberg were writing the same music – not a view one would like to defend before the shade of Richard Wagner, even though these composers were indeed all using much the same basic musical resources. Although Rorty's tendency to equate very different thinkers may be misleading since it is often the 'spin' that is interesting, it is none the less a valuable counterbalance to those postmodernists whose work is based on a claim of complete originality.

Rorty's anti-foundationalism is undiluted, more radical in its import than that of one of his intellectual heroes, Thomas Kuhn, but his style of reasoning and his apparent ability to demonstrate that figures who look like opposites are in fact on the same side is rather reassuring and comforting. Similar adjectives could be used to describe Rorty's politics. His self-description – quoted above – as a postmodern bourgeois liberal is perhaps not to be taken too seriously; better is the term 'liberal ironist' from his later work, *Contingency, Irony and Solidarity*.[36] What does this mean? It may be useful to return at this point to *Dialectic of Enlightenment*, a text Rorty himself uses to make his point.[37] His reading of this work is that it demonstrates that the various elements of the Enlightenment project do not cohere. The foundations of the social institutions of the liberal Enlightenment rest on an account of rationality that can no longer be accepted. The rationality promoted by the Enlightenment undermines itself, reveals its own limits. Rorty accepts this diagnosis; the key question is what follows from the destruction of these foundations? For Horkheimer and Adorno it is a deep pessimism of the left, for Daniel Bell a pessimism of the right;[38] for Habermas it is a desire to find new foundations in the ideal speech situation and for most postmoderns it is a new politics altogether, a politics in which the institutions of the liberal state are denied their status as fora within which human liberation is possible and seen instead as forces which bear down upon human subjects. Rorty rejects all these options. Instead, he believes it is possible to support the social institutions of liberalism while rejecting the epistemological foundations upon which it has been assumed that these institutions rest.

A key term here is 'redescription'. What Rorty is arguing is that we do, indeed need to *redescribe* liberal institutions, we need to find new metaphors to replace those that the undermining of the Enlightenment world-view have left without force, but he argues that this process of redescription need not involve the sort of wholesale rejection of liberalism that most postmoderns suggest it must. Rorty's redescriptions will be 'ironic' – that is to say, aware of their contingent character, their ungrounded nature – and this contrasts with Habermas and other Critical Theorists, who are trying to find foundations for their 'liberalism' (Rorty's broad characterisation of the goals of Critical Theory); but Rorty's redescriptions will also be liberal, in contrast to the ironic formulations of, for example, Michael Foucault, who sees liberal institutions as standing in the way of the sort of ungrounded desire for autonomy which he promotes. Rorty sees this latter position – a longing for a self-creating autonomy shared by Nietzsche, and his followers Derrida and Foucault – as simply unattainable within *any* set of institutions, a desire that should be confined to the private sphere.[39] In the public sphere, the liberal desire to diminish suffering should be endorsed.

An important text for understanding Rorty's politics is his 'Method, social science and social hope', and a key sentence in this text runs as follows: 'There is no inferential connection between the disappearance of the transcendental subject – of "man" as something having a nature which society can repress or understand – and the disappearance of human solidarity.' The reason this is such an interesting sentence is because most writers, both those who accept and those who deny the disappearance of the transcendental subject, would say that there is such a connection. But in the text Rorty continues, 'Bourgeois liberalism seems to me the best example of this solidarity we have yet achieved', and this is, perhaps, even more controversial.[40] Rorty's communitarianism is extraordinarily eclectic in its roots. He endorses Michael Oakeshott's idea of a 'practice' as something that operates within a community, and adopts the Hegelian position that there is no frame of reference outside the community, no relevant notion of humanity, which would allow us to ask ourselves whether ours is a moral society.[41] The contrast between our private interests and the public interests of the community remains, but 'it is impossible to think that there is something that stands to my community as my community stands to me, some larger community called "humanity" which has an intrinsic nature'.[42] The human solidarity which Rorty proclaims is a solidarity based on human communities which embody liberal social institutions; in another revealing remark he comments that 'we should be more willing to celebrate bourgeois capitalist society as the best polity actualised so far, while regretting that it is irrelevant to most of the problems of most of the population of the planet.'[43]

Rorty's position is that when we realise that communities are human creations, not something given by nature but something made by our identification with them, that identification will be stronger. His is a naturalised, demythologised, liberal Hegelianism which he argues works better for being anti-foundationalist; most modern Hegelians are vulnerable to the charge of relativism and lack Hegel's own defence against this charge because they are unwilling to endorse his notion of self-positing spirit. Rorty simply refuses to take the charge of relativism seriously, arguing that it makes sense only on the assumption that some defensible non-relativist position could exist, an assumption that he believes to be wholly false. Of course, there is no non-relativist argument in favour of solidarity with one's community, there is no non-relativist argument in favour of *anything*. Our community is ours and that is that – although this does not mean that we cannot propose changes to the way in which our community handles its general arrangements.

In a review evocatively titled 'The mirror of America' William Connolly remarks that Rorty 'comforts and tranquilizes'.[44] Rorty's endorsement of Western science, technology, capitalist and bourgeois society is altogether too complacent. The assumption, for example, that capitalism is irrelevant to the problems of most inhabitants of the planet seems to act as a kind of political anaesthetic, simultaneously denying both the possibility that liberal society might have something to say to all mankind, and the, perhaps rather more plausible, possibility that capitalism has had something to do with creating at least some of the world's problems.

These criticisms hit the mark – particularly coming from a writer who comes closer to being a liberal ironist than most of Rorty's critics – but they do not affect Rorty's status as one of the most interesting communitarian thinkers writing today. Just as Habermas' Critical Theory can be seen as a version of post-Enlightenment cosmopolitanism which can be placed alongside the version of a more conventional theorist such as Beitz, so Rorty's communitarianism stands in relationship to thinkers such as Sandel or Walzer. Rorty is a figure who contributes to two different discourses: on the one hand, he is a central figure in modern communitarianism, defending his position from a radical anti-foundationalist philosophical stance; on the other hand, he is a key figure of postmodernism, but here a figure whose effect is to domesticate, to tame, the insights of postmodernism. This is an uneasy position brilliantly defended. As yet, there are no explicitly Rortian works on international relations but it can be predicted that if the trends towards postmodernist thought continue over the next decade Rorty's defence of human solidarity and community will come to be increasingly of importance to international theorists. However, it is some of the undomesticated variants of postmodernism, such as Foucaultian genealogy and Derridean deconstruction that have already inspired postmodernist international relations theory, and it is to these works we now turn.

INTERNATIONAL, INTERTEXTUAL

Rorty is a postmodernist to liberals, and a liberal to postmodernists.[45] His account of the postmodern is radical in implications, but presented in a reassuring and comfortable manner. Reading Rorty is not a disturbing experience. Reading the papers in the recent collections *International/Intertextual Relations: Postmodern readings of world politics* and *Speaking the Language of Exile, Dissidence in International Studies* is a different matter.[46] These readings are designed to disturb, to disorient, to resist incorporation by conventional scholarship. They call for a different kind of response from that given to most of the rest of the materials discussed in this book. The titles and subjects of these papers are in themselves challenging. International/intertextual? The sport/war intertext? Textual strategies of the military? The intertextual power of international intrigue? A deconstruction of Waltz's *Man, The State and War?*[47] A point is being made with these titles, which are designed to signal to the reader that something unusual is going on here. It is not simply that these texts are 'difficult'. In principle postmodernism is no more difficult to grasp than, say, Hegel's theory of the modern state, or Nash and Braithwaite's account of 'fair division' as outlined by Barry; the point is that postmodern writing requires a different *kind* of reading from these samples of modernist theory – a reading more akin to that which might be given to a work of 'literature' rather than a work of 'social science'; of course, part of the postmodernist project is to undermine oppositions of this kind.

One of the implications of this position is that postmodernist discourse is resistant to the sort of examination that modernist discourse invites. A brief summary of Rawls' theory of justice is, in principle, possible and valuable – although in practice rather difficult, as chapter 7 no doubt demonstrates – but a brief summary of Ashley's deconstruction of Waltz's text would be of little value, akin to the sort of account of Shakespeare that tells us simply that *King Lear* is about ingratitude (or, in the social science version, homelessness). Moreover, there are so many postmodernisms, each resistant to definition and summary, that to provide a background that would throw light on even the texts collected in the *International/Intertextual* reader – and this is only one collection, albeit the best – would require a book-length study.[48] The response to this problem of exposition adopted in the rest of this chapter will be as follows: first, an account will be given of the idea of 'textuality' and 'intertextuality'; one way or another textuality raises most of the metathemes of postmodern thought, such as the disappearnce of the subject/object distinction and the death of the author. The idea of the text opens up into a discussion of the reading of texts, with some brief and rather hostile comments on deconstruction. The next sections of the chapter will examine two of the more promising areas of postmodernist writing; the cultural and political economy of postmodernism, and, more important, postmodern accounts of the nature of human identity which, by challenging us to rethink our own natures outside the assumption of sovereign man built into Western thought, may offer a route into a post-Western and postpatriarchal (international) politics.

First, the text and intertextuality. Consider a three-part, common-sense model of knowledge consisting of the knowing subject, the object of knowledge and the words, sentences, laws, theories and so on produced by the former to account for or represent the latter. Thus, for example, Darwin's theory of evolution accounts for the origins of species. Now, this is a simple but powerful scientific theory, but there are a great many other kinds of sentences produced by subjects in response to objects, and it may be a mistake – at least initially – to divide off 'scientific' statements from other kinds of statements. We need a word which describes all the different possibilities here, and 'text' seems convenient; all sentences, laws, theories and so on are in some sense 'texts'; even if they are not written down in the way that common sense (an overworked but essential notion) usually expects them to be, they are attempts to make fixed statements representing the world. A reasonable revision of this three-part model would thus be that 'subjects produce texts representing objects'.

Now, at least since the eighteenth century, we have known that there is a problem here. Hume demonstrated the impossibility of knowing that a text represents its object, and Kant suggested that the order implied by the creation of texts is a feature of the human mind not the unknowable 'thing-in-itself'.[49] Studies such as the philosophy of science have been designed to find ways of getting round these problems. As we saw in the last section one response – the pragmatic and neo-pragmatic approach exemplified by James and Rorty – is to abandon the idea of representation and correspondence theories of truth. To say that a text truthfully represents an object is to say no more than that it is a useful way of approaching the object.

Another and different approach to these problems of knowledge, influential especially in France, is 'structuralism', which emerged out of structural linguistics.[50] The basic idea of structural linguistics is that languages operate as relations of difference. The word 'cat' has no necessary relation to a small furry quadruped; any set of sounds could be used as a signifier here. Instead of thinking of the signifier 'cat' as representing a signified it is better to think of its meaning as emerging from its relationship to other signifiers in the structure of a language. Thus the point about 'cat' is not that it is *the same as* a furry quadruped, but that it is *different from* 'car' or 'cot' or 'bat'. Meaning emerges not from the relationship between a signifier and signified, but *in the relationship between signifiers*. This is only one account of language – and a controversial account at that – but is has become the basis for structuralist accounts of literature and society, and out of these accounts post-structuralism emerged.

Just as the relationship between signifiers is taken to replace the relationship between signifier and signified, so, on a broader canvas, the relationship between texts – intertextuality – replaces the common-sense notion that texts are produced by subjects and represent objects. The object of knowledge – the 'transcendental signified' – disappears from view; this is not a particularly unusual position but what is more startling is that the knowing subject also disappears. If a text is to be understood in relation to other texts, then the figure of the supposed 'author' of the text becomes redundant. The (in)famous slogan 'There is nothing outside the text' is not simply a reference to the disappearance of the transcendentally signified, but also a rejection of the idea that texts have creators or authors.[51] Intertextuality has deep implications not simply for how we understand texts but for how we understand ourselves as human beings; it leads naturally to rhetorics which refer to the end of 'man'; thus 'As the archaeology of our thought easily shows, man is an invention of recent date. And perhaps one nearing its end', and from the same work in a lasting image, we can envisage man erased 'like a face drawn in the sand at the edge of the sea'.[52]

This is only one possible implication of intertextuality, but before following up just a few post-structuralist and postmodern writings, it may be useful here to address one of the two most common critiques of this work, which is that it is essentially irrationlist. The supposed death of the author is a good way into this problem since it seems that here we have a position which is, on the face of it, nonsense, and self-evidently so. What can it mean to say that a text has no author? Surely 'I' wrote this sentence at 12.40 p.m. on 18 June 1990, on a Canon Typestar 7 electronic typewriter and am rewriting it a year later with a ballpoint pen; moreover, this is a sentence which is *about* something, viz the postmodern notion that texts are not produced by knowing subjects and have no objects? How can this apparent contradiction be, if not overcome, at least coped with?

There are several ways in which one can make sense of the idea of the death of the author. In the first place, it is clear that there is a conventional sense in which every text is dependent directly on other texts. Nothing can come of nothing, and even the most 'creative' of writers cannot create a whole vocabulary or a new syntax. As Wittgenstein insists, there is no such thing as a private language.[53] This particular text is the product of other texts, unavoidably so. Now, this in itself does not eliminate the author; after all, it is, apparently, my work as an author that produced the selection of texts presented here as a new text. A second point is needed here, which concerns the role of the author in conventional discourse, and in particular the privileged status which the author is usually granted as interpreter of the text. Normally, the author is seen as having a degree of control over the meaning of the text he or she has produced. One sense in which the author has disappeared is that this control can clearly be seen to be ineffective. I have no control over what people make of these sentences. I know that some will read them in one way, some in another, some as 'for' some as 'against' the position they are attempting to characterise. I have no *authority* over these readings. I may (mildy) express a view about a particular interpretation but I cannot control it or prevent it.

Both these points are fairly obvious and trivial; there is a third sense in which the author disappears, which is rather more fundamental. The points made above assume that I as author know what I mean to say in a particular text, even if I cannot find ways of saying it that are genuinely my own, and even if I am unable to make my self-knowledge compelling to others. A more fundamental sense in which the author disappears occurs when this self-knowledge cannot be assumed, and one of the effects of a number of writers over the last century, including modernists such as Freud as well as proto-postmoderns such as Nietzsche, has been to undermine the confidence with which anyone can assess their own motives and meanings. However much I may think I know what I meant to write when I wrote the above sentences a few minutes ago, I cannot be sure either of being able to recapture the context of what I thought at the time or of knowing that what I took to be my meaning was in fact what I meant.[54] It is here, I think, that the idea of the death of the author, the disappearance of the knowing subject, begins to make some kind of sense. The common-sense position that someone is writing these lines need not be denied, but the model of what a 'someone' is is changing radically. The idea of 'man' as a sovereign being, in control of self and self-expression, of thought and the products of thought, is what is alleged to be disappearing. Intertextuality is one way of expressing the erasure of this account of what it is to be human; and since the picture of man as a rational sovereign being is so deeply embedded in what is usually termed 'modernity', the idea of the postmodern as one characterisation of intertextuality makes sense.

None of this, of course, amounts to more than a sketch of an argument; no-one not already receptive will find this position remotely convincing without the sort of back-up that a book of this scale cannot provide. However, perhaps it will be accepted for the sake of argument that the idea of intertextuality is intelligible, that the notion that texts can only be read by reference to other texts is not obviously nonsensical. If this be accepted, what follows? What kind of international thought might be stimulated by this position? Clearly, there is not one answer to this question, but some lines for development can be identified. The dethronement of the Western notion of humans as the sovereign creators of texts clearly has implications which need to be investigated. The breaking of the link between subject and object opens a space for new meanings of time and space which could have major implications for international theory. These points will be addressed below; for the moment a more literal account of the text and the intertext deserves examination. When Der Derian writes of the 'intertextual power of international intrigue', what can this mean? Likewise, how are we to understand the idea of a 'deconstruction' of Waltz's *Man, the State and War?* Combining these questions, we might ask 'How do we read which texts?'

Which texts? The key point here is that the texts which we need to understand can no longer be regarded as predetermined by the subject matter of their discourse. Such a predetermination would imply precisely that linkage between the knowing subject and the object of knowledge which the root idea of intertextuality denies. If we think of the intertext as a chain of texts, then the principle upon which the chain is constructed cannot be determined in advance by considerations of genre or apparent appropriateness. The idea, for example, that diplomacy as an activity is to be understood in terms of a given account of what it is to be a diplomat – an account constructed upon a series of authorative texts – is precisely what Der Derian's path-breaking study, *On Diplomacy: A genealogy of Western estrangement,* works to undermine; the mytho-diplomatic role of angels in the biblical texts generally escapes the attention of those whose studies of diplomacy are self-limited by the availability of the 'appropriate' texts contained in state archives, the memoirs of diplomats and so on.[55] The same author's account of espionage and terrorism in the *International/Intertextual* reader again draws upon the resources of spy fiction as well as the more generally accepted (and, in this case, quite limited) official sources.[56]

A key question immediately arises: if the chain of texts is not predetermined, does this mean that any text can be read in the light of any other text or set of texts? Are there limits here, and if so, how can they be justified? Der Derian in his account of the intrigue intertext makes a point of stressing that spy stories draw on contemporary spy scandals and, conversely, that actual spies seem to read a lot of spy fiction – and, indeed, political candidates employ popular fiction to legitimate their defence policies.[57] This makes for an entertaining and instructive text, but it does seem to subvert the idea of intertextuality by re-introducing the notion of the 'transcendental signified' – that is, the 'real world' of terror and espionage that the fictional texts that Der Derian discusses are believed to illuminate. If these fictional texts are interesting because they tell us something about the 'real world', then it is good that we should have our attention drawn to them; what is not clear is why we should abandon such modern procedures as the identification of 'influence' or 'contributing factors' in favour of the postmodern language of intertextuality. It is possible, of course, that without this language we would not have noticed the connection, but postmodernism claims more than this sort of heuristic role for its constructions. Stress on intertextuality leads to the making of connections that might not otherwise have been made, but it seems to be unavoidably the case that the context that makes a particular intertextual reading a contribution to international relations theory has to be established by reference to criteria that are not internal to the intertext.

The problems here outlined recur when it comes to the reading of a particular text. Deconstruction is/is not a way of reading a text, which emerges from the work of Derrida and is employed by Ashley in the *International/Intertextual* collection in his reading of *Man, the State and War*.[58] Impossible to summarise, even in a book of impossible summaries, Derrida's deconstructions involve a reading of a text in which it is shown that the author fails to produce the logical, rational construction of thought that was intended.[59] Texts collapse under their own weight once it is demonstrated that the 'truth' they attempt to convey is no more than the 'mobile army of metaphors' identified by Nietzsche, the oppositions they contain work in ways contrary to intention and so on. In the case of Waltz, Ashley attempts in the course of a long and complex argument to show that *Man, the State and War* is not a 'monological' text, whose meaning Waltz is able to control, but a polysemic intertext at one time privileging 'man' as the sovereign provider of order, at another time reversing itself and assigning to 'war' the role of defining and constituting humankind.

It is quite impossible here even to give a brief account of Ashley's argument, let alone an evaluation of his reading of Waltz – to do this it would be necessary to retrace the steps of the argument, producing a map on the scale of one to one and a deconstruction of the deconstruction which would be longer that the (rather long) original. However, it is possible to ask what status is to be attached to this reading. It seems clear that Ashley cannot possibly claim that his is the 'true' reading of *Man, the State and War*; having denied to the author of this text sovereignty over its interpretation, he cannot claim this for himself. Going to the other extreme, is any interpretation as good as any other? Some of the more imaginative of Derrida's American literary-critical disciples seem to want to claim that the freeplay of interpretation should not be constrained, but presumably Ashley would resist the notion that Waltz's text could be about whatever we want it to be about. The final pages of Ashley's text defend the asking of irresponsible questions, the pursuit of lines of enquiry which do not seem to meet the needs of people in a dangerous world, but this justifiable resistance to the acceptance of a predetermined agenda need not imply a total free-for-all. Presumably Ashley, while not claiming that his account of Waltz is 'true', would want to argue that it is in some sense a 'better' account of the text than others currently available, just as Der

Derian would want to argue that his account of spy fiction in some sense illuminates the 'real world' of international espionage. The problem each author has is in reconciling this (implicit) claim of relevance to an account of the world which seems to deny the possibility of making such claims.

Ashley's own account of what he is doing – which, of course, from his perspective has no particular status but which is, none the less quite interesting – denies any intent to produce a post-structuralist theory of international relations. The role of post-structuralist readings is to bring to the surface the contradictions to be found within non-poststructuralist theory, from a perspective which is neither within nor without the regime of modernity – hence the 'borderlines' in Ashley's title. This self-denying ordinance with respect to theory is indeed mandated by the approach to intertextuality adopted by Ashley which draws most heavily on Derrida, but there are other branches of post-structuralism – not to mention the wider field of postmodernism – which are less restrained. Ashley's account of himself as a post-structuralist begs the more important question of what kind of post-structuralist he is; certainly, Michael Foucault's work could be described as post-structuralist, but leads in very different directions from that of Derrida; indeed, it leads precisely towards the production of post-structuralist social theory, even if this is not a term used by Foucault.[60]

If one of the two most frequent charges laid against postmodernism is irrationalism, the other is conservatism. Habermas, in *The Philosphical Discourses of Modernity*, refers to the 'young conservatives' of postmodernism, and other critics, such as Charles Taylor, have developed similar points.[61] Derrida's notion of deconstruction is particulary vulnerable to the criticism that, by refusing any task more positive than that of undermining existing theory, it effectively leaves the world as it is. It is difficult to see what effect Ashley's deconstruction of Waltz will have, could have or even is supposed to have on the dominance of realist thought in much contemporary theoretical discourse on international relations. The unwillingness to think in terms of alternative theories in effect leaves the situation where it was before Ashley wrote. However, to reiterate, a great deal of postmodernist thought does not turn away from theory and does not merit the description conservative; some postmodern (even post-structuralist) theory is just that, theory – an attempt not simply to undermine the modern but also to develop a positive sense of the postmodern. This is the subject of the next sections of this chapter.

POSTMODERNISM, CULTURE AND POLITICAL ECONOMY

For much of the last section an identification of postmodernism and post-structuralism was permitted - partly for purposes of exposition, partly because at least some of the authors under consideration appear to use the terms synonymously. This is, however, misleading. Post-structuralism was a particular phase in (French) intellectual life, a response, unsurprisingly, to (French) structuralism. Authors such as Derrida, Kristeva, the later Barthes and the earlier Foucault developed post-structuralist themes in response to structuralists such as Saussure, Lacan and the early Barthes - in the process moving away from abstraction and formalism and returning to the text while hanging on to some characteristic structuralist themes such as the death of the author. It is these post-structuralists, in particular Barthes and Derrida, whom Ashley follows in the work discussed above. However, the post-structuralist position is only one variant of postmodernism. Even in France a number of thinkers such as Lyotard, Baudrillard and Virilio have moved beyond the structuralist/post-structuralist moment, and in any event it would be a mistake to think of postmodernism as something intrinsically French.[62] There is a clear sense in which, since Descartes, 'modernism' has been so firmly entrenched in French thought that it is unsurprising that some of the most dramatic rejections of this position have also been French, but this should not mislead us into disregarding some of the less flamboyant thinkers of the non-French world who are equally sceptical of the great totalising narratives of modernity and of the politics of representation. One such, Richard Rorty, has been discussed above specifically as a postmodernist, but two other figures who have appeared elsewhere in this text could equally be so identified - Michael Oakeshott and Quentin Skinner. Postmodernism may be a strange tag to hang on these pillars of Western scholarship, but only because we have come to associate the idea of the postmodern with a particular intellectual style.

The *Modern-Day Dictionary of Received Ideas* helpfully tells us of postmodernism: 'This word has no meaning. Use it as often as possible.'[63] In fact, the commonest usages of the word have probably been aesthetic - as in postmodern architecture, or postmodern cinema - and one of the most interesting features of postmodernism (generally and for the international theorist) is the link between postmodernist political economy, aesthetics and philosophy. There is now a growing literature linking these themes; this section will examine some of this material, focussing on writers such as Harvey and Jameson - who, in the end, must be seen as sympathetic critics of the postmodern - while, briefly, bringing into the argument some more anarchic voices.

In 1984 Frederic Jameson produced an influential paper in the *New Left Review* entitled 'Postmodernism, or the cultural logic of late capitalism', recently forming the lead chapter in a book of the same title.[64] More recently, the urbanist and social scientist David Harvey published *The Condition of Postmodernity: An enquiry into the origins of Cultural Change.*[65] These titles have been quoted in full to make the point that what these authors are responding to is a sense that 'something has happened' recently to the ways in which we understand the world and that this 'something' is not simply(?) a matter of the loss of the transcendentally signified (although movement in the realm of philosophy may be part of the 'something'). What is at stake is culture in the wide sense. Harvey's summary of this argument makes the point succinctly and with (extraordinary) precision. 'There has been', he suggests, 'a sea-change in cultural as well as in political–economic practices since around 1972. This sea-change is bound up with the emergence of new dominant ways in which we experience space and time.'[66] Following Charles Jencks, the architect and critic, he offers even more precision; at 3.32 p.m. on 15 July 1972 the passage to the postmodern took place with the destruction of a prize-winning modernist housing development in St Louis, blown up as an uninhabitable environment.[67] In the same year the title of a work of architectural criticism gives a clue to the nature of the coming postmodern aesthetic; *Learning from Las Vegas* points to an aesthetic populism, an enjoyment of the vernacular, the reproducible, the disposable.[68] The collapse of the grand 'metanarratives' of human liberation is mirrored in the destruction of the aesthetic edifices which gave cultural form to these metanarratives. As Jameson puts it, 'pastiche eclipses parody'; both parody and pastiche eclectically draw on historical materials, mimicry and simulation, but parody intends to lead back to a modernist narrative while pastiche is a 'neutral practice of such mimicry, without any of parody's ulterior motives, . . . devoid . . . of any conviction that alongside the abnormal tongue you have momentarily borrowed, some healthy linguistic normality still exists'.[69] Pastiche is exemplified by Stravinsky's neo-classical concertos, parody by Mahler's use of *Ländler* and military marches in his symphonies.

Reproducing from Hassan a table reproduced here as an appendix to this chapter (a suitably postmodernist sequence), Harvey suggests that the movement from modern to postmodern is an incredibly complex and wide-ranging process, involving some of the shifts discussed in the last section of this chapter (from signified to signifier, from lisible/readerly to scriptible/writerly), but others less easily related to post-structuralism (God the Father to the Holy Ghost, purpose to play). Not directly confronted in this schema is an issue that both Harvey and Jameson take to be critical, the ways in which we understand space and time. Modernity privileges time over space; while both are taken to be unalterable forces of nature, it is in time that development takes place while the spatial order for this temporal development is taken for granted. Postmodern geographies sometimes reverse this privileging – but more to the point is that both time and space need to be understood in different ways in the postmodèrn world. Electronic systems that allow instantaneous transmission of information and money annihilate both space and time. Electronic news-gathering techniques combined with communication satellites and inexpensive video and sound recorders allow a degree of access to events anywhere, anytime that is unprecedented – with political consequences that are, in the long run, still to be determined.

The geostrategic implications of these new understandings of time and space have yet to be worked through. Foucault, in an interview in 1976, spoke of linking the geographer's interest in time and space to his own investigations of power/knowledge to create a new geopolitics which would involve a study of the army as a matrix of organisation and knowledge, and the study of 'the history of the fortress, the "campaign", the "movement", the colony, the territory'.[70] Foucault himself never brought this to fruition. Soja's examinations of Los Angeles' attempt to introduce fortress themes, building on the fact that Los Angeles sprawls within a sixty-mile circle that touches on its circumference a series of military bases, but without ever making of this more than a coincidence.[71] Paul Virilio, in *Speed and Politics* and in conversation with Sylvere Lotringer in *Pure War*, writes of the centrality of logistics and war systems based on the new meanings of time and space, but again without producing a convincing account of what this might mean.[72] Der Derian's forthcoming work on *Antidiplomacy: Speed, spies and terror in international relations* may answer some of these questions, although his paper 'The (s)pace of international relations: simulation, survelliance and speed', does not give much of a hint as to where the significance of these phenomena for international studies might be.[73]

Another key term of postmodernism, intimately connected to new understandings of time and space, is 'simulation' and 'simulacra'. A major source here is Jean Baudrillard, whose *Simulacra and Simulation* and later *America* give an account of a culture devoid of reality, composed entirely of models which are models of nothing other than themselves – tracing a movement from a real economy of commodities via the sort of unreal economy stigmatised by the Frankfurt School as the product of advertising, to a 'hyperreal' world of self-referential signs.[74] It is difficult to take Baudrillard's *America* seriously; however, the implications for a culture of a technology that is capable of creating exact replicas of virtually anything have not been thought through, save perhaps in the realm of art. Ridley Scott's postmodernism film *Bladerunner* is, as Harvey suggests, as good a way of raising these themes as any other. The spirit of simulacra is well caught by a recent proposal to protect the English prehistoric site at Stonehenge from the physical and spiritual degradation created by the apparatus of modern tourism by creating an exact replica – made of plastic, to be known as Foamhenge – a few miles away, around which souvenir shops, druids and daytrippers can congregate.[75] The fact that it is not clear whether this is supposed to be a joke is also in keeping with the postmodern condition.[76]

These few paragraphs have attempted to give some kind of substance to the view that 'something has happened' to signal a shift from the modern to the postmodern. Obviously, one can only skate over the surface here but it does seem that something of substance has happened. The next question may or may not be 'Why has this happened?' May or may not be, because this question implies a return to notions of cause and effect that are irredeemably modernist in their thrust. One of the features of writers such as Virilio and Baudrillard is their refusal to place their insights within a framework of cause and effect. More generally, to single out one feature of a cluster of phenomena and describe this as a cause of its companions is to recreate a narrative of the sort that postmodernism in principle denies can exist. However, Harvey certainly, and less clearly Jameson, in the end does trace back postmodernism to a 'cause'. Harvey looks to changes in the mode of production, away from what he calls the Fordist model of factory-based assembly-line production towards the 'flexible accumulation' he identifies as the political economy of postmodernism:

> It [flexible accumulation] rests on flexibility with respect to labour processes, labour markets, products, and patterns of consumption. It is characterised by the emergence of entirely new sectors of production, new ways of providing financial services, new markets, and, above all, greatly intensified rates of commercial, technological and organisational innovation.[77]

Harvey sees the politics and culture of postmodernism as a reflection of this flexibility – albeit not in a simple way, and without the processes of causation being entirely one way, since part of the attraction of the notion of flexible accumulation is that it reflects and reinforces as well as creates the cultural changes of postmodernism.

Harvey would also wish to argue that although the shift from

Fordism to flexible accumulation is quite fundamental, it does not represent a move away from the underlying logic of capitalist and, more generally, industrial society. Jameson's combination of postmodernity with 'late' capitalism makes the same point. Both writers in the end remain within a historical materialism that, however unorthodox, is to be contrasted with the rejection of Marxism by, say Baudrillard, who regards an emphasis on production and materialism as a source of error, common to Marxism and the bourgeois theories it proposes to replace.[78] Perhaps the term 'late modernity' rather than 'postmodernity' would be more appropriate for Harvey; certainly, his work involves a return to 'metanarrative' in Lyotard's sense of the term, even if this metanarrative is about the way in which metanarratives no longer correspond to the material conditions of production.[79]

For many, Harvey's late modernism will be more congenial than the postmodernism of a Virilio or a Baudrillard, easier to relate to stories with which they are familiar. This, of course, is a rather bad reason for accrediting this position. However, from the perspective of a postmodern international theory a late modern reading of the postmodern may be extremely useful. Certainly, Harvey does attempt to offer something that Ashley does not, namely a positive postmodern social theory, even if the price is the re-institution of some element of metanarrative. Many would see this as a reasonable trade-off. However, a late modern reading of the postmodern is not the only alternative to Ashley's negativism, and at least some writers have attempted to produce a theory that is not simply negative but which does not re-introduce the narratives of modernity; to this we now turn.

INTERNATIONAL RELATIONS THEORY AND THE END OF WESTERN MAN

One of the most consistent themes of postmodern writing works to undermine the picture of Western man as the sovereign master of the universe, the source of rationality and identity, the standard against which everything else is judged. This theme may occur in deconstruction and lead nowhere, but other texts exist which work to produce new notions of identity and difference without giving up the ambition of creating theory. The implications of this work for international relations theory are direct and of great moment – nothing less than the possibility of transcending the Western and gendered nature of contemporary theory is promised. These implications will be followed up in the conclusion of this book after a brief and eclectic examination of some of the writers whose work may eventually coalesce into a genuinely postmodern social theory.

Tsvetan Todorov's extraordinary work, *The Conquest of America*, featured in chapter 6 above in the context of the study of violence in international relations; the main theme of this book is an account of how the Western conquerers of the New World came to terms with the Otherness they encountered there.[80] The civilisations they encountered were Different, and the story Todorov tells is of the two reactions to this difference which between them encompassed the possibilities allowed by Western thought, while excluding a third and better way. The conquistadors experienced difference as inferiority and conquered in the name of a superior civilisation, raping, murdering, pillaging and spreading disease – depopulating a continent – under the banner of suppressing the tyranny of human sacrifice, a practice stressed as the paradigm of an unbearable otherness. The defenders of the Indians – priests such as Las Casas – abhorred the practices of the conquistadors and condemned them in the name of a universalism that recognised the Indian as a being with an immortal soul to be saved; the Indians were defended by giving them a place within the schemas of the West, an identity as potential Christians.[81] These two approaches – the preservation of difference within a superior–inferior relationship and the assertion of equality by the elimination of difference – have been a recurrent feature of the meeting of Western and non-Western societies throughout the centuries of empire. The district officer and the missionary, the East India Company and the Society for the Abolition of the Slave Trade, these binary pairs have been the way in which the West has coped with otherness.

What this excludes is the possibility of difference without hierarchy, an equality that recognises and celebrates difference. Todorov's point is that even the most sympathetic of the defenders of the Indians were unable to conceive of an opposition to the barbarism of the conquistadors which would allow the preservation of otherness. One way or another, as inferiors or equals the Indians had to be brought within the Western framework. Todorov's background is that of a student of literature, of poetics, and the author of a study of the Russian critic M. M. Bakhtin.[82] Bakhtin's work stresses the value of 'The dialogic imagination'; the novel is the paradigm of a work of art because it contains a constant interaction of meanings, of points of view, of otherness, resisting any reduction to a single position, a monologue. Todorov, in *The Conquest of America*, is pointing to the failure of the Spaniards to develop a dialogic understanding of what was happening – a failure repeated throughout the history of empire.

A similar story can be told of the role of gender in Western social thought. Again, for at least two hundred years – since Mary Wollstone-craft's *Vindication of the Right of Women* – challenges to a hierarchical understanding of women as different and inferior to men have been delivered, but again it is only more recently that understandings of identity and difference have allowed for the category of different and equal. Again, as with the impact of the non-Western world, the replacement of implicit or explicit monologue by the dialogic imagination does not simply leave the original categories as they were. An understanding of femininity that escapes stereotypes demands a changed understanding of masculinity. Jean Bethke Elshtain's *Women and War* addresses these themes; patriarchy and (some) modernist feminism create stereotypes of the role of men and women in war – the 'just warrior' and the 'beautiful soul' – which underpin notions of civic virtue based on the right to bear arms.[83] Although examples that reverse these stereotypes can be found, this would simply create a new monologic understanding. Elshtain's aim is to point to a politics in which there are neither warriors nor victims, but in which difference is not replaced by identity.

Sex and gender are major themes of the later work of Michel Foucault.[84] What Foucault was concerned to challenge was the modernist story of man as a being with a nature that is shaped and repressed by society. At one level this is a 'true' story – his own work on the disciplinary society and surveillance had demonstrated the ways in which the self is constrained by power – but at another level it is profoundly misleading in so far as this story implies the existence of an unrepressed self under the layers of conditioning. Foucault's study of the sexual practices of classical Greece and Christianity is designed to shake this notion that there is somewhere a natural self – even those aspects of the self we consider to be most basic have to be understood as created; Foucault sees this attack on the hypothesis of sexual repression in a wider context as part of his examination of the 'technologies of the self'. *The History of Sexuality* is about the art of living; the desire to master oneself and others and the form this desire takes, which Foucault discusses generically under the title of 'The will to know' – *La Volonté de Savoir*, the title of the book translated into English as *The History of Sexuality: An introduction*.

Foucault's desire to undermine the notion that there is such a thing as a natural self finds an echo in a strange place, the work of the Oxford philosopher Derek Parfit. Parfit's *Reasons and Persons* is a study in the utilitarian tradition which faces up squarely to the standard critique of utilitarianism, delivered by, for example, Rawls and Williams, that it does not, in Rawls' words, 'take seriously the distinction between persons.'[85] Parfit's response is to reduce this distinction. His argument is that the reductionist view that we are simply physical and/or psychological continuity – a set of embodied memories, which fade over time, and many of which we share with others – is correct. There is no 'further fact' about identity, no deeper non-reductionist sense of what it is to be me.[86] The gap between one person and another is thereby rendered less significant – indeed, it may be no more significant than the gap between the 'I' of today and the 'I' of ten years ago or ten years' time. One of Parfit's points is that if this counterintuitive view came to be widely accepted it would have enormous implications for the way in which we handle a whole range of ethical issues, and this is surely true. The interesting point in this context is that although Parfit's interests are incommensurable with those of Foucault, his account of the nature of 'man' is quite compatible with the sort of things Foucault is saying in his later work; in both cases the received Western account of this nature lies in ruins.

It is not the aim of this discussion to suggest that the authors introduced in this section are all saying the same thing, or even that they are saying different but ultimately compatible things – although, allowing for the difficulties involved in translation (literally and metaphorically), it may be that this is the case, and that some future theorist of identity and difference will be able to incorporate all these positions into a common frame of reference.[87] The more important point is that each of these writers is signposting the end of a conception of 'man' that has been basic to the social theory of modernity. In the current international context, with the end of (formal) empire and the emergence of a world no longer dominated by Europeans – and indeed, a world in which gender is an increasingly important focus of interest – this is a challenge of great significance, heralding the arrival of a change in consciousness which surely merits the description 'postmodern'. The politicised understanding of identity and difference which may emerge from these attacks on these notions of 'man' which constrain our thinking could be the most important shift in social thinking of our era.

What is also interesting about this work is that it does promote a particular way of looking at the world as well as provide a critique of existing modernist thought. In this it differs from 'deconstruction'. The latter can do nothing other than show the weaknesses of the regime of modernity; a deconstructed text is a text which can no longer perform the function it once had, and if it be accepted that quite frequently the function of the texts of modernity is to close down discussion the negative role of deconstruction may have a positive value. But work such as that of Todorov and Bakhtin goes beyond this in actually promoting a positive sense of what ought to replace the closure of modernity. All the texts discussed in this section, one way or another, either explicitly or implicitly promote the idea of plurality of meanings, an openness to dialogue. The literary concerns of Bakhtin seem a long way from the subject matter of international theory, and yet the idea of the 'dialogic imagination' has potential applications that are very wide ranging. Bakhtin's notion of 'heteroglossia' – that the social, historical and so on conditions governing at any one time insure that sentences uttered at that time will have meanings different from those uttered at any other time – may seem to be close to Derrida's thought, but leads in Bakhtin's case towards 'dialogism' – 'the characteristic epistemological mode of a world dominated by heteroglossia' – rather than towards deconstruction. [88] Whether Bakhtin's formulations, or some other existing or yet-to-be-created notion comes to be at the centre of future thought, the root idea of the replacement of monologue by dialogue, of the sovereignty of Western rational man by a more pluralistic understanding of what it is to be human would be a positive move of great significance.

APPENDIX: SCHEMATIC DIFFERENCES BETWEEN MODERNISM AND POSTMODERNISM

Modernism	*Postmodernism*
romanticism/Symbolism	paraphysics/Dadaism
form (conjunctive, closed)	antiform (disjunctive, open)
purpose	play
design	chance
hierarchy	anarchy
mastery/logos	exhaustion/silence
art object/finished work	process/performance/happening
distance	participation
creation/totalisation/synthesis	decreation/deconstruction/antithesis
presence	absence
centring	dispersal
genre/boundary	text/intertex
semantics	rhetoric
paradigm	syntagm
hypotaxis	parataxis
metaphor	metonymy
selection	combination
root/depth	rhizome/surface
interpretation/reading	against interpretation/misreading

signified	signifier
lisible (readerly)	scriptible (writerly)
narrative/*grande histoire*	anti-narrative/*petite histoire*
master code	idiolect
symptom	desire
type	mutant
genital/phallic	polymorphous/androgynous
paranoia	schizophrenia
origin/cause	difference–*différance*/trance
God the Father	The Holy Ghost
metaphysics	irony
determinacy	indeterminacy
transcendance	immanence

Source: Harvey, *op. cit.*, p. 43, citing I. Hassan, 'The culture of postmodernism', *Theory Culture and Society*, vol. 2, no. 3 (1985), pp. 123–4.

NOTES

1. M. Weber, *The Protestant Ethic and the Spirit of Capitalism*, 20th impression (Unwin Hyman, 1989), p. 181.
2. Q. Skinner (ed.) *The Return of Grand Theory in the Human Sciences* (Cambridge University Press, Cambridge, 1985), is a collection of radio talks, ideal as an introduction to these theorists. R. Bernstein's *The Restructuring of Social and Political Theory* (Methuen, London, 1979) is also excellent.
3. On these matters see below, and V. Descombes, *Modern French Philosophy*, trans. L. Scott-Fox and J. M. Harding, orginal title *Le Même et l'autre* (Cambridge University Press, Cambridge, 1980).
4. Again see below, and M. Jay, *The Dialectical Imagination* (Little Brown, Boston, Mass. 1973).
5. M. Oakeshott, *Rationalism in Politics and Other Essays* (Methuen, London, 1962); R. Rorty, *Philosophy and the Mirror of Nature* (Blackwell, Oxford, 1980); A. MacIntyre, *After Virtue* (Duckworth, London, 1981); and J. Tully (ed.) *Meaning and Context: Quentin Skinner and his critics* (Polity Press, Cambridge, 1988).
6. See, for example, L. Appignamesi (ed.) *Postmodernism: ICA documents* (Free Association Books, London, 1989).
7. The best account of writing under erasure is G. C. Spivak, Introduction to J. Derrida, *Of Grammatolgoy*, trans. Spivak (Johns Hopkins University Press, Baltimore, Md. 1976), pp. xiv ff
8. Cited from C. Norris, *Derrida* (Fontana, London, 1987), p. 16.
9. 'Postmodern bourgeois liberalism', *Journal of Philosphy*, (1983), pp. 583–9, and collected in R. Rorty, *Objectivity, Relativism and Truth:*

Philosophical papers, vol. I (Cambridge University Press, Cambridge, 1991).

10. For an account of political thought giving pride of place to Nietzsche see W. E. Connolly, *Political Theory and Modernity* (Blackwell, Oxford, 1988), esp. ch. 5; Nietzsche scholarship has advanced dramatically in the last generation: for a useful collection of writing up to the mid-1970s see D. B. Allison (ed.) *The New Nietzsche* (MIT Press, Cambridge, Mass., 1977); and for a recent reading of Nietzsche as a political theorist, M. Warren *Nietzsche and Political Thought* (MIT Press, Cambridge, Mass., 1988). Heideggerian influences are possibly less important to (most of) the writers discussed here; for an excellent recent account see D. Kolb, *The Critique of Pure Modernity: Hegel, Heidegger and after* (Chicago University Press, Chicago, 1986).

11. For more on Marxist ethics, C. Brown 'Marxism and international ethics', in T. Nardin and D. Mapel (eds) *Traditions of International Ethics* (Cambridge University Press, Cambridge, 1992).

12. Jay, *op. cit.* and Bernstein, *op. cit.* provide excellent general accounts of the Frankfurt School.

13. Trans. John Cumming (Verso, London, 1979).

14. Beacon Hill Press, Boston, 1964.

15. On Habermas see Bernstein, *op. cit.*; A. Giddens in Skinner (ed.) *op. cit.*; T. McCarthy, *The Critical Theory of Jurgen Habermas* (Hutchinson, London, 1978); and R. Bernstein (ed.) *Habermas and Modernity* (Polity Press, Cambridge, 1985). Critical Theory, when capitalised in the text, refers to Habermas' project, in distinction from the great many other areas which often fall under this rubric.

16. P. Winch, *The Idea of a Social Science and its Relation to Philosophy* (Routledge and Kegan Paul, London, 1958). A different presentation of a similar position is C. Taylor, 'Interpretation and the sciences of man', *Review of Metaphysics*, vol. 25 (1971) pp. 3–51.

17. See J. Habermas, *Knowledge and Human Interests*, trans. J. Shapiro (Heinemann, London, 1972), appendix, pp. 301–51. Giddens, *op. cit.*, is used extensively in the following summary.

18. R. Cox, 'Social forces states and world order: beyond international theory', *Millennium: Journal of International Studies*, vol. 10, no. 2 (1981), (collected in R. Keohane (ed.) *Neo-Realism and its Critics* (Columbia University Press, New York, 1986)); see also Cox, *Production Power and World Order* (Columbia University Press, New York, 1987).

19. *Beyond Realism and Marxism: Critical theory and international relations* (Macmillan, London, 1990).

20. See Cox's Postscript in Keohane (ed.) *op. cit.*

21. M. Hoffman's 'Critical theory and the inter-paradigm debate', *Millennium: Journal of International Studies*, vol. 16, no. 2 (1987), refers to a wider range of 'critical' theory; for example, the World Order Models Project.

22. See Habermas, *Legitimation Crisis*, (Heinemann, London, 1976).

23. These ideas are discussed in *The Theory of Communicative Action*, vols I and II (Polity Press, Cambridge, 1984).
24. See Giddens in Skinner (ed.) *op. cit.*, for a brief elaboration of these distinctions.
25. W. E. Connolly, 'The Critical Theory of Jurgen Habermas', in his *Politics and Ambiguity* (Wisconsin University Press, Madison, 1987), p. 71.
26. Polity Press, Cambridge, 1987.
27. W. James, 'What pragmatism means', in his *Selected Papers on Philosophy*, (Dent, London, 1917), p. 215.
28. A. MacIntyre, *A Short History of Ethics*, (Routledge and Kegan Paul, London, 1967), p. 253.
29. (Penguin, Harmondsworth, 1952), pp. 22, 26.
30. Rorty, *op. cit.*
31. The argument here is very technical: Rorty argues that the work of Sellars and Quine considered together rather than separately, undermines the premises of analytical philosophy. Fortunately, the details of this argument are unimportant for our purposes.
32. *ibid.*, ch. VIII, section 2, pp. 365ff.
33. *ibid.*, p. 367.
34. See M. Oakeshott, 'The role of poetry in the conversation of mankind', in his *Rationalism and Politics*.
35. 'Method, social science and social hope', in *Consequences of Pragmatism* (Harvester Wheatsheaf, Hemel Hempstead, 1982), pp. 205ff.
36. Cambridge University Press, Cambridge, 1989.
37. *ibid.*, pp. 56ff.
38. D. Bell, *The Cultural Contradictions of Capitalism* (Heinemann, London, 1976).
39. *Contingency*, pp. 63ff.
40. 'Method', p. 207.
41. *Contingency*, pp. 58ff.
42. *ibid.*, p. 59.
43. 'Method', note p. 210.
44. *Politics and Ambiguity*, pp. 116ff.
45. Anne Norton's turn of phrase; see 'A response to Henry S. Kariel', *Political Theory*, vol. 18, no. 2. (May 1990), p. 273.
46. Eds J. Der Derian and M. J Shapiro (Lexington Books, Lexington, Mass., 1989), and *International Studies Quarterly*, special issue, vol. 34, no. 3 (1990), ed. R. K. Ashley and R. B. J. Walker respectively. It has to be said that 'exile' and 'dissidence' seem terms inappropriately used in the official journal of the International Studies Association.
47. International intrigue and the deconstruction of Waltz are discussed below; other papers referred to here are M. J. Shapiro, 'Representing world politics: the sport war intertext', and B. S. Klein, 'The textual strategies of the military, or have you read any good defence manuals recently?' both in Der Derian and Shapiro (eds), *op. cit.*
48. Other postmodern international relations can be found in the journals

Alternatives and *Millennium: Journal of International Studies*. O. Waever, *Beyond the Beyond of Critical International Theory* (Working Paper 1/ 1989 of Centre for Peace and Conflict Research in Copenhagen) is a substantial study of this work.

49. See the brief account in ch. 2.

50. What follows is very inadequate. For a better account see Descombes, *op. cit.*; Norris, *op. cit.*; Norris, *The Contest of Faculties: Philosophy and theory after deconstruction* (Methuen, London 1985); J. Culler, *On Deconstruction: Theory and criticism after structuralism* (Cornell University Press, Ithaca, N.Y. 1982); and for less sympathetic accounts, T. Eagleton, *Literary Theory: An introduction* (Blackwell, Oxford, 1983); P. Dews, *Logics of Disintegration: Poststructuralist thought and the claims of critical theory* (Verso, London, 1987).

51. Norris, in *Derrida*, argues that this slogan ('Il n'y a pas de hors-texte') from *Of Grammatology* has been misunderstood. 'There is no excuse for the sloppy misreading of Derrida that represents him as some kind of transcendental solipsist who believes that nothing "real" exists outside the written text' (p. 158). If this is a sloppy reading it is one that Derrida himself has done much to promote.

52. M. Foucault, *The Order of Things*, trans. Alan Sheridan (Tavistock, London, 1970), p. 387.

53. More accurately 'Sound which no one else understands but which I "appear to understand" might be called a private language' (*Philosophical Investigations*, trans. G. E. M. Anscombe (Blackwell, Oxford, 1968), part 1, section 269, p. 94e).

54. The most dramatic/amusing/silly illustration of this point of undecidability is Derrida's account of a note of Nietzsche's isolated on a scrap of paper, 'I have forgotten my umbrella'. In the absence of context this note cannot be interpreted *Spurs: Nietzsche's styles*, trans. B. Harlow (Chicago University Press, Chicago, 1979).

55. Blackwell, Oxford, 1987.

56. 'Spy versus spy: the intertextual power of international intrigue', *Interna-tional/Intertextual*, pp. 163ff.

57. p. 172. Admittedly, the fact that it was Senator (now Vice President) Quayle who referred to Tom Clancy's *Red Storm Rising* does somewhat weaken the point.

58. 'Living on border lines: man, poststructuralism and war', pp. 259ff. See also R. Ashley, 'The geopolitics of geopolitical space', *Alternatives*, vol. 12 (October 1987), and the controversy this generated with papers by Roy, Walker and a reply from Ashley, *Alternatives*, vol. 13 (January 1988); O. Waever *Tradition and Transgression in International Relations: A post-Ashleyan position* (Working Paper 24/1989), Centre for Peace and Conflict Research, Copenhagen) is a detailed account of the evolution of Ashley's thought.

59. See Norris, *Derrida*, and Spivak's long Introduction to *On Grammatology* for the most accessible accounts of deconstruction.

60. For a critique of Ashley on similar lines see W. E. Connolly 'Identity and Difference in Global Politics' in *International/Intertextual*, pp. 323ff.

61. Habermas, *Philosophical Discourses*. Taylor, 'Foucault on freedom and truth', *Political Theory*, vol. 2 (1984), and the debate between Connolly, 'Taylor, Foucault and otherness', and Taylor, 'Connolly, Foucault and truth', in *Political Theory*, vol. 13, no. 3. (August 1985).

62. See, for example, J. E. Lyotard, *The Postmodern Condition: A report on knowledge*, trans. G. Bennington and B. Massumi (Manchester University Press, Manchester, 1986); M. Poster (ed.) *Jean Baudrillard: Selected writings* (Polity Press, Cambridge, 1988); P. Virilio, *Speed and Politics*, trans. M. Poltzotti (Semiotext(e) New York, 1986).

63. Cited from M. Featherstone, 'In pursuit of the postmodern: an introduction', in *Theory, Culture and Society*, vol. 5, nos 2 and 3 (June 1988), special issue on Postmodernism, p. 195.

64. No. 146 (July/August 1984) and Verso, London, 1991.

65. Blackwell, Oxford, 1989.

66. *ibid.*, p. vii.

67. *ibid.*, p. 39.

68. R. Venturi, D. Scott-Brown, S. Izenour (MIT Press, Cambridge, Mass., 1972).

69. Jameson, *op. cit.*, p. 65.

70. 'Questions on geography', in M. Foucault *Power/Knowledge: Selected interviews and other writings 1972–1977*, ed. and trans. Colin Gordon (Harvester Wheatsheaf, Hemel Hempstead, 1980), p. 77.

71. E. Soja, *Postmodern Geographies: The reassertion of space in critical social theory* (Verso, London, 1989), pp. 223ff.

72. Virilio, *op. cit.*, and (with Lotringer) Semiotext(e), New York, 1983.

73. See *International Studies Quarterly*, vol. 34, no. 3 (1990).

74. See Poster (ed.) *op. cit.*, for extracts from *Simulacra and Simulation; America* (New Left Books, London, 1988).

75. *The Independent Magazine*, 16 June 1990.

76. However, the suggestion in the same article that this and other replicas (of, for example, the Eiffel Tower) be set in areas of high unemployment does indicate a somewhat frivolous attitude to the matter.

77. Harvey, *op. cit.*, p. 147.

78. A position articulated most effectively in *The Mirror of Production*, extracts in Poster (ed.) *op. cit.*

79. Lyotard's definition of the postmodern as 'incredulity towards meta-narratives' is the best one-liner available on the subject: see Lyotard, *op. cit.*, p. xxiv.

80. Trans. R. Howard (Harper Torchbooks, New York, 1987).

81. Todorov makes the point that Las Casas comes close to accepting the spirituality of the Indians on their own terms (pp. 186ff).

82. See Todorov, *Mikhail Bakhtin: The dialogic principle* (Manchester University Press, Manchester, 1984). Bakhtin's most important work is *The Dialogic Imagination* (University of Texas Press, Austin, 1981). A

good guide is the collection R. Kirschkop and D. Shepherd (eds) *Bakhtin and Cultural Theory* (Manchester University Press, Manchester, 1989).

83. Harvester Wheatsheaf, Hemel Hempstead, 1987. The literature on feminist approaches to international relations is growing rapidly – see the special issue, 'Women and international relations', of *Millennium: Journal of International Studies*, vol. 17, no. 3 (1988).

84. *The History of Sexuality*, vols I–III, trans. R. Hurley (Penguin, Harmondsworth, 1981, 1987). As often seems to be the case with Foucault translations, the original titles (used in the English version as sub-titles) are more informative, viz, 'The will to know', 'The use of pleasure' and 'The care of the self'.

85. Oxford University Press, Oxford, 1984.

86. *ibid.*, pp. 210ff.

87. W. E. Connolly's forthcoming study, *Identity and Difference: A political analysis*, will pull some of these themes together. This whole section owes a lot to Connolly's thought.

88. These formulations come largely from the glossary of *The Dialogic Imagination*, pp. 426, 428.

Chapter 9
Conclusion?

In part I of this book cosmopolitan and communitarian approaches to the theory of international relations were set out; in part II the focus was on contemporary thinkers working within these broad categories – and if there is one feature common to both parts it is the clear impossibility of bringing either to any kind of conclusion. The arguments and discussions set out therein simply resist closure. Majority opinion may form in the short run and take the argument in one direction, but a comeback is always possible for the losing side. The best example of this is the recent revival of Hegelian ideas of the nature of political community. A generation or so ago Hegel was widely regarded as a thinker of no significance, or whose importance rested on the extent to which he provided an agenda for the early work of Karl Marx. Now, at the end of the century, it is coming to seem more likely that Marx will be regarded as the minor figure, and that the 'great thinkers' of the nineteenth century will be Hegel, Mill and Nietzsche. Who can tell where the weight of critical opinion will be in fifty years' time?

It may be that this continual change is not a contingent feature of this particular branch of political theory, but is built into the nature of normative theory as such. W. B. Gallie's notion of an 'essentially contested concept' – given, perhaps, its most elaborate political-science exposition in William Connolly's *The Terms of Political Discourse* – is possibly relevant.[1] Gallie posits that thinkers coming from different positions and perspectives may share concepts for some purposes but employ these shared concepts differently for other purposes. Thus, to take an example highly relevant to chapters 6 and 7 above, neo-liberals and social democrats may possess a shared notion of justice when the frame of reference is procedural, while differing radically on whether or not to extend the idea of justice to distributive issues. Gallie's and Connolly's point is that this contest over the meaning of justice is not reconcilable because reconciliation can only take place within a common frame of reference and in this case the issue is precisely whether the frame of reference should or should not be extended.

Clearly, there is something to this, but the extent to which the point is more than semantic can be exaggerated. After all, to take the example employed above, what is at stake here is in essence political rather than conceptual. Neo-liberals take 'justice' to be a good thing but are opposed to the idea of resources and wealth being subject to social distribution and redistribution; they therefore resist the idea of extending the notion of justice to cover these activities. Social democrats also value justice, but have a different view of the worth of distribution and redistribution and are therefore prepared to extend the idea of justice in this direction. This is not a contest over concepts but a contest over real political values. Extending the point, the reason why the argument between cosmopolitans and communitarians cannot be brought to a conclusion is not that there is some feature of these concepts that makes this impossible, but rather that the people who espouse these views see the world in different ways and from different perspectives.

In any event, whether because of essential contestability or simply because human beings espouse different values, the positions outlined in parts I and II – the arguments of conventional political theory as applied to the agendas of international relations – remain in an unresolved state. As will have been apparent, one of the aims of the writers examined in part III is to transcend these conventions and their agendas and thus to reach a kind of conclusion to all these questions, but, again, this attempt to bring about an end to philosophy must be ajudged a failure. As was suggested in chapter 8, the more extreme statements of the death of an author and the end of conventional theory are difficult to take too seriously – even if one accepts that certain features of contemporary thought do give credence to the idea of postmodernity. The wilder shores of deconstruction point to an end of representation and the collapse of all the grand theories of social action considered in parts I and II of this book, but the very extremism of this claim tells against it; rather better reasons than those offered by Derrida or Barthes would be required before most people would be prepared to throw overboard the social thought of two-and-a-half millennia.

However, there are some features of the thought of late modernity which do point in the direction of the closure of a particular agenda, and these are those features identified in chapter 1 as limiting conditions of the writers surveyed in this book, namely their gendered and Western origin. Foucaultian accounts of the undermining of Westerners' sense of identity as the reasoning sovereign of all they survey can be made to relate to the demand for post-Western international thought emanating from the non-Western world, while the feminist critique of gendered politics can, without great difficulty, be seen as part of the same wider postmodern critique. As suggested in Chapter 1, the materials are as yet lacking for a reasoned assessment of the projects of post-western, post-patriarchal international relations theory, but in these concluding pages some further comment may be helpful, especially if, as seems quite likely, these are issues which will loom larger in the years ahead.

The essential point made by critics of international relations theory as set out in parts I and II (and, to a considerable extent, part III) of this book is that this is theory created by writers who, for the most part, hale from the minority – but privileged – sex, a minority – but privileged – culture and a minority – but dominant – position within the world economy. Putting this in language that could fit on a badge or bumper sticker, international relations theory is produced by (comparatively) rich, white men. As an empirical propostion this is clearly true, and, to repeat a point made in chapter 1 above, there is no need to apologise for the fact that the writers who dominate this book fit the description. This is where international relations theory has come from in the past and that is what this book reflects; what is interesting is whether this will continue to be the case in the future, and, if not, what difference a change of emphasis here will make.

Feminist writers in international relations theory such as those collected in a recent *Millennium* special issue are clearly determined to assert that the situation will change and that this will make a difference.[2] The question is how far this challenge can move beyond rhetoric towards substance – much the same question is frequently asked of postmodernist international relations theory, and with equal legitimacy. To answer this question it is necessary to try to read the signs of the times – both current intellectual trends and the movements in real-world politics – and the problem here is that these signs seem profoundly ambiguous: phenomena that can be read as dethroning conventional categories of thought and opening space for new characterisations of experience can usually be read from another direction as relegitimising the older perspectives. Two examples may be useful here.

Consider Lyotard's simplified definition of the postmodern as 'incredulity towards metanarratives' – a 'metanarrative' being characteristic of the modern, and exemplified by such grand narratives as 'the dialectics of Spirit, the hermeneutics of meaning, the emancipation of the rational or working subject, or the creation of wealth'.[3] The idea is that the big stories we tell ourselves about justice, reason and human nature simply do not stand up to scrutiny. The Enlightenment project identified by Kant as man's emergence from self-incurred immaturity is simply incredible – not wrong or mistaken, simply impossible to believe in. The international relations theory of the Enlightenment and post-Enlightenment falls victim to the same scepticism: it is no longer possible to believe in the sort of stories that back up cosmopolitan or communitarian accounts of the world; such at least is the way the new story goes.

However, the truly subversive nature of this thought becomes clear when incredulity is directed towards not only the old Enlightenment metanarratives but also the new stories of liberation told by feminists, Third-Worlders – and postmodernists themselves when their guard is down. Grand stories which are told about notions such as 'patriarchy', or 'Africa' or 'Islam' are every bit as incredible to those who do not wish to believe in them as are the metanarratives of modernity. If all metanarratives are to be cleared away, then what is left is a kind of open-ended pluralism based on the principle that no particular position has a monopoly of truth, and that trial and error is the only appropriate scientific technique – and this, roughly speaking, is the position Lyotard ends up with in *The Post-Modern Condition*. But such an eclectic position is very little different from the piecemeal social engineering taken by Popper and others to be wholly characteristic of the best side of contemporary liberalism, and all the old forms of social thought excluded as incredible in their metanarrative form regain credibility if recast in what Rorty would call an 'ironic' mould – that is, aware of their own contingency. Feminist positions on partriarchy, or Islamic critiques of the Western-dominated international system can no longer claim to be able to recast thought; at best, they enter into the intellectual marketplace in competition with existing ideas – which is exactly where conventional theory has always seen these approaches.

It might be argued that Lyotard's postmodernism is particularly susceptible to this kind of reversal, and that other variants are less readily domesticated into the frameworks of conventional thought. This is true enough in the sense that other postmodernists use different languages and are less willing to quote Popper, but the basic point about the ambiguity of postmodern positions remains: in order to deliver a fundamental critique of the thought of modernity, postmodernists and post-structuralists adopt stances which are self-subverting, which prevent any new thought taking the place from which the old categories have been ejected. Of course, by no means all feminists want to think within postmodernity and it is perfectly possible to understand feminist claims from the perspective of the older frameworks of thought; but in this case these older frameworks are reinforced rather than subverted by the new learning, and the debates discussed in parts I and II of this book remain both central and unresolvable.

The ambiguities of postmodernity occur in the realm of theory, but similar ambiguities can be seen in the realm of practice – in the practical implications of real-world changes. Consider the collapse of Soviet communism, the re-emergence of Russia and the end of the Soviet empire. This is clearly a key event of the modern era but the interpretation thereof is by no means without ambiguity. These great changes can be read as signalling a return to the 'metanarratives' of the Enlightenment or as clearing the space for the establishment of new stories more alien to the West than that of Soviet communism.

Fukuyama's 'End of history' is perhaps the most extreme example of a line of argument that suggests that the collapse of communism represents a triumph for liberal–democratic principles. Fukuyama argues that communism was the last in a line of challengers to the basic principles of liberalism established in the early nineteenth century by Hegel.[4] The basic terms of the debates that have dominated Western political thought over the last two centuries are now, finally, recognised to be of universal significance; to put the matter in different language, the great 'Other' of the West has fallen, the defeat of communism is a defeat for 'difference' as a normative principle. Although the Hegelian way in which Fukuyama expresses these thoughts is controversial, the position he argues receives support from a number of other directions. Perhaps most significant here is the debate taking place in Russia on the significance of the end of communism. A commonplace of this debate is a celebration of Russia's return to being a 'normal' society.[5] This is at one and the same time both a rejection of the experiments of socialism and an affirmation of the values of the West, seen not as specific to a region or culture, but as universals.

On the other hand, a number of the features of the collapse of communism can be seen in a very different light. From the perspective of Soviet Central Asia, communism was a Western doctrine acting as the advance guard of the Enlightenment rather than as its greatest opponent. The end of communism is likely here to lead not to the establishment of liberal institutions but to Islamic republics or oriental despotisms, and a genuine 'otherness' may come to take the place of the communist version of the West. The ending of a wide-ranging ideological conflict between different interpretations of the inheritance of the West may be replaced by a series of new conflicts between ways of life that are genuinely alien to one another. It is already the case that the popular mass media in the West are casting 'Islam' in the oppositional role previously occupied by communism.

Deciding between these two models of the future – a rallying to the alleged normality of Western modes of thought, or the emergence of a genuine Other in the place of the phoney otherness of communism – is made virtually impossible by the ambiguous nature of the evidence. The end of the Soviet empire is clearly leading to a great many regional conflicts, in the Caucasus, in Central Asia and, possibly, between Russia and the Ukraine: meanwhile, the end of communism in eastern Europe has directly or indirectly led to a state of civil war in the former territory of Yugoslavia and major refugee problems in Germany, Italy and Greece. How are these events to be interpreted? As the first, rather unpleasant, symptoms of a new, pluralistic, world order, or as a reversion to the old patterns of pre-Cold-War world politics? It simply is not possible to say whether we are now witnessing the return of an old world or the birth of a new.

The point of this extended digression has been to ask whether there is reason to believe that the issues discussed in this book are finally either reaching some kind of conclusion or slipping into relative insignificance, and the burden of the argument is that there is insufficient reason to think that this is so. New modes of thought can be seen either as genuinely revolutionary or they can be subsumed within the old categories; new trends in world politics may be genuinely new or they may be re-acquisitions of the old trends. There is no conclusive way of deciding between these positions, and thus the older debate between cosmopolitanism and communitarianism remains unresolved.

This ought not to be a source of concern or embarrassment for international relations theory. The idea that the role of theory is to settle questions once and for all – to reach conclusions – is fundamentally mistaken, the products of a misreading of the nature of science and a misapplication of this misreading to the social sciences. In a famous essay Oakeshott writes of the 'Voice of poetry in the conversation of mankind':[6] extending this metaphor, the idea that the role of normative international relations theory is to contribute a voice to such a conversation seems more to the point than the scientistic notion that the role of theory is to reach a finding, to come to a conclusion. Good conversation does not involve the reaching of conclusions. It simply stops, to be taken up again the next time an occasion arises.

NOTES

1. W. B. Gallie, 'Essentially contested concepts', *Proceedings of the Aristotelean Society*, vol. 56 (1955-6). Connolly, 2nd edn (Martin Robertson, Oxford, 1983).
2. Special issue, 'Women and internatinal relations', *Millennium: Journal of International Studies*, vol. 17, no. 3 (1988).
3. J. F. Lyotard, *The Postmodern Condition: A report on knowledge* (Manchester University Press, Manchester, 1986), p. xxiii.
4. F. Fukuyama, 'The end of history?', *The National Interest*, (Summer 1988).
5. I am grateful to Dr Richard Sakwa for this point.
6. M. Oakeshott, *Rationalism in Politics and other Essays* (Methuen, London, 1962), pp. 197ff.

Bibliography

Ackerman, B., *Social Justice and the Liberal State*, Yale University Press, New Haven, Conn., 1980.

Adorno, T. and Horkheimer, M., *Dialectic of Enlightenment*, Verso, London, 1979.

Allison, D.B. (ed.) *The New Nietzsche*, MIT Press, Cambridge, MA., 1977.

Anscombe, G.E.M., *The Collected Philosophical Papers of G.E.M. Anscombe: vol. 3: Ethics, Religion and Politics* Blackwell, Oxford, 1981.

Appignamesi, L. (ed.) *Postmodernism: ICA documents*, Free Association Books, London, 1989.

Aristotle, *The Politics*, ed. S. Everson, Cambridge University Press, Cambridge, 1988.

Aristotle, *The Nichomachean Ethics*, ed. and trans. D. Ross (The World's Classics), Oxford University Press, Oxford, 1969.

Aron, R., *Peace and War*, Weidenfeld and Nicholson, London, 1962.

Ashley, R.K. and R.B.J. Walker (eds) 'Speaking the language of exile: dissidence in international studies', special issue *International Studies Quarterly*, vol. 34, no. 3 (1990).

Ashley R. 'The geopolitics of geopolitical space', *Alternatives*, vol. 12 (1987).

Austin, J.L., *How To Do Things With Words*, Oxford University Press, Oxford, 1962.

Avineri, S., *Hegel's Theory of the Modern State*, Cambridge University Press, Cambridge, 1972.

Ayer, A.J., *Language, Truth and Logic*, Gollancz, London, 1936.

Ayer, A.J., *Wittgenstein*, Penguin, Harmondsworth, 1985.

Bhagwati, J.N. and Ruggie, J.G. (eds), *Power, Passion and Purpose*, MIT Press, Cambridge, MA, 1984.

Bailey, S.D., *Prohibitions and Restraints in War*, Oxford University Press/ RIIA, Oxford, 1972.

Bakhtin, M., *The Dialogic Imagination*, University of Texas Press, Austin, 1981.

Banks, M., 'Two meanings of theory in the study of international relations', *Yearbook of World Affairs*, vol. 20, (1966).

Banks, M., 'The inter-paradigm debate', in M. Light and A.J.R. Groom (eds) *International Relations: A handbook of current theory*, Frances Pinter, London, 1985.

Baran, P., *The Political Economy of Growth*, Penguin, Harmondsworth, 1973.

Barber, B., *The Conquest of Politics: Liberal philosophy in democratic times*, Princeton University Press, Princeton, N.J., 1988.

Barnard, F.M., (ed.) *J.G. Herder on Social and Political Culture*, Cambridge University Press, Cambridge, 1969.

Barnard, F.M., *Herder's Social and Political Thought: From Enlightenment to nationalism*, Clarendon, Oxford, 1965.

Barry, B., *The Liberal Theory of Justice: A critical examination of the principle doctrines in 'A Theory of Justice' by John Rawls*, Clarendon, Oxford, 1973.

Barry B., 'Circumstances of justice and future generations', in R. Sikora and B. Barry, *Obligations to Future Generations*, Temple University Press, Philadelphia, 1978.

Barry, B., 'Humanity and justice in global perspective', in J.R. Pennock and J.W. Chapman (eds) *Nomos XXIL*, New York University Press, New York, 1982.

Barry, B. *Democracy, Power and Justice: Essays in political theory*, Clarendon, Oxford, 1989.

Barry, B. *Theories of Justice* Harvester Wheatsheaf, Hemel Hempstead, 1989.

Baudrillard, J., *America*, New Left Books, London, 1988.

Bauer, P.T., *Equality, the Third World and Economic Delusion*, Weidenfeld and Nicholson, London, 1981.

Beck, L.W., *Kant: Selections*, Scribner Macmillan, New York, 1988.

Beitz, C.R., *Political Theory and International Relations*, Princeton University Press, Princeton, N.J., 1979.

Beitz, C.R., 'Bounded morality: justice and the state in world politics', *International Organisation*, vol. 33, no. 3 (1979).

Beitz, C.R., 'Cosmopolitan ideals and national sentiment', *Journal of Philosophy*, vol. 80 (1983).

Beitz, C.R. M. Cohen, T. Scanlon and A.J. Simmons (eds) *International Ethics*, Princeton University Press, Princeton, N.J., 1985.

Bell, D., *The Cultural Contradictions of Capitalism*, Heinemann, London, 1976.

Bentham, J., *An Introduction to the Principles of Morals and Legislation: A fragment on government*, ed. W. Harrison, Blackwell, Oxford, 1960.

Bentham, J., 'Principles of international law', in *Works*, vol. 2, Russell and Russell, New York, 1962.

Bernstein, R., *The Restructuring of Social and Political Theory*, Methuen, London, 1979.

Bernstein, R., (ed.) *Habermas and Modernity* Polity Press, Cambridge, 1985.

Best, G., *Humanity in Warfare*, Weidenfeld and Nicholson, London, 1980.

Bosanquet, B., *The Philosophical Theory of the State*, 4th edn, Macmillan, London, 1965.

Bradley, F.H., *Ethical Studies*, Oxford University Press, Oxford, 1988.

Brandt, R.B., 'Utilitarianism and the rules of war', *Philosophy and Public Affairs*, vol. 1, no. 2 (1972).

Braudel, F., *Capitalism and Material Life 1400-1800*, Fontana, London, 1973.

Brown, C., 'Development and dependency', in M. Light and A.J.R. Groom (eds) *International Relations: A handbook of current theory*, Frances Pinter, London, 1985.

Brown, C., 'Not my department: normative theory and international relations' *Paradigms; The Kent Journal of International Relations*, vol. 1, no. 2 (1987).

Brown, C., 'Ethics of co-existence: the international theory of Terry Nardin', *Review of International Studies*, vol. 14, no. 3 (1988).

Brown, C., 'Cosmopolitan confusions – a reply to Hoffman', *Paradigms: The Kent Journal of International Relations*, vol. 2, no. 2 (1988).

Brown, C., 'Marxist approaches to international political economy', in R.J.B. Jones (ed.) *The Worlds of Political Economy*, Frances Pinter, London, 1988.

Brown, C., 'Marxism and international ethics', in T. Nardin and D. Mapel (eds) *Traditions of International Ethics*, Cambridge University Press, Cambridge, 1992.

Brown, C., 'Hegel and international ethics', *Ethics and International Affairs*, vol. 5 (1991).

Brown D., *Bury My Heart at Wounded Knee*, Barrie and Jenkins, London, 1970.

Bull, H., 'International theory: the case for a classical approach', in K. Knorr and J.N. Rosenau (eds) *Contending Approaches to International Politics*, Princeton University Press, Princeton, N.J., 1969.

Bull, H., 'Martin Wight and the theory of international relations', *British Journal of International Studies*, vol. 2, no. 2 (1976).

Bull, H., *The Anarchical Society: A study of order in world politics*, Macmillan, London, 1977.

Bull, H., 'Recapturing the Just War for political theory', *World Politics*, vol. 31, no. 4 (1979).

Bull, H., (ed.) *Intervention in World Politics*, Clarendon, Oxford, 1984.

Bull, H. and A. Watson (eds) *The Expansion of International Society*, Clarendon, Oxford, 1984.

Burke, E., *Writings and Speeches*, vol. VI (The World's Classics), Oxford University Press, Oxford, 1907.

Butterfield, H. and M. Wight (eds) *Diplomatic Investigations: Essays in the theory of international politics*, Allen and Unwin, London, 1966.

Carr, E.H., *The Twenty Years Crisis*, Macmillan, London, 1939.

Carter, C.J., *Rousseau and the Problem of War*, Garland, New York, 1987.

Charvet, J., *A Critique of Freedom and Equality*, Cambridge University Press, Cambridge, 1981.

Charvet, J., *Feminism*, Dent, London, 1982.

Clark, I., *The Hierarchy of States: Reform and resistance in the international order*, Cambridge University Press, Cambridge, 1989.

Cohen, M., T. Nagel and T. Scanlon (eds) *War and Moral Responsibility*, Princeton University Press, Princeton, N.J., 1974.

Connolly, W.E., *The Terms of Political Discourse*, 2nd edn, Martin Robertson, Oxford, 1983.

Connolly, W.E., 'Taylor, Foucault and otherness', *Political Theory*, vol. 13, no. 3 (1985).

Connolly, W.E., *Political Theory and Modernity*, Blackwell, Oxford, 1988.

Cox, R., 'Social forces, states and world order: beyond international theory', *Millennium: Journal of International Studies*, vol. 10, no. 2 (1981).

Cox, R., *Production Power and World Order*, Columbia University Press, New York, 1987.

Culler, J., *On Deconstruction: Theory and criticism after structuralism*, Cornell University Press, Ithaca, N.Y., 1982.

Daniels, N., (ed.) *Reading Rawls: Critical studies of 'A Theory of Justice'*, Blackwell, Oxford, 1975.

Der Derian, J., *On Diplomacy: A genealogy of Western estrangement* Blackwell, Oxford, 1987.

Der Derian, J. and M.J. Shapiro (eds) *International/Intertextual Relations: Postmodern readings in world politics*, Lexington Books, Lexington, Mass., 1989.

Derrida, J., *Of Grammatology*, trans. and with an Introduction by G. Spivak, Johns Hopkins University Press, Baltimore, Md., 1976.

Derrida, J., *Spurs: Nietzsche's styles*, trans. B. Harlow, Chicago University Press, Chicago, 1979.

Descombes, V., *Modern French Philosophy*, trans. L. Scott-Fox and J.M. Harding, Cambridge University Press, Cambridge, 1980.

Deutsch, K., *Political Community and the North Atlantic Area*, Princeton University Press, Princeton, N.J., 1957.

Dews, P., *Logics of Disintegration: Poststructuralist thought and the claims of critical theory*, Verso, London, 1987.

Donagan, A., *The Theory of Morality*, University of Chicago Press, Chicago, 1977.

Donagan, A., 'Comments on Dan Brock and Terence Reynolds', *Ethics*, vol. 95, no. 4 (1985).

Donaldson, T., 'Kant's global rationalism', in T. Nardin and D. Mapel (eds) *Traditions of International Ethics*, Cambridge University Press, Cambridge, 1992.

Donelan, M., (ed.) *The Reason of States: A study in international political theory*, Allen and Unwin, London, 1978.

Donelan, M., 'Reason in war', *Review of International Studies*, vol. 8, no. 1 (1982).

Donelan, M., *Elements of International Political Theory*, Clarendon, Oxford, 1990.

Donnelly, J., 'Humanitarian intervention', *Journal of International Affairs*, vol. 37 (Winter 1984).

Doppelt, G. 'Walzer's theory of morality in international relations', *Philosophy and Public Affairs*, vol. 8, no. 1 (1979).

Doyle, M., 'Kant, liberal legacies and foreign affairs', parts 1 and 2, *Philosophy and Public Affairs*, vol. 12, nos 3/4 (1983).

Dworkin, R., *Taking Rights Seriously*, Duckworth, London, 1977.

Eagleton, T., *Literary Theory: An introduction*, Blackwell, Oxford, 1983.

Easton, D., 'The new revolution in political science', *American Political Science Review*, vol. 63, no. 4 (1969).

Ellis, A., (ed.) *Ethics and International Relations*, Manchester University Press, Manchester, 1986.

Ellis, A., 'Utilitarianism and international ethics' in Nardin, T. and Mapel, D., *Traditions of International Ethics*.

Elshtain, J.B., *Women and War*, Harvester Press, Brighton, 1987.

Emmanuel, A., *Unequal Exchange*, New Left Books, London, 1982.

Engels, F., *The Condition of the Working Class in England*, Grafton, London, 1969.

Enloe, C., *Bananas, Beaches and Bases: Making Feminist Sense of International Politics*, Pandora Books, London, 1989.

Evans, D., 'A Critical Assessment of some Neo-marxist Trade Theories' *Journal of Development Studies*, vol. 20, no. 2 (1984).

Evans, P., *Dependent Development*, Princeton University Press, Princeton, N.J., 1979.

Falk, R., *Revolutionaries and Functionaries: The Dual Face of Terrorism*, Dutton, New York, 1988.

Featherstone, M., (ed.), 'In pursuit of the postmodern: an introduction', Special Issue of *Theory, Culture and Society*, Vol. 5, Nos 2/3 (1988).

Finnis, J., Boyle, J. and Grisez, G., *Nuclear Deterrence, Morality and Realism*, Clarendon Press, Oxford, 1987.

Foot, P., (ed.), *Theories of Ethics*, Oxford University Press, Oxford, 1967.

Forsythe, M., Keen-Soper, H.M.A. and Savigear, P. (eds), *The Theory of International Relations*, Allen and Unwin, London, 1970.

Foucault, M., *The Order of Things*, (trans. Alan Sheridan), Tavistock, London, 1970.

Foucault, M., *Power/Knowledge: Selected Interviews and Writings 1972–1977*, (Edited and trans. Colin Gordon) Harvester, Brighton, 1980.

Foucault, M., *The History of Sexuality*, vols I–III, (trans. Robert Hurley) Penguin, Harmondsworth, 1981/87.

Frank, A.G., *Capitalism and Underdevelopment in Latin America*, Penguin, Harmondsworth, 1971.

Freedman, L., *The Evolution of Nuclear Strategy*, Macmillan, London, 1981.

Friedman, M., 'The Methodology of Positive Economics' in *Essays in Positive Economics*, Chicago University Press, Chicago, 1953.

Frost, M., *Towards a Normative Theory of International Relations*, Cambridge University Press, Cambridge, 1986.

Fukuyama, F., 'The end of history?', *The National Interest*, (Summer 1989).

Gallie, W.B., *Pierce and Pragmatism*, Penguin, Harmondsworth, 1952.

Gallie, W.B., 'Essentially contested concepts', *Proceedings of the Aristotelean Society*, vol. 56 (1955/6).

Gallie, W.B., *Philosophers of War and Peace*, Cambridge University Press, Cambridge, 1978.

Gallie, W.B., 'Wanted: a philosophy of international relations', *Political Studies*, vol. 27, no. 3 (1979).

Galston, W.A., *Justice and the Human Good*, University of Chicago Press, Chicago, 1980.

Galtung, J., 'A structural theory of imperialism', *Journal of Peace Research*, vol. 13, no. 2 (1971).

Gauthier, D., 'Deterrence, maximisation and rationality', *Ethics*, vol. 94, no. 3 (1984).

Gauthier, D., *Morals by Agreement*, Clarendon, Oxford, 1986.

Gellner, E., *Nations and Nationalism*, Blackwell, Oxford, 1983.

Gewirth, A., *Reason and Morality*, University of Chicago Press, Chicago, 1978.

Gilpin, R., 'The richness of the tradition of political realism', in R.O. Keohane (ed.) *Neo-Realism and its Critics*, Columbia University Press, New York, 1986.

Gilpin, R., *War and Change in World Politics*, Cambridge University Press, Cambridge, 1981.

Goodin, R., *Political Theory and Public Policy*, University of Chicago Press, Chicago, 1982.

Gong, G.C., *The Standard of 'Civilisation' in International Society*, Oxford University Press, Oxford, 1984.

Goulet, D., *The Cruel Choice*, Atheneum Press, London, 1973.

Grader, S., 'The English School of international relations: evidence and evaluation', *Review of International Studies*, vol. 14, no. 1 (1988).

Gramsci, A., Selection from the *Prison Notebooks of Antonio Gramsci*, ed. and trans. Q. Hoare and G. Nowell Smith, Lawrence and Wishart, London, 1971.

Gray, C., 'Nuclear strategy: the case for a theory for victory', *International Security*, vol. 4 (1979).

Green, T.H., *Lectures on the Principles of Political Obligation*, Longman, London, 1941.

Habermas, J., *Knowledge and Human Interests*, trans J. Shapiro, Heinemann, London, 1972.

Habermas, J., *Legitimation Crisis*, Heinemann, London, 1976.

Habermas, J., *The Theory of Communicative Action*, vols I and II, Polity Press, Cambridge, 1984.

Habermas, J., *The Philosophical Discourses of Modernity*, Polity Press, Cambridge, 1987.

Hall, S., Critcher, C., Jefferson, T., Clarke, J. and Roberts, B. (eds) *Policing the Crisis*, Macmillan, London, 1978.

Hampson, N., *The Enlightenment*, Penguin, Harmondsworth, 1968.

Hancock, G., *Lords of Poverty*, Atlantic Monthly Press, New York, 1989.

Hardin, G., 'Lifeboat ethics: the case against helping the poor', *Psychology Today*, vol. 8 (1974).

Hardin, R., 'Unilateral vs. mutual disarmament', *Philosophy and Public Affairs*, vol. 11, no. 3 (1982).

Hardin R. and Mearsheimer, J.J., (eds) special issue on Nuclear Deterrence and Disarmament, *Ethics*, vol. 95, no. 3 (1985).

Hare, R.M., *The Language of Morals*, Oxford University Press, Oxford, 1952.

Hare, R.M., *Freedom and Reason*, Oxford University Press, Oxford, 1963.

Hare, R.M., 'The rules of war and moral reasoning', *Philosophy and Public Affairs*, vol. 1, no. 2 (1972).

Harries, R., 'The path to a Just War', *The Independent*, 31 October 1990.

Harries, R., 'A Just War not a crusade', *The Observer*, 20 January 1991.

Harvey, D., *The Condition of Postmodernity: An enquiry into the origins of cultural change*, Blackwell, Oxford, 1989.

Hastings, M., *Bomber Command*, Pan, London, 1981.

Hazard, P., *The European Mind 1680–1715*, Penguin, Harmondsworth, 1964.

Hazard, P., *European Thought in the Eighteenth Century*, Penguin, Harmondsworth, 1965.

Hegel, W.F.G., *Philosophy of Right*, trans. with notes by T.M. Knox, Oxford University Press, Oxford, 1967.

Hegel, W.F.G., *Philosophy of History*, trans. J. Sibree, Dover, New York, 1956.

Herz, J., *International Politics in the Atomic Age*, Columbia University Press, New York, 1959.

Hill, B.W., *Edmund Burke on Government, Politics and Society*, Fontana, London, 1975.

Hinsley, F.H., *Power and the Pursuit of Peace*, Cambridge University Press, Cambridge, 1963.

Hinsley, F.H., *Sovereignty*, Watts, London, 1966.

Hobhouse, L.T., *The Metaphysical Theory of the State: A criticism*, Allen and Unwin, London, 1918.

Hoffman, M., 'Critical theory and the inter-paradigm debate', *Millennium: Journal of International Studies*, vol. 16, no. 2 (1987).

Hoffman, M., 'Cosmopolitanism and normative international theory', *Paradigms: The Kent Journal of International Relations*, vol. 2, no. 1 (1988).

Hoffman, S., *The State of War*, Praeger, New York, 1965.

Hume, D., *A Treatise on Human Nature*, Penguin, Harmondsworth, 1969.

Hume, D., *Enquiries Concerning Human Nature and Concerning the Principles of Morals*, ed. L.A. Selby-Bigge, Clarendon, Oxford, 1975.

Hume, D., *Political Essays*, Bobbs Merrill, New York, 1953.

Hurrell, A., 'Kant and the Kantian paradigm in international relations', *Review of International Studies*, vol. 16, no. 3 (1990).

Ignatief, M., *The Needs of Strangers*, Chatto, London, 1984.

Independent Commission on International Development, *North–South: A programme for survival*, (The 'Brandt Report'), Pan, London, 1988.

Independent Commission on International Development, *Common Crisis*, Pan, London, 1984.

Jackson, R.H., *Quasi-States: Sovereignty, international relations and the Third World*, Cambridge University Press, Cambridge, 1990.

James, W., *Selected Papers on Philosophy*, Dent, London, 1917.

Jameson, F., 'Postmodernism or the cultural logic of late capitalism', *New Left Review*, vol. 146 (1984).

Jameson, F., *Postmodernism, Or the Cultural Logic of Late Capitalism*, Verso, London, 1991.

Jay, M., *The Dialectical Imagination*, Little Brown, Boston, Mass., 1973.

Johnson, J.T., *Ideology, Reason and the Limitation of War: Religious and secular concepts 1200-1740*, Princeton University Press, Princeton, N.J., 1975.

Johnson, J.T., *Just War Tradition and the Restraint of War*, Princeton University Press, Princeton, N.J., 1981.

Jones, R.J.B., (ed.) *The Worlds of Political Economy*, Frances Pinter, London, 1988.

Kamenka, E. and T. Ehr-Soon (eds) *Justice*, Edward Arnold, London, 1979.

Kaufman, W., (ed.) *Hegel's Political Philosophy*, Atherton Press, New York, 1970.

Kavka, G., *Moral Paradoxes of Nuclear Deterrence*, Cambridge University Press, Cambridge, 1987.

Keane, J., (ed.) *Civil Society and the State: New European perspectives*, Verso, London, 1988.

Keane, J., *Democracy and Civil Society*, Verso, London, 1988.

Kedourie, E., *Nationalism*, Hutchinson University Library, London, 1960.

Keegan, J., *The Face of Battle*, Cape, London, 1976.

Kennan, G., *American Diplomacy 1900-1950*, Mentor, New York, 1951.

Kenwood, A.K. and A.L. Lougheed, *The Growth of the International Economy 18209-1980*, Allen and Unwin, London, 1983.

Keohane, R.O., (ed.) *Neo-Realism and its Critics*, Columbia University Press, New York, 1986.

Keohane, R.O., *International Institutions and State Power*, Westview Press, Boulder, Colo., 1989.

Kirschkop, R. and D. Shepherd (eds) *Bakhtin and Cultural Theory*, Manchester University Press, Manchester, 1989.

Knorr, K. and J.N. Rosenau (eds) *Contending Approaches to International Politics*, Princeton University Press, Princeton, N.J., 1969.

Kolb, D., *The Critique of Pure Modernity: Hegel, Heidegger and after*, Chicago University Press, Chicago, 1986.

Korner, S., *Kant*, Penguin, Harmondsworth, 1955.

Krasner, S., *Structural Conflict: The Third World against global liberalism*, University of California Press, Berkeley, 1985.

Kratochwil, F., *Rules, Norms and Decisions*, Cambridge University Press, Cambridge, 1989.

Kymlicka, W., *Liberalism, Community and Culture*, Clarendon, Oxford, 1989.

Lal, D., *The Poverty of Development Economics*, (Hobart Paperback no. 16), Institute of Economic Affairs, London, 1983.

Laslett, P., (ed.) *Philosophy, Politics and Society*, 1st series, Blackwell, Oxford, 1956.

Lawrence, D.H., *The Rainbow*, Penguin, Harmondsworth, 1986.

Leff, G., *Medieval Thought from St Augustine to Ockham*, Penguin, Harmondsworth, 1958.

Lenin, V.I., *Selected Works*, Progress, Moscow, 1968.

Lenin, V.I., *Socialism and War*, Progress, Moscow, 1972.

Levinson, S., 'Responsibilities for crimes of war', in M. Cohen *et al.* (eds) *War and Moral Responsibility*, Princeton University Press, Princeton, N.J., 1974.

Light, M. and A.J.R. Groom (eds) *International Relations: A handbook of current theory*, Frances Pinter, London, 1985.

Linklater, A., *Men and Citizens in the Theory of International Relations*, Macmillan, London, 1990.

Linklater, A., *Beyond Realism and Marxism: Critical theory and international relations*, Macmillan, London, 1990.

Little, I., *Economic Development*, Basic Books, New York, 1982.

Little, R., *Intervention: External involvement in civil wars*, Martin Robertson, London, 1975.

Little, R. and M. Smith, (eds) *Perspectives on World Politics*, 2nd edn, Routledge, London, 1991.

Longley, C., 'Going by the Aquinas Book', *The Times*, 3 November 1990.

Luban, D., 'Just War and human rights', *Philosophy and Public Affairs*, vol. 9, no. 2 (1980).

Luban, D., 'The romance of the nation–state', *Philosophy and Public Affairs*, vol. 9, no. 4 (1980).

Lukes, S., *Marxism and Morality*, Oxford University Press, Oxford, 1985.

Luper-Foy, S. (ed), *Problems of International Justice*, Westview Press, Boulder, Colo., 1988.

Lyotard, J.F., *The Postmodern Condition: A report on knowledge*, trans. G. Bennington and B. Massumi, Manchester University Press, Manchester, 1986.

MacIntyre, A., *A Short History of Ethics*, Routledge and Kegan Paul, London, 1967.

MacIntyre, A., (ed.) *Hegel: A collection of critical essays*, Anchor, New York, 1972.

MacIntyre, A., *After Virtue*, University of Notre Dame Press, Notre Dame, In., 1981.

MacIntyre, A., *Whose Justice, Which Rationality?*, Duckworth, London, 1988.

Mackie, J.L., *Ethics: Inventing right and wrong*, Penguin, Harmondsworth, 1977.

Manning, C.A.W., *The Nature of International Society* (re-issue), Macmillan/ London School of Economics, London, 1975.

Marx, K., *The Eastern Question*, ed. E. Marx Aveling and E. Aveling, Cass Reprints of the Economic Classics, London, 1969.

Mayall, J., (ed.) *The Community of States*, Allen and Unwin, London, 1982.

Mayall, J., *Nationalism and International Society*, Cambridge University Press, Cambridge, 1989.

Mazzini, G., *Essays*, ed. B. King, Dent, London, 1884.

McCarthy, T., *The Critical Theory of Jurgen Habermas*, Hutchinson, London, 1978.

250 *Bibliography*

McLellan, D., *The Young Hegelians and Karl Marx*, Macmillan, London, 1969.
McLellan, D., *Marx Before Marxism*, Macmillan, London, 1970.
McLellan, D., (ed.) *Karl Marx: Selected writings*, Oxford University Press, Oxford, 1977.
Meinecke, F., *Machiavellism*, Routledge and Kegan Paul, London, 1956.
Mill, J.S., *Essays on Politics and Culture*, ed. G. Himmelfarb, Anchor Doubleday, New York, 1963.
Mill, J.S., *Utilitarianism, On Liberty and Representative Government*, Dent, London, 1972.
Monty Python's 'Life of Brian', Eyre Methuen, London, 1979.
Moore, G.E., *Principia Ethica*, Cambridge University Press, Cambridge, 1903.
Morgenthau, H.J., *Politics Among Nations*, 1st edn, Alfred A. Knopf, New York, 1948.
Mosley, P., *Overseas Aid*, Harvester Wheatsheaf, Hemel Hempstead, 1987.
Nagel, T., *Mortal Questions*, Cambridge University Press, Cambridge, 1979.
Nairn, T., *The Break-up of Britain*, New Left Books, London, 1977.
Nardin, T., *Law, Morality and the Relations of States*, Princeton Univerity Press, Princeton, N.J., 1983.
Nardin, T., 'The problem of relativism in international ethics', *Millennium: Journal of International Studies* vol. 18, no. 2 (1989).
Nardin, T. and D. Mapel (eds) *Traditions of International Ethics*, Cambridge University Press, Cambridge, 1992.
Navari, C., (ed.) *The Condition of States*, Open University Press, London, 1991.
Nicholson, M., 'Methodology' in M. Light and A.J.R. Groom (eds) *International Relations: A handbook of current theory*, Frances Pinter, London, 1985.
Norman, R., *Hegel's Phonomenology: A philosophical introduction*, Sussex University Press, Brighton, 1976.
Norman, R., *The Moral Philosophers*, Clarendon, Oxford, 1983.
Norris, C., *The Contest of Faculties: Philosophy and theory after deconstruction*, Methuen, London, 1985.
Norris, C., *Derrida*, Fontana, London, 1987.
Norton, A., 'A response to Henry Kariel', *Political Theory*, vol. 18, no. 2 (1990).
Nozick, R., *Anarchy, State and Utopia*, Basic Books, New York, 1974.
Oakeshott, M., *Rationalism in Politics and other Essays*, Methuen, London, 1962.
Oakeshott, M., *On Human Conduct*, Oxford University Press, Oxford, 1975.
O'Neill, O., *Faces of Hunger: An essay on poverty, justice and development*, Allen and Unwin, London, 1986.
O'Neill, O., 'Hunger, needs and rights', in S. Luper-Foy (ed.) *Problems of International Justice*, Westview Press, Boulder, Colo., 1988.
Parfit, D., *Reasons and Persons*, Clarendon Press, Oxford, 1984.
Parkinson, F., *The Philosophy of International Relations*, Sage, Beverly Hills, Calif., 1977.
Paskins, B. and M. Dockrill, *The Ethics of War*, Duckworth, London, 1979.

Paton, H.J., *The Moral Law: Kant's groundwork of the metaphysics of morals*, Hutchinson University Library, London, 1948.

Pears, D., *The False Prison: A study in the development of Wittgenstein's philosophy*, 2 vols, Oxford University Press, Oxford, 1987 and 1989.

Pelczynski, Z., *Hegel's Political Writings*, Oxford University Press, Oxford, 1964.

Pelczynski, Z., (ed.) *Hegel's Political Philosophy*, Cambridge University Press, Cambridge, 1971.

Pennock, R.J. and J.W. Chapman (eds) *Nomos XXIL: Ethics, economics and the law*, New York University Press, New York, 1982.

Plamenatz, J., *On Alien Rule and Self-Government*, Longman, London, 1961.

Plant, R., *Hegel: An introduction*, 2nd edn, Blackwell, Oxford, 1983.

Plant, R., *Modern Political Thought*, Blackwell, Oxford, 1991.

Pogge, T., *Realising Rawls*, Cornell University Press, Ithaca, N.Y., 1989.

Popper, K.R., *The Open Society and its Enemies*, Routledge and Kegan Paul, London, 1945.

Porter, B., 'Patterns of thought and practice in Martin Wight's international theory', in M. Donelan (ed.) *The Reason of States: A study in international political theory*, Allen and Unwin, London, 1978.

Poster, M. (ed.) *Jean Baudrillard: Selected writings*, Polity Press, Cambridge, 1988.

Rabinow, P., (ed.) *The Foucault Reader*, Penguin, Harmondworth, 1986.

Ramsey, P., *The Just War*, Charles Scribner's Sons, New York, 1968.

Rawls, J., *A Theory of Justice*, Oxford University Press, Oxford, 1971.

Rawls, J., 'Kantian constructivism in moral theory', *Journal of Philosophy*, vol. 27 (1980).

Redman, B.R., *The Portable Voltaire*, Penguin Viking, New York, 1949.

Reiss, H.J., (ed.) *The Political Thought of the German Romantics 1793–1815*, Blackwell, Oxford, 1955.

Reiss, H.J., (ed.) *Kant's Political Writings*, trans. H.B. Nisbet, Cambridge University Press, Cambridge, 1970.

Rengger, N.J., 'Serpents and doves in classical international theory', *Millennium: Journal of International Studies*, vol. 17, no. 2 (1988).

Richards, D., 'International distributive justice', in J.R. Pennock and J.W. Chapman (eds) *Nomos XXIL: Ethics, economics and the law*, New York University Press, New York, 1982.

Riley, P., *Kant's Political Philosophy*, Rowman Littlefield, Totawa, N.J., 1983.

Rodney, W., *How Europe Underdeveloped Africa*, Tanzania Publishing House, Dar es Salaam, 1971.

Rorty, R., *Philosophy and the Mirror of Nature*, Blackwell, Oxford, 1980.

Rorty, R., *Consequences of Pragmatism*, Harvester Wheatsheaf, Hemel Hempstead, 1982.

Rorty, R., 'Postmodern bourgeois liberalism', *Journal of Philosophy*, vol. 80, pp. 583–9 (1983).

Rorty, R., *Contingency, Irony and Solidarity*, Cambridge University Press, Cambridge, 1989.

Rorty, R., *Objectivity, Relativism and Truth: Philosophical Papers*, vol. I, Cambridge University Press, Cambridge, 1991.

Ross, W.D., *The Right and the Good*, Oxford University Press, Oxford, 1930.

Rousseau, J.-J., *The Social Contract and the Discourses*, ed. and trans. G.D.H. Cole, Dent, London, 1973.

Rousseau, J.-J., *The Social Contract and other Writings*, ed. and trans. F. Watkins, Nelson, London, 1953.

Rousseau, J.-J., *Emile*, trans. B. Foxley, Dent, London, 1969.

Sagan, S.D., *et.al.* (Harvard Nuclear Study Group), *Living with Nuclear Weapons*, Harvard University Press, Cambridge, Mass., 1983.

Sandel, M.J., *Liberalism and the Limits of Justice*, Cambridge University Press, Cambridge, 1982.

Sandel, M.J., 'The procedural republic and the unencumbered self', *Political Theory*, vol. 12, no. 1 (1984).

Savigear, P., 'Philosophical idealism and international politics: Bosanquet, Treitschke and war', *British Journal of International Studies*, vol. 1, no. 1 (1975).

Scheffler, S., (ed.) *Consequentialism and its Critics*, Oxford University Press, Oxford, 1988.

Schell, J., *The Fate of the Earth*, Knopf, New York, 1982.

Shama, S., *Citizens*, Viking Penguin, London, 1989.

Shue, H., *Basic Rights*, Princeton University Press, Princeton, N.J., 1980.

Sikora, R. and B. Barry (eds) *Obligations to Future Generations*, Temple University Press, Philadelphia, Pa., 1978.

Singer, J.D., (ed.) *Quantitative International Politics*, Free Press, New York, 1967.

Singer, J.D. and M. Small, *The Wages of War 1816–1965*, Wiley, London, 1972.

Singer, P., 'Famine, affluence, and morality', *Philosophy and Public Affairs*, vol. 1, no. 1 (1972).

Singer, P., *Hegel*, Oxford University Press, Oxford, 1973.

Singer P., *Practical Ethics*, Cambridge University Press, Cambridge, 1979.

Singer, P., (ed.) *Applied Ethics*, Oxford University Press, Oxford, 1986.

Skinner, Q., (ed.) *The Return of Grand Theory in the Human Sciences*, Cambridge University Press, Cambridge, 1985.

Smart, J.J.C. and B. Williams, *Utilitarianism: For and against*, Cambridge University Press, Cambridge, 1973.

Smith, A.D., *Theories of Nationalism*, Duckworth, London, 1971.

Soja, E., *Postmodern Geographies: The reassertion of space in critical social theory*, Verso, London, 1989.

Solomon, R., *Continental Philosophy Since 1750*, Oxford University Press, Oxford, 1988.

Spykman, N., *America's Strategy in World Affairs*, Harcourt Brace, New York, 1942.

Stawell, F.M., *The Growth of International Thought*, Butterworth, London, 1929.

Stevenson, C.L., *Ethics and Language*, Yale University Press, New Haven, Conn., 1944.

Sullivan, M.P., *International Relations: Theories and evidence*, Prentice Hall, N.J., 1976.

Talmon, J.L., *The Origins of Totalitarian Democracy*, Sphere, London, 1970.

Taylor, C., 'Interpretation and the sciences of man', *Review of Metaphysics*, vol. 25 (1971).

Taylor, C., *Hegel*, Cambridge University Press, Cambridge, 1975.

Taylor, C., 'Foucault on freedom and truth', *Political Theory*, vol. 12, no. 2 (1984).

Taylor, C., 'Connolly, Foucault and truth', *Political Theory*, vol. 13, no. 3 (1985).

Taylor, I., Walton, P., Young, J., (eds) *Critical Criminology*, Routledge and Kegan Paul, London, 1975.

Terraine, J., *The Right of the Line*, Hodder, London, 1985.

Thompson, E.P. and D. Smith (eds) *Protest and Survive*, Penguin, Harmondsworth, 1980.

Todorov, T., *Mikhail Bakhtin: The dialogic principle*, Manchester University Press, Manchester, 1984.

Todorov, R., *The Conquest of America*, trans. R. Howard, Harper Torchbooks, New York, 1987.

Tucker, R.C., *Philosophy and Myth in Karl Marx*, Cambridge University Press, Cambridge, 1961.

Tucker, R.C., *The Inequality of Nations*, Basic Books, New York, 1979.

Tully, J., (ed.) *Meaning and Context: Quentin Skinner and his critics*, Polity Press, Cambridge, 1988.

Urmson, J.O., *Philosophical Analysis*, Oxford University Press, Oxford, 1956.

Vasquez, J.A., *The Power of Power-Politics*, Frances Pinter, London, 1982.

Venturi, R., D. Scott-Brown and S. Izenour, *Learning from Las Vegas*, MIT Press, Cambridge, Mass., 1972.

Vincent, R.J., *Nonintervention and International Order*, Princeton University Press, Princeton, N.J., 1974.

Vincent, R.J., 'Edmund Burke and the theory of international relations', *Review of International Studies*, vol. 10, no. 3 (1984).

Vincent, R.J., *Human Rights and International Relations*, Cambridge University Press, Cambridge, 1986.

Virilio, P., *Speed and Politics*, trans. M. Poltzotti, Semiotext(e), New York, 1986.

Waever, O., *Beyond the Beyond of Critical International Theory*, Centre for Peace and Conflict Research, Copenhagen, 1989.

Waever, O., *Tradition and Transgression in International Relations: A post-Ashleyan position*, Centre for Peace and Conflict Research, Copenhagen, 1989.

Walker, R.B.J. and S.H. Mendlovitz (eds) *Contending Sovereignties: Redefining political community*, Lynn Reimer, Boulder, Colo., 1990.

Wallerstein, I., *The Modern World System*, 2 vols, Academic Press, New York, 1974 and 1980.

Wallerstein, I., *The Politics of the World Economy*, Cambridge University Press, Cambridge, 1984.

Walsh, W.H., *Hegelian Ethics*, Macmillan, London, 1969.

Waltz, K., *Man, the State, and War*, Columbia University Press, New York, 1959.

Waltz, K., *Theory of International Politics*, Addison-Wesley, Reading, Mass., 1979.

Walzer, M., *Just and Unjust Wars: A moral argument with historical illustrations*, Penguin, Harmondsworth, 1980.

Walzer, M., 'The moral standing of states: A response to four critics', *Philosophy and Public Affairs*, vol. 9, no. 3 (1980).

Walzer, M., *Spheres of Justice*, Martin Robertson, Oxford, 1983.

Walzer, M., 'The communitarian critique of liberalism', *Political Theory*, vol. 8, no. 1 (1990).

Walzer, M., 'Perplexed', *The New Republic*, 28 January 1991.

Warnock, G.J., *Contemporary Moral Philosophy*, Macmillan, London, 1967.

Warnock, M. (ed.) *Utilitatianism*, Fontana, London, 1962.

Warren, B., *Imperialism: Pioneer of capitalism*, Verso, London, 1980.

Warren, M., *Nietzsche and Political Thought*, MIT Press, Cambridge, Mass., 1988.

Wasserstrom, R., 'The relevance of Nuremburg', in M. Cohen *et al.* (eds) *War and Moral Responsibility*, Princeton University Press, Princeton, N.J., 1974.

Watson, H.S., *Nations and States*, Methuen, London, 1977.

Weber, M., *The Protestant Ethic and the Spirit of Capitalism*, 20th impression, Unwin Hyman, London, 1989.

Wight, M., 'Why is there no international theory' in H. Butterfield and M. Wight (eds) *Diplomatic Investigations: Essays in the theory of international politics*, Allen and Unwin, London, 1966.

Wight, M., *Systems of States*, ed. H. Bull, Leicester University Press/London School of Economics, Leicester, 1977.

Wight, M., *Power Politics*, 2nd edn, Leicester University Press/RIIA, Leicester, 1978.

Williams, R., *The Long Revolution*, Penguin, Harmondsworth, 1961.

Williams, R., 'Onward Chritian soldiers?', *The Guardian*, 1 November 1990.

Wilson, P., 'The English School of international relations: a reply to Sheila Grader', *Review of International Studies*, vol. 15, no. 1 (1989).

Winch, P., *The Idea of a Social Science and its Relation to Philosophy*, Routledge and Kegan Paul, London, 1958.

Wittgenstein, L., *Philosophical Investigations*, trans. G.E.M. Anscombe, Blackwell, Oxford, 1968.

Wolfers, A., *Discord and Collaboration*, Johns Hopkins University Press, Baltimore, Md., 1962.

World Bank, *World Development Report*, Oxford University Press, New York, 1991.

Wright, Q., *A Study of War*, Chicago University Press, Chicago, 1942.

Zimmern, A., *Greek Commonwealth*, Oxford University Press, Oxford, 1931.

Zimmern, A., *The League of Nations and the Rule of Law, 1918-1935*, Macmillan, London, 1939.

Zinnes, D.A., *Contemporary Research in International Relations*, Free Press, New York, 1976.

Name index

257

General index